Ethiopian Christianity

Ethiopian Christianity

History, Theology, Practice

Philip F. Esler

BAYLOR UNIVERSITY PRESS

© 2019 by Baylor University Press
Waco, Texas 76798

All Rights Reserved. No part of this publication may be reproduced, stored in a retrieval system, or transmitted, in any form or by any means, electronic, mechanical, photocopying, recording, or otherwise, without the prior permission in writing of Baylor University Press.

Cover Design by Aaron Cobbs and Savanah N. Landerholm
Cover image: Woman praying before the church of Dabra Sahay Maryam in Qwesqwam Abbey in Gondar during Lent, March 2017. Photograph courtesy of Angus Pryor.

The Library of Congress has cataloged this book under ISBN 978-1-4813-0674-4.

First issued in paperback in 2021 under ISBN 978-1-4813-0675-1

Contents

List of Figures   vii
Acknowledgments   xi
Abbreviations   xv

PART ONE
INTRODUCTION

1   Locating Ethiopian Christianity   3

PART TWO
THE HISTORY OF ORTHODOX ETHIOPIAN CHRISTIANITY

2   The Advent of Christianity in Ethiopia   27

3   Fifth to Seventeenth Centuries   43

4   Mid-seventeenth Century to the Present   75

PART THREE
ETHIOPIAN ORTHODOXY

5	Intellectual and Literary Traditions	101
6	Art, Architecture, and Music	133
7	Theology	171

PART FOUR
OTHER ETHIOPIAN CHRISTIANITIES

8	Protestantism	195
9	Catholicism	223

PART FIVE
CONCLUSION

10	The Future of Christianity in Ethiopia	239

Notes	257
Bibliography	279
Index	293

Figures

1.1	Map of Ethiopia. Created by Tessa Rickards.	9
1.2	Ploughing near Adwa, March 2017. Photo by Philip F. Esler.	11
1.3	The Great Temple of Almaqah at Yeha. Photo by Philip F. Esler.	14
1.4	Crescent and moon symbol of Almaqah on an incense burner from Yeha, currently in the museum in Yeha. Photo by Philip F. Esler.	15
1.5	The libation altar of the Temple at Maqaber Ga'ewa. Photo courtesy of P. Wolf, © German Archaeological Institute, Oriental Department, Wuqro Project.	16
1.6	Coin of King Endubis. Public domain.	22

Figures

2.1	Gold coin of King Ebana, fifth century CE. Public domain.	36
3.1	Painting of the Nine Saints in the Arbat Ensesa Church in Aksum. Photo by Philip F. Esler.	47
3.2	The hill (amba) on which is built the monastery of Dabra Damo. Photo courtesy of Wikimedia / A. Savin.	49
3.3	The pillar of Vasco da Gama, at Malindi, Kenya. Photo courtesy of Wikimedia/Mgiganteus.	63
4.1	The Palace of Fasilidas in Gondar. Photo by Philip F. Esler.	77
4.2	The Library and Chancellery of Yohannes I at Gondar. Photo courtesy of Wikimedia / Bernard Gagnon.	78
4.3	Tewodros (Theodore) II. Public domain.	80
4.4	Dabra Berhan Selassie Church, Gondar. Photo by Philip F. Esler.	84
4.5	Ethiopian painting of the Battle of Adwa. Photo courtesy of the Tropenmuseum, the Netherlands.	85
4.6	Memorial to the Italian dead at Adwa. Photo by Philip F. Esler.	85
4.7	A *beta salot* in an ex-Falasha village outside Gondar. Photo by Philip F. Esler.	95
5.1	Colored reproduction of the canon table from Garima Gospel book I, from a wall poster in the Abba Garima Monastery. Photo by Philip F. Esler.	105
5.2	Chapel of the Ark of the Covenant, adjacent to the Cathedral of St. Mary of Zion, Aksum. Photo by Philip F. Esler.	113
5.3	St. Walatta Petros, from a manuscript dated 1721. Photo courtesy of Wikimedia.	121
6.1	Two leaves from the Gunde Gospels, ca. 1540. Photo courtesy of the Walters Art Museum, Baltimore.	134

Figures   ix

6.2   Ethiopian handcrafted crosses used by priests on staffs.
      Property of and photo by Philip F. Esler.   136

6.3   Church of the monastery of Dabra Damo.
      Photo courtesy of Wikimedia / A. Savin.   136

6.4   Mark the Evangelist from Garima Gospel book III.
      Photo courtesy of Wikimedia.   137

6.5   Diptych with Mary and her son, flanked by archangels,
      apostles, and a saint, likely by a follower of fifteenth-
      century painter Fre Seyon, late fifteenth century.
      Photo courtesy of the Walters Art Museum, Baltimore.   141

6.6   Ethiopian engraved processional cross from the late
      eighteenth century. Photo courtesy of the Walters Art
      Museum, Baltimore.   142

6.7   Right half of a diptych with the virgin and child,
      by Niccolò Brancaleon, ca. 1500. Photo courtesy of
      the Walters Art Museum, Baltimore.   144

6.8   Marian icon, known as *Salus Populi Romani*, Basilica di
      Santa Maria Maggiore, Rome, perhaps sixth century CE.
      Photo courtesy of Wikimedia/SeoulKing.   145

6.9   Detail of a *Great Triptych*, ca. 1700, Museum Rietberg,
      Zurich. Photo courtesy of Wikimedia / Andreas Praefcke.   146

6.10 Engraving by Antonio Tempesta of Christ curing a leper,
      ca. 1591. Photo courtesy of the Wellcome Collection.   147

6.11 The archangels Michael and Gabriel, from a *Homiliary
      of the Archangel Michael*, late seventeenth century.
      Photo courtesy of the Walters Art Museum, Baltimore.   148

6.12 Painting of the Trinity in the Arbat Ensesa Church
      in Aksum. Photo by Philip F. Esler.   153

6.13 A detail of the ceiling of the Dabra Berhan Selassie
      Church in Gondar, illuminated with angels.
      Photo courtesy of Wikimedia/dsg-photo.   153

6.14 Ethiopian prayer scroll. Property of and photo
      by Philip F. Esler.   155

6.15	Stele at Aksum carved to imitate wooden beam and stone block Aksumite construction style. Photo by Philip F. Esler.	160
6.16	Beta Maryam in Lalibela. Photo by Philip F. Esler.	162
6.17	The cruciform church of Saint George (Beta Giyorgis) in Lalibela. Photo by Philip F. Esler.	163
6.18	Round church of a monastery, near Gorgora, on Lake Tana. Photo by Philip F. Esler.	164
6.19	St. Yared stabbed in the foot by the emperor while performing. Photo courtesy of Wikimedia / A. Davey.	167
7.1	The festival of Timkat in the baths of Fasilidas, Gondar. Photo courtesy of Wikimedia / Jialiang Gao.	178
7.2	The festival of Mesqel in Mesqel Square, Addis Ababa. Photo courtesy of Wikimedia/DanielGrimaTsige.	179
8.1	Samuel Gobat. Photo courtesy of Wikimedia.	198

Acknowledgments

My interest in the history and character of Christianity in Ethiopia has grown from earlier research on the historical meaning and also the contemporary significance of 1 Enoch, an ancient Jewish apocryphal text that survived in toto from antiquity only in Ethiopia in Ge'ez versions. This research culminated in my monograph *God's Court and Courtiers in the Book of the Watchers: Re-interpreting Heaven in 1 Enoch* and my edited volume *The Blessing of Enoch: 1 Enoch and Contemporary Theology*, both published by Cascade Books (Eugene, Oregon) in 2017. My visits to Ethiopia in relation to these two projects in the company of my friend and colleague, Angus Pryor, a practicing artist and head of the School of Art and Design in our highly supportive institutional base, the University of Gloucestershire, fired my interest in the history and character of Christianity in the country. We were both struck by the deep religiosity of the people of Ethiopia and by the remarkable and still insufficiently appreciated intellectual and artistic traditions of Ethiopian Orthodoxy. I found it reassuring that at times when I sensed, as a nonexpert, that a centuries-old wall painting in an Orthodox church was a towering masterpiece of religious art, Angus was having the same thought. Indeed, his experience of Ethiopia and its artistic tradition has become a major influence on a series of twenty-one 2 × 2 meter paintings and a large-scale model of an Ethiopian church illuminating scenes from 1 Enoch that he is currently creating for exhibition in 2020.

The idea to write this book, however, came not from me but from Professor Francis Watson of the University of Durham. I am grateful to him for the stimulus that led to its production. I am also grateful to Dr. Carey Newman, director of Baylor University Press, for accepting the book for publication so readily and for his strong interest in it throughout the writing process. Mr. Cade Jarrell at Baylor University Press has provided timely and expert advice whenever it was needed.

I have greatly profited from information and advice supplied to me by people who know far more about Ethiopia than I ever will. Rev. Dr. Daniel Assefa, director of the Capuchin Franciscan Research and Retreat Center in Addis Ababa, has provided invaluable advice on many occasions, both personally in Addis Ababa and in Cheltenham, by e-mail, and in the form of printed material not readily available outside Ethiopia. Dr. Girma Mohammed, now resident in the UK, has given me the benefit of his expert views on the political and religious situation in Ethiopia on a number of issues. Fr. Daniel Seyfe Michael, of the Ethiopian Orthodox Church, explained issues relating to the means being undertaken by the church to preserve its historical and artistic legacy. Ms. Sofanit Abebe, a graduate of the impressive Ethiopian Graduate School of Theology in Addis Ababa who is now undertaking a doctorate in the University of Edinburgh, also supplied me with helpful information. I have learned much about Ethiopian Christianity from Professor Loren Stuckenbruck, of the University of Munich, during conversations in Addis Ababa and Cheltenham. Dr. Ralph Lee, who lived in Ethiopia for many years and now resides in Cambridge, offered valuable insights into the shape of the project and into particular details. Dr. Pawel Wolf, of the German Archaeological Institute in Berlin, kindly allowed me to use a photo of the altar from the well-preserved temple of Almaqah near Wukro, which he and his Ethiopian and German colleagues excavated recently. Professor Alessandro Bausi, of the University of Hamburg, supplied me with an important article that I might otherwise have overlooked. Archaeological illustrator Tessa Rickards prepared the map of Ethiopia that is Figure 1.1. My daughter-in-law, Lauren Esler, helped me understand aspects of Ethiopian music. Finally, an anonymous reader of the proposal for Baylor University Press also made very useful suggestions. I am immensely grateful to all of them for their help. All views expressed, and any errors made, in the volume, however, are solely my responsibility.

Abbreviations

EA   *Encyclopaedia Aethiopica*, vols. 1–3 (2003, 2005, and 2007), edited by Siegbert Uhlig, vol. 4 (2010), edited by Siegbert Uhlig, in cooperation with Alessandro Bausi, and Vol. 5 (2014), edited by Alessandro Bausi, in cooperation with Siegbert Uhlig. Wiesbaden: Harrassowitz Verlag.

RIE   *Recueil des inscriptions de l'Éthiopie des périodes pré-axoumite et axoumite*, 3 vols., edited by E. Bernand, A. J. Drewes, and R. Schneider. Académie des Inscriptions et Belles-Lettres. Paris: Diffusion de Boccard 1991–2000.

PART ONE

INTRODUCTION

1

Locating Ethiopian Christianity

The image on the front cover of this volume depicts a scene of contemporary Christianity in Ethiopia. On a cool but sunny morning in mid-March 2017, and thus during Lent, in Gondar, northern Ethiopia, a woman stands praying intensely outside the round church of Dabra Sahay Maryam in the Qwesqwam Abbey. Wearing the *netela*, the white Ethiopian prayer shawl over her head, shoulders, and back, she is positioned in front of a contemporary painting in traditional Ethiopian style of the flight into Egypt (Matt 2:13-15), her attention fixed on the faces of Jesus and Mary. In the painting, with an airborne Saint Gabriel pointing the way, Joseph leads a contented donkey bearing the nimbed Mary and Jesus, the focus of the painting, to Egypt, while a female figure identified as Salome, whom some ancient sources describe as accompanying the Holy Family,[1] brings up the rear. The abbey is named after Qus Qam or Qwesqwam in middle Egypt, south of Asyut, where tradition has it that the Holy Family rested on their flight into Egypt.[2] This connection is an example of the common Ethiopian practice of naming churches after places with a biblical reference so that, in a sense, to live in Ethiopia is to live in the Holy Land. But this is Lent, and, across the church's heartland in the north of the country, Orthodox Christians, like this woman, are flocking to the churches, monasteries, and holy places in Aksum, Lalibela, Gondar, and elsewhere. The Ethiopian Lent lasts for fifty-five days, and during this period the faithful abstain from animal foods during weekdays, attend Mass more frequently, and lengthen their daily prayers.[3] Half an hour later, the woman is still standing there, in fervent prayer.

To encounter Christianity in Ethiopia is to experience forms of the faith without parallel elsewhere. The predominant reason is that, from the arrival of Christianity in the country, then manifested as the powerful and highly civilized Kingdom of Aksum, in around 335 CE, until 1974, the Ethiopian Church and the Ethiopian monarchy existed continuously and in close relationship with one another. For most of that period the emperor of the day regarded himself as the protector of Orthodox Christianity and was regularly active in its affairs and organization. Only between 1936 and 1941, when Emperor Haile Selassie was forced into exile by the brief Italian occupation, was this chain of power and authority broken. An earlier Italian attempt to take control of the country in 1895 and 1896 ended at the Battle of Adwa on March 1, 1896, when the army of Menelik II inflicted a massive defeat on the Italians, killing or wounding more than half their army of fifteen thousand. Ethiopians are proud of the fact that apart from the Italian period they were never defeated by a foreign power (although a Muslim leader came close in the early sixteenth century) and were never colonized. The Christian monarchy came to an end only with the death of its last emperor, Haile Selassie, in 1974.

Added to this unique continuity of the dominant political and religious institutions for sixteen centuries, the comparative geographic isolation of Ethiopia (see the current chapter, below) has allowed the persistence of traditions in ways that, again, are unparalleled. To this very day, for example, Ethiopian monks copy texts onto vellum manuscripts resting on their knees, just like the scribes of ancient Greece and Rome, while these same monks and their predecessors, over some sixty generations, have preserved ancient texts, like 1 Enoch, Jubilees, and the Ascension of Isaiah, which disappeared elsewhere in the Christian world. Just as significant, however, is that in the Orthodox segment of Ethiopian Christianity so many of the faithful live with a profound sense of the Israelite and Christian past—its thought and its culture, in liturgy, text, images, and music—that they regard their homeland as a new Holy Land and themselves as active participants in the drama of redemption, with all its plots and subplots. Ethiopian Orthodoxy shows a variety of cultural influences, including Judaism, African religion, the Syriac tradition, and Coptic Christianity. "As an old, African, Orthodox church it occupies a unique place in the history of Christianity."[4] The character of Ethiopian intellectual and literary traditions, and of its pictorial, architectural, and musical heritage, deserves close attention (chapters 5 and 6).

The defining aspect of Ethiopian Orthodoxy, which is expressed in its official name, the Ethiopian Orthodox Tewahedo Church, is that it rejects the view taken at the Council of Chalcedon in 451 CE that Christ had two natures, one divine and one human, and insists instead that in Christ the divine and the human are fully fused in one nature (a notion encapsulated in the word "miaphysite" or, sometimes, less accurately "monophysite"). "Tewahedo" means "made one" in Ge'ez, the ancient language of Ethiopia (also called Ethiopic) still used for liturgical and other purposes by the Ethiopian Orthodox Church, and it refers to this unity of nature in Christ. Ethiopian Orthodoxy shares this view with five other "Oriental" Orthodox Churches: the Coptic Orthodox Church of Alexandria, the Syriac Orthodox Church of Antioch, the Armenian Apostolic Church, the Malankara Syrian Orthodox Church of India, and the Eritrean Orthodox Tewahedo Church. These churches refer to their theological position on Christ as miaphysitism (not monophysitism).

The continual and vigorous activation of collective memory in Ethiopia, extending back to the fourth century CE and earlier, in a context where the church and the ruling dynasty were so closely intertwined, makes serious attention to its history (in chapters 1,

2, 3, and 4 below) essential to understanding the current situation. No other country comes close to matching Ethiopia in the extent to which understanding the church entails understanding the state and vice versa. One prominent example is the tradition that Solomon and the queen of Sheba had a son (Menelik I), who stole the ark of the covenant and brought it to Ethiopia, where it remains to this day, in a building in Aksum. From the thirteenth century CE until Emperor Haile Selassie's death in 1974, the ruling dynasty in Ethiopia, by claiming physical descent from Menelik, deployed this tradition to cement its grip on power. Another example is the lingering dislike of Catholicism among Ethiopians stemming from the disastrous errors the Jesuits committed in attempting to bring Ethiopian Orthodoxy under the authority of Rome in the late sixteenth and early seventeenth centuries.

Accordingly, it is fair to say that the central national institutions that sustained Ethiopia for so long were the monarchy and the church, while the theological, intellectual, literary, and artistic traditions of Ethiopian Orthodoxy constituted the core of a national culture that provided a distinctive and durable identity, even when faced with major external or internal challenges.

But Christianity in Ethiopia is bigger than Orthodoxy. Since the nineteenth century the country has seen Protestant churches and Pentecostalism arrive and flourish. Now roughly one-quarter of the country's sixty million Christians are Protestant. Many have been attracted by the dynamic, personal, and less formal nature of Protestant Christianity. Over the same period the Roman Catholic Church has made converts but in much smaller numbers, and its adherents total only one-twentieth the number of Protestants. The Protestant churches offer a striking alternative to Orthodoxy both in theology and in modes of ecclesial organization. The Catholics, on the contrary, are virtually identical to Orthodox Christians in terms of doctrine and offer liturgies in both an Eastern form (very similar to the Orthodox one) and a Roman rite. Accordingly, separate chapters below will consider the nature of Orthodoxy, Protestantism, and Catholicism in Ethiopia today (chapters 7,

8, and 9). These various Christian churches must coexist in a rapidly changing Ethiopia, where the Muslim minority, which has been disadvantaged and looked down on for centuries, is beginning to enter the heart of national life. What might the future hold? That is the subject of chapter 10.

Throughout this book I will refer to Ethiopia as Ethiopia and not use the name Abyssinia except where I am citing some other writer. Abyssinia was widely used to refer to the country until about the middle of the twentieth century. Where it is used today, it tends to have a very specific reference to the northern, predominantly Christian and Semitic-language highland of Ethiopia and Eritrea. The word has a three-thousand-year-old lineage, being found in hieroglyphic Egyptian in the form Hbsty to designate a region near the Red Sea in south Arabia or east Africa that produced incense. In Sabaean inscriptions from the first millennium BCE it appears as HBST (perhaps to be vocalized as Habasat) in connection with Aksum, the ancient pre-Christian and then Christian kingdom, the history of which is covered in chapter 2. As such it is a self-designation by the people who lived there. In Arabic texts the name appears in the form Al-Habasa and is applied to what we know, roughly speaking, as Ethiopia. This form, with minor modifications, came into English as Abyssinia (and in French as Abyssinie and German as Abessinien).[5]

Finally, it is worth noting as we explore the contours of Christianity in this volume that Ethiopia is an extraordinarily diverse country in terms of ethnic groups, languages, and religious affiliations. Thus, the Federal Democratic Republic of Ethiopia officially recognizes some ninety ethnic groups, of which the largest is the Oromo and the second largest the Amhara. Almost eighty languages are spoken in the country. As well as large populations of Ethiopian Orthodox, Protestants, and Muslims, there are some two million people practicing traditional religions and about seven hundred thousand Roman Catholics. Abiy Ahmed, the prime minister appointed on April 2, 2018, sees it as key to his leadership to develop and embed a national narrative and value system to which all Ethiopians can subscribe, whatever their ethnic, linguistic, or religious identity.

The Geographical and Historical Setting

The aim of the remainder of this chapter is to outline the geography and relevant aspects of the history of Ethiopia prior to the arrival of Christianity, since both aspects provide the context within which Christianity was born and shaped in the centuries that followed.

Geography

Ethiopia is a landlocked country of some 103 million inhabitants situated in the Horn of Africa (see figure 1.1). Eritrea stretches along its northern border. On its eastern border lie Djibouti and Somalia, to the south Somalia and Kenya, and to the west Sudan and South Sudan. It stretches from 14°53′ in the north to 3°527′ in the south, and from 48°0′ in the east to 33°0′ in the west, and it occupies 1.106 million square kilometers. The Great Rift Valley, running from the northeast to the southwest, dissects the country roughly in half. Much of the country north of the Great Rift consists of an elevated region consisting of mountains and plateaus divided by valleys. The highest mountains approach 4,500 meters in height. The main cities in this area tend to be located at high altitudes: Addis Ababa 2,355 meters (7,726 feet), Aksum 2,131 meters, Gondar 2,133 meters, and Lalibela 2,600 meters. In the northwestern part of the Ethiopian highlands lies Lake Tana (Tana Hayq), roughly 85 kilometers long and 65 kilometers wide. A number of rivers flow into it, and it is, in turn, the source of the mighty Blue Nile that joins the White Nile a thousand miles downstream near Khartoum. There is a lower region in the northeastern corner, the Afar Triangle or Depression, through which the Awash River flows, although it runs dry in the annual dry season and terminates in a chain of salt lakes.

Locating Ethiopian Christianity 9

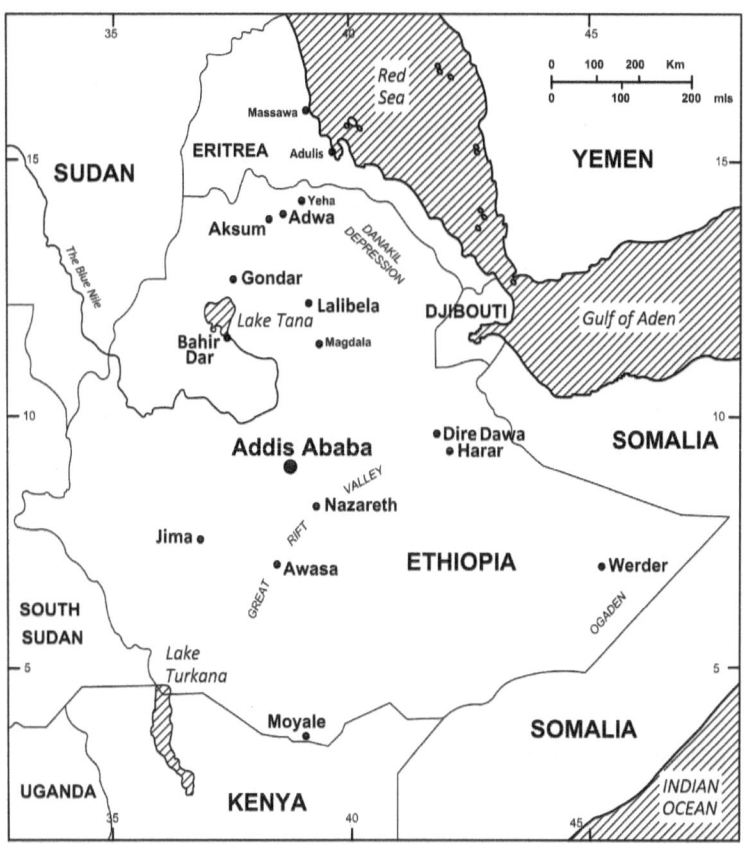

Figure 1.1. *Map of Ethiopia*

The northern part of the Afar Triangle is the fiercely hot Danakil Depression, about 100 meters below sea level. It was in the Awash Valley in the Afar Triangle in 1974 that Donald Johanson and his colleagues found the 3.2-million-year-old skeleton of an *Australopithecus afarensis* woman only 1.1 meters tall whom they called Lucy. Ethiopians are very proud of Lucy and refer to her in Amharic as Dinkinesh, meaning "you are marvelous." South of the rift there are mountains of similar height, plateaus, and valleys drained by rivers.

But on the eastern side of this mountainous area, the land drops to extensive lower regions, with the Ogaden Desert forming the sharp eastern point of the country that pushes into Somalia. Along the western side the mountains give way to lower territory that borders Sudan and South Sudan.

The extremely mountainous nature of the country means that it is difficult to traverse and, therefore, to govern. This topography explains why Ethiopian monarchs used to spend much of their time traveling around the country.[6] These characteristics also make the country difficult to invade.[7]

The fact that Ethiopia embraces large stretches of territory from very high to very low altitudes is reflected in similarly varied climatic regions. Ethiopians speak of three zones: the *quolla* is the low-lying and hot area, up to 5,000 feet; the *woyna dega* (highlands of the vine) is the intermediate zone, from 5,000 to 7,000 feet; and the *dega* is the temperate zone of the highlands, above 7,000 feet.[8] Average annual temperatures in the highlands (the *dega*) are in the low 60s Fahrenheit (mid-10s Celsius), whereas in the lowlands (the *quolla*) the average is in the low 80s Fahrenheit (upper 20s Celsius).[9] The highlands, moreover, "show a remarkably even temperature throughout the year."[10] In the high country rain falls predominantly in the hot months, from June to September, with another, short rain season from February to March. The coastal lowlands, however, have a more Mediterranean climate, receiving rain in December and January. Annual rainfall in the mountainous region ranges from 1 to 2.5 meters (or 98.5 inches). Addis Ababa has an average annual precipitation of 1.143 meters (or 45 inches). Some of this abundant rain ends up in Lake Tana and from there drains into the Blue Nile before flowing to the Mediterranean.

The highlands (the area of principal interest in this volume) tend to be very or reasonably fertile for agricultural purposes. There are two dominant types of soil. The first is based on volcanic material and has a medium to high potential for rain-fed agriculture. The second has a subsurface accumulation of clay, which causes problems in nutrient retention, surface crusting, and erosion; this type has medium agricultural potential if it is properly managed.[11] Across the country agriculture is still carried out using traditional methods, including the use of iron-tipped wooden ploughs drawn by oxen (see figure 1.2).

The country has been divided into administrative regions by the government. The capital, Addis Ababa, falls within the region of Oromia, which is named after the Oromo ethnic group.

Pre-Christian History

It was in this highly distinctive geomorphic and climatic setting that literate civilization began in Ethiopia at about 1000 BCE. Much of the evidence is archaeological, enriched by some inscriptions, but there are also references to what was happening there in ancient historical and literary texts.

Figure 1.2. *Ploughing near Adwa, March 2017*

The First Millennium BCE

African Origins

From even before the classical period, the Greeks knew of a people whom they called the Aithiopes, a name meaning "burned faces." The earliest references to them are in Homer (dating to about the eighth to seventh centuries BCE), and the picture given is a very favorable one. At one point in the *Iliad* Thetis tells Achilles that on the previous day Zeus and all the gods went off to the Ocean River, which was the river believed to surround the flat disk of the earth,[12] to feast with the excellent (*amumones*) Aithiopes (1.423–424). This area lay in the far south (*Odyssey* 4.81–84), apparently in the region we call Africa. Elsewhere in the *Iliad*, the goddess Iris announces her intention to return to the Ocean River and the land of the Aithiopes; they were making a splendid sacrifice to the gods, and she did not want to miss her share (23.205–207)! Other reports in the *Odyssey* (1.21–25; 5.281–287) mention visits Poseidon paid to the Aithiopes, the first to receive a generous sacrifice. As well as living at the farthest limits of humankind, the Aithiopes were thought to be a people split in two, with a western part and an eastern part (*Odyssey* 1.21–25). Yet it would be risky to identify the people that Homer called the Aithiopes specifically with the Ethiopians as we know them. More likely, and this is confirmed by Herodotus, to whom we will return below, Aithiopes was a way of referring to all of the people south of Egypt. Our first knowledge of the people living in Ethiopia specifically comes from material remains, not from literary sources, which, coincidentally, date to a period reasonably close to the time of the composition of Homer.

It is early in the first millennium BCE that we find the beginnings of a high level of material culture in what is now northern Ethiopia (which roughly corresponds to the present regional state of Tigray) and Eritrea, a culture of which Aksum, the kingdom that first embraced Christianity in the mid-fourth century CE, was in part an heir. The evidence is mainly archaeological, with a handful of inscriptions augmenting our understanding. But recent research has largely dispelled the earlier picture of foreign influence from the

Sabaean culture of southern Arabia, which is today Yemen, as being overwhelmingly dominant in the northern Ethiopian highlands. Although the evidence is limited, it is now clear that by 1000 BCE there were (and perhaps long had been) farming communities scattered across the North that cultivated emmer wheat and barley, and also herded cattle, sheep, and goats. These people made pottery and used flaked-stone tools, and some of them lived in rectangular stone houses such as have been found at Ona, near Asmara, in Eritrea. South Semitic languages (related to Ge'ez) are likely to have been spoken in the region at this period.[13] This character of the indigenous population, its agriculture, and its culture persisted into the Aksumite period, and more recent writing on Ethiopia stresses this underlying continuity, while acknowledging some discontinuities, the latter often occurring on the back of influences from abroad. Non-elite sites from early in the first millennium BCE showing very few signs of external influence have been discovered (although in many cases not yet excavated) at Ona in Eritrea, at Aksum, and at Yeha (in north-central Tigray near modern-day Adwa and about 50 kilometers northeast of Aksum). Phillipson observes that in these sites "strong continuity is apparent from earlier times, notably in pottery, flaked-stone artefacts and farming economy."[14]

The Ethio-Sabaean Period

Nevertheless, during this period a major discontinuity did occur. Until very recently this change was demonstrated mainly in the arrival of large, monumental architecture, clearly at the service of elite elements in the population. The major and impressive evidence for this is to be found in Yeha, where, after traversing a winding road down into a valley from the highway from Adwa, one discovers some remarkable ruins. The most impressive of these is what has long been referred to as the Great Temple of Almaqah (see figure 1.3), a well-preserved rectangular structure, measuring 18.6 × 15.0 meters with some parts of its walls 13 meters high.

It is probably to be dated to the seventh century BCE and is clearly built in the Sabaean style of southern Arabia, as its strong

Figure 1.3. *The Great Temple of Almaqah at Yeha*

resemblance to Sabaean temples at Marib and Baraqish indicates. Furthermore, neatly carved stone inscriptions originally from the altar in the temple reveal that it was dedicated to Almaqah, the southern Arabian moon god.[15] A standard symbol of Almaqah was a crescent above which was an orb, a symbol that appears on an incense burner found at Yeha (see figure 1.4). As we will see below, this symbol persisted in use in this region for at least one thousand years.

The other major building at Yeha is the Grat Be'al Gebri, currently under careful excavation and conservation by a French team. This appears to have been a palace, probably built in the eighth century and later deliberately emptied and burned.[16] These architectural remains are amenable to a variety of explanations, ranging from conquest by Sabaean invaders to the establishment of significant trade links with southern Arabia by wealthy merchants who brought their religious practices and beliefs with them.

Figure 1.4. *Crescent and moon symbol of Almaqah on an incense burner, currently in the museum in Yeha*

A recent archaeological excavation has greatly enhanced our knowledge of Ethiopia during this period. In 2008 excavations were conducted by an Ethiopian-German team on a site at Maqaber Ga'ewa near Wukro, about 90 kilometers southeast of Yeha (or 160 kilometers by road). They revealed a temple precinct from the eighth century BCE, with substantial stone remains of the temple and other buildings, a superbly preserved libation altar in that temple (see figure 1.5), a statue of a seated woman, and carved stone blocks and incense burners. Also found were numerous objects believed to be votive offerings and various types of pottery.[17] Perhaps most remarkable was the fact that preserved on the altar (in finely carved monumental Sabaean written from right to left) was its dedicatory inscription:

> Waran, the king, who throws down [enemies], son of Radium and Shakkatum, the companion, rebuilt [the altar] for Almaqah, when he was appointed the Lord of the temple of Almaqah in Yeha, on the instruction of Attar and Almaqah and Dat Hamyin and Dat Ba'dan.[18]

Figure 1.5. *The libation altar of the Temple at Maqaber Ga'ewa*

Another inscription reads, "On the instruction of Waran has Hayrhumu, the stone mason, from the clan of Hadan, dedicated (this wall) to Almaqah."[19] The name of the mason and his clan are south Arabian in origin.[20]

We now know that a king with strong Sabaean links ruled in the area, which suggests a movement of Sabaeans into the area that probably went beyond increased trade. This knowledge amplifies the inscriptional evidence for kings in the region farther north, around Aksum and Yeha, kings whose names may suggest they were related to this one.[21] Where one has kings, one has courts and courtiers and armies, and a peasantry who support the system in various ways, through taxes and levies and so on. From the altar inscription, we not only have confirmation that the temple at Yeha was dedicated to Almaqah but also the clearest sign that this was the central cult site in the area, and that it legitimated royal authority.[22] Waran claims no fewer than four Sabaean gods were responsible for his appointment as lord of temple of Almaqah in Yeha. Sabaean influence is also proven by the fact that the master mason for the stonework and the inscriptions came from southern Arabia.

Yet what is perhaps most remarkable about this temple site is that it provides evidence for cultural transfer between, and even the integration of, indigenous and Sabaean cultures. The fact that the inscription names Waran a destroyer of enemies and names his mother as well as his father does not reflect south Arabian culture.[23] The reference to his mother seems instead to relate to neighboring Kushite culture, where kings based their claim on the matriline and statues of queens as well as kings were common.[24] Even if the craftsmen and style were Sabaean, for whom were they working? People from south Arabia or members of a local elite heavily influenced by Sabaean influences?[25] Equally noteworthy is that the non-elite indigenous population also adopted the cult of Almaqah.[26] Compelling evidence for this exists in the fact that many of the numerous examples of pottery discovered at the site reflect African, not Sabaean, forms and traditions. They were shaped by molding and coiling techniques that still prevail in the region.[27] Also worth mentioning is that Yeha has borne that name for some three thousand years.

In short, the architectural, sculptural, and inscriptional remains from Yeha, Maqaber Ga'ewa, and other places in the North almost certainly reflect the arrival of incomers, possibly few in number and with an elite component, from southern Arabia.[28] While the manner of their arrival remains uncertain, they left a legacy in terms of architecture, literacy, and aspects of religious belief and practice that were taken up by the indigenous population.[29] Indeed, the northern indigenous people's adoption of the Arabian cult of Almaqah practiced by local kings will find an echo a thousand years later in the way Ezana leads his subjects into Christianity.

The Proto-Aksumite Period

Psalm 68:31 states, "Let bronze be brought from Egypt; let Ethiopia hasten to stretch out her arms to God" (RSV). In this verse Ethiopia actually refers to ancient Kush (roughly equivalent to today's Sudan). Many Ethiopians today, however, proudly regard this passage as a reference to their homeland. The Greek historian Herodotus, writing about 430 BCE, was someone who had visited Egypt as far south as Elephantine (*Histories*, 2.29). He states that south of Elephantine the country is inhabited by Aithiopes. He has a reasonable amount to say about this area, but it is clear that he is largely talking about Nubia, or Kush,[30] in what is modern-day Sudan, not Ethiopia as we understand it, a country farther south (see above). He states that Meroe is the capital of all Aithiopia and that the people of the place worship Zeus and Dionysus, the equivalents of Amun and Osiris (2.29). Meroe, however, located in modern Sudan about 200 kilometers northeast of Khartoum, was the capital of Kush.[31] He is aware of claims that the annual flooding of the Nile is a result of snows melting in the far south yet observes that he cannot understand how there could be snow in Africa, the hottest part of the known world (*Histories*, 2.22). He has also heard that the Nile flows through Aithiopia and that the Nile runs into a lake (2.29). According to Herodotus, the Aithiopes are said to be the tallest and most handsome of all men and that, uniquely, they choose as their king the tallest among them, having strength proportionate to his stature (3.20). Finally, he also records Aithiopia is in the southwest and it produces abundant gold, huge elephants, all sorts of trees, ebony, and the most handsome and long-living of all people (3.114). Herodotus appears to have Kush in mind.

Pliny the Elder, writing in about 77 CE, stated that the queen of the Ethiopians bore the title of candace (*Natural History* 6.29). Archaeological excavations at Meroe[32] have confirmed that candace (or kandake) was the title of the queens of Kush and a number are known. This allows us to interpret the following passage from the Acts of the Apostles concerning Philip:

> He rose and went. And behold, an Ethiopian, a eunuch, a minister of Candace, queen of the Ethiopians, in charge of all her treasure, had come to Jerusalem to worship and was returning; seated in his chariot, he was reading the prophet Isaiah. (8:27-28)

The text really concerns an official from Kush in modern Sudan, not in Ethiopia, and the author appears to have mistaken the title of the queen for her name. Nevertheless, the fact that an "Ethiopian" eunuch appears in Acts 8:27 no doubt explains the tradition among Ethiopians today that he was an ancestor in Christ. Fragmentary Aksumite inscriptions in Greek on the site of Meroe, erected by an Aksumite king (thought to be King Ezana or his predecessor), show that the city was conquered by the Aksumites in the first half of the fourth century CE.[33] This may have led to the decline of Meroe, which had ceased to exist by the fifth century CE. Since the literary sources, while important for understanding the traditions connected with Aithiopia and the Aithiopes, fall short of taking us into the area of Africa that we know today as Ethiopia, we need to turn to archaeological evidence for assistance.

During the last four centuries of the first millennium BCE, there were developments occurring in parts of northern Ethiopia that to an extent justify the description "proto-Aksumite" since there is some measure of continuity between them and what would later appear in Aksum. The best evidence comes from Beta Giyorgis hill, adjacent to Aksum itself, in the form of residential and funerary structures, the latter marked by stone stelae that would later become (and remain) so visually prominent in Aksum. In particular, the cult of Almaqah (or something very like it) and Sabaean architectural styles persisted from the Ethio-Sabaean period into that of Aksum. Nevertheless, the continuance of indigenous pottery traditions indicates that the occupation on Beta Giyorgis remained within a local tradition. Barley, emmer wheat, some free threshing wheat, and possibly teff were cultivated, and cattle, sheep, and goats were raised, with dogs also present. Such imported artifacts as were found originated in the Nile valley rather than in southern Arabia. This is interesting in the light of increased activity in the Red Sea area by the Ptolemaic Egyptians at this time, partly in pursuit of elephant ivory, with an inscription of Ptolemy III (reigned 246–222 BCE) visible in the port of Adulis (a place on the western shore of the Red Sea) in the sixth century CE.[34] Putting all this together, David

Phillipson concludes that the proto-Aksumite inhabitants of Beta Giyorgis were the ancestors of the people subsequently responsible for the establishment and expansion of the Aksumite kingdom.[35]

The Rise of Aksum

The evidence for the kings and kingdom of Aksum, which grew, flourished, and declined during the first seven centuries CE, consists of archaeology, coinage, some inscriptions, and a handful of literary references. Later Ethiopian tradition generally does not know the original names of the kings and uses others. It also appears that several names could be used to designate the same king.[36]

The initial development of Aksum in this period is signaled by archaeological evidence for the commencement of significant building activity between the hills of Beta Giyorgis and Mai Qoho, which probably occurred between 50 BCE and 50 CE.[37] There is little doubt that the major reason for the expansion of Aksum was its role in moving African products and animals from the interior of the continent to the Mediterranean countries and India through the port of Adulis. Precious literary evidence relating to Aksum and this trade in the mid-first century CE is provided by a work from that time known as the *Periplus Maris Erythraei* (A voyage around the Red Sea).[38] It describes various routes between ports in the Red Sea region and in India and the goods that could be bought and sold in each. The author was a Greek-speaking merchant from Egypt who had sailed these routes for trading purposes and composed a handbook on the subject, as a guide for other merchants.[39] In describing the progression southward along the western side of the Red Sea, he mentions Adulis, "a legally limited port of trade," and a fair-sized village. From Adulis it was a three-day journey to Koloē and then another five days to the mother city (Greek: *metropolis*) called Axōmitēs, which is now called Aksum. The reference to Aksum as the mother city indicates that Adulis was located within a kingdom ruled from Aksum. The author explains that all the ivory (from elephants and rhinoceroses) from beyond the Nile is brought to Aksum and thence to Adulis.[40] Writing about twenty-five years later (ca. 77 CE) the Roman author

Pliny the Elder (who died in the eruption of Vesuvius in 79 CE) provided a much more ample list of exports from Adulis: ivory in large quantities, horns of the rhinoceros, hides of the hippopotamus, tortoise shell, sphingiæ (a kind of ape), and slaves.[41] This longer list probably testifies to an expansion of the export trade.

Immediately after describing Adulis, the author of the *Periplus* says that about 800 stades (south) there is another bay, and the ruler of these regions is Zōskalēs, a tough negotiator but nevertheless a fine person "well versed in reading and writing Greek." Yet 800 stades is about 144 kilometers, and although it is often stated that Zōskalēs was the king of Aksum, he may have been the monarch of a different kingdom.[42] On the basis that Zōskalēs was not a king of Aksum, the earliest king is known from the words inscribed in unvocalized Ge'ez on a copper-alloy object from about 200 CE: GDR, king of Aksum.[43] The names of other kings are known from inscriptions and coins.[44]

As the wealth of the Aksumite kingdom expanded into the second and third centuries CE, so too did its political ambitions. Various inscriptions reveal that Aksumite kings waged war against other peoples in Africa to their north and east and, from about 200 CE, in southern Arabia.[45] There is evidence that as early as 240 CE Aksum was a powerful state in a statement attributed to Mani: "There are four great kingdoms in the world: the first is that of Babylon and Persia; the second is the Roman Empire; the third is the kingdom of the Aksumites and the fourth is the kingdom of Sileos (?).'"[46] An inscription on a throne at Adulis from the second half of the third century CE reported by Cosmas in the sixth century CE shows Aksum to be very powerful in the region.[47] It records how an Aksumite king who revered Ares (so this was in the pre-Christian period) had conquered a long list of peoples on both sides of the Red Sea.[48] Much of the inscriptional evidence, however, relates to campaigns conducted by King Ezana in the early to mid-fourth century.[49]

In matters of religious practice and belief, Aksum had inherited a pantheon of deities from the earlier Ethio-Sabaean period. But it was also subject to Egyptian influences via Nubia, and it was aware of the Greek gods from the Greek merchants who traded among the Mediterranean, the Red Sea, and India.[50] Such of these gods as were official gods of the state are known from inscriptions in stone commissioned by Ethiopian kings, typically to celebrate victories over neighboring states.[51] Many of these inscriptions are trilingual: in Greek, (pseudo-)Sabaean, and Ge'ez. The principal state god of this pre-Christian period was the war god, known as Ares in Greek and Mahrem in Ge'ez. He was associated with the moon and is represented on coins and inscriptions by a horizontal crescent and, above it, a disc. This god, and as a god of the state, stretches back to the Sabaean period, where he was known as Almaqah, as discussed above. On the pre-Christian Aksumite coinage, as we will see below, the symbol of the crescent and the disk regularly appears above the king's head. Other important gods were Astar, Meder, and Beher, who appear to have been the gods of heaven, earth, and sea. On many Aksumite coins ears of wheat encircle the bust of the king, and in the pre-Christian period these probably represented Meder as god of the earth.[52]

Coins were minted by twenty Aksumite kings from about 290 to 640 CE, beginning with Endubis, who reigned from about 270 to 300 CE (see figure 1.6), and ending with Armah

Figure 1.6. *Coin of King Endubis*

(although the ordering of some of the kings is disputed). The ability of the Aksumite kings to mint coins is a testimony to their wealth and power for some 350 years.

This is quite a sophisticated coin. It shows the sign of the orb and the crescent at the top, now associated with the god Mahrem (previously Almaqah). It also has two wheat stalks emerging from the king's shoulders. The coin reads in Greek Endubis Basileus (King Endubis).

The coins minted by Ezana (reigned ca. 330–365) early in his reign continue the imagery of his predecessors' coinage. Thus, on one coin he is depicted wearing an arcaded tiara, holding a spear that interrupts the legend (Azanas Basileus, "Azanas the King"), while from shoulder level the bust is framed by two wheat sheaves and at the top of the coin is the well-established Aksumite image of a crescent within which is a disk (which may symbolize a planet).[53]

We will see in chapter 2 how the conversion of King Ezana to Christianity led to startling transformations in Aksumite coinage. But that forms part of the larger story of the coming of Christianity to Aksum, which meant moving away from religious practices and beliefs that had characterized the area we know as northern Ethiopia for roughly a thousand years. We now proceed to that subject.

PART TWO

THE HISTORY OF ORTHODOX ETHIOPIAN CHRISTIANITY

2

The Advent of Christianity in Ethiopia

The long history of Christianity in Ethiopia and the pervasive collective memories it has stimulated assume a starting point. It is impossible to know when the first Christian reached Ethiopia—those days in the form of Aksum—although we can surmise that the person in question was probably a Greek-speaking merchant engaged in trade around the Red Sea. Nevertheless, we do have information on the circumstances in which Ezana, the king of Aksum, became a Christian and then encouraged his people to follow him in the new faith, even if the conversion of the population beyond his family and court, from the old gods to the Christian triune God, did not occur overnight. How this happened is the subject of the present chapter of this volume, and we will see that the evidence comes from a mixture of Christian texts and Aksumite coins and inscriptions.

The Ancient Account of Saint Frumentius

The story begins with a certain Frumentius, as recorded in the *Ecclesiastical History* of Rufinus of Aquileia, a work written in Latin about 400 CE. Here is the relevant passage that, given its importance, is worth quoting in full:

> A certain philosopher, Metrodorus, is said to have penetrated Further India [sc. including Ethiopia][1] for the sake of inspecting places and examining the world. Inspired by his example, a certain Meropius, a philosopher from Tyre, wished to journey to India for a similar reason. He had with him two young boys, whose education he had taken in hand since they were relatives. The younger of them was called Edesius and the older Frumentius. Therefore when, having surveyed and brought to notice that by which his spirit was nourished, the philosopher had begun to return, the ship in which he was being conveyed put into a certain port for water or other necessities. It is the custom of the barbarians in those parts that if neighboring peoples announce that the treaty between themselves and the Romans has been broken, then all Romans who are found among them should be slain. The philosopher's ship was boarded and everyone, including the philosopher, was killed. The young boys, who were found under a tree studying and preparing their lessons, were spared by the mercy of the barbarians and led to the king. Of these he made one, that is, Edesius, his cupbearer. But Frumentius, whom he judged to be clever and prudent, he appointed his treasurer and secretary. As a result they were held in great honor and love by the king. Upon his death, the king appointed his wife, who had a young son, as heir of the kingdom. To the young men he gave the free faculty of doing whatever they wished. The queen, however, suppliantly prevailed upon them, as if she had no one more faithful in the whole kingdom, that they might share with her the worry of ruling the kingdom until her son had grown up—especially Frumentius, who was capable enough to manage the kingdom, while the other simply exhibited a pure faith and a sober mind.
>
> While they lived there and Frumentius had the control of the kingdom in his hands, God stirred up his mind and spirit so that he began unceasingly to inquire whether there were Christians among the Roman merchants. He gave them the greatest power and urged them to establish meeting places in various sites where they might come together for the sake of

prayer in the Roman rite. He himself did the same, but to a greater extent, and encouraged the others, alluring them with his favor and with benefits and undertaking whatever was opportune, supplying places for buildings and other necessary things and acting passionately in every respect so that the seed of Christians might grow there. But when the prince, for whom they were conducting the management of the kingdom, came of age, and they had completed and faithfully handed everything over, although the queen and her son greatly detained them and begged them to remain, they nevertheless returned once more to our world.

Edesius hastened to Tyre to meet again his parents and relatives. Frumentius proceeded to Alexandria saying it was not righteous to hide the work of the Lord. Therefore he explained everything that had happened to the bishop and advised him to provide some suitable worthy person to send as a bishop to the numerous Christians already in congregations and the churches built on barbarian soil. Then indeed Athanasius—for he had recently taken up the episcopate—when he had attentively and carefully weighed up what Frumentius had said and done, declared in the council of priests, "And what other man will we find of such a kind, in whom is the Spirit of God as in you yourself, who can thus accomplish this?" So when he had consecrated him as bishop, he bade him return with the Spirit of God from where he had come.

When he returned to India [sc. Ethiopia] as bishop, it is said that the God of virtue gave him so much grace that miracles like those of the apostles were worked through him and an immense number of pagans were converted to the faith. It was through him that in parts of India [sc. Ethiopia] both Christian peoples and churches were created and the episcopacy was begun. We learned these things that were done not by public rumor but through the account of Edesius himself, who had previously been the companion of Frumentius and who was later ordained a priest of Tyre.[2]

No literary document independent of this account exists to compare it with.[3] Because the name Aksum is not mentioned and "Further India" (India ulterior) is mentioned, some authors reject this account concerning Frumentius and suggest that Christianity did not reach Ethiopia before the fifth century CE.[4] This is an extreme and untenable view, given the evidence of the coinage and inscriptions of Ezana and a letter that survives from 356 CE that will be considered below. Moreover, Rufinus insists it is based on the firsthand account of Edesius and there is no good reason to doubt this.[5] It "is simply told and involves no incredible miracles or impossible situations,"[6] at least not in the period before the departure of Frumentius for Alexandria when Edesius was an eyewitness to what happened. Other factors support its reliability. The Tyrians were tireless traders and operated in the Red Sea, and it would have been easy for a philosopher like Meropius to embark on a voyage with them. Second, the existence and journey to the East of the philosopher Metrodorus, in whose footsteps Meropius was said to be following, has independent attestation in the Roman author Ammianus Marcellinus and the Byzantine historian Cedrenus.[7] Third, Rufinus lived in Jerusalem from 380 to 397 CE, and Edesius may still have been alive at that time and not far away, in Tyre, and could have come to one or more of the many religious festivals held in Jerusalem.

There is a homily in honor of Frumentius, in two Ge'ez manuscripts from the fourteenth century CE that appear to be based on Greek sources dependent on the account of Rufinus from the early fourth century CE, so that it could be a text composed in the Aksumite period, between the fourth and the seventh centuries CE.[8] In this document the Ethiopia is referred to as "the land of the Agāzi" (free men), a popular way for Ethiopians to describe themselves.[9] The king to whom the two boys are given is called Ella Allada, which brings us to the task of identifying that king and his son. In Ethiopian tradition St. Frumentius is also referred to as Abba Salama (Father Salama). He is also called Kasate Berhan (Revealer of Light).[10]

Dating the Events in Rufinus' Account of Frumentius

Unfortunately, Rufinus provides not a single date for the events he describes, the critical one being the year in which Frumentius was ordained by Athanasius and returned to Aksum. Yet he does situate this account "in the times of Constantine" (temporibus Constantini), who reigned from 306 to 337 CE.[11] Frumentius was ordained by Athanasius, who had himself been consecrated to the see of Alexandria "recently" (nuper), with this latter event occurring in 328 CE. Some scholars date the elevation of Frumentius to 329–330 CE. The difficulty with this view is that there is independent evidence as to the date of the return of Metrodorus from his travels to the East: the twenty-first year of the reign of Constantine, that is, 324 CE.[12] Assuming that Meropius set out on his voyage soon afterward, say in 325 CE, we need to assume that Frumentius and Edesius were in Aksum for at least ten years to accord with the data.[13] This in turn means that Athanasius would have consecrated Frumentius as bishop in circa 335 CE, seven years after his own elevation. For some scholars such an elevation could not be said to have occurred "recently." However, in the context of Athanasius' episcopacy lasting forty-five years (328–373 CE), it is not such a stretch to describe his episcopal consecration as "recent" with respect to an event that occurred only seven years into such a long term in office. Another advantage of this date is that it allows time for Frumentius to return to Aksum and become involved in the activities attributed to him by Rufinus, so that the entirety of the events he records fits within "the times of Constantine."[14] It also accords with the fact that we know from other sources that Athanasius was in Alexandria from June 8, 328, to July 11, 335.[15] It should be noted that the patriarch of Alexandria continued to appoint the bishop for Ethiopia, with a few interruptions, until 1959. To conclude, therefore, Frumentius is likely to have returned to Aksum as its first bishop in about 335 CE.

Identifying the Kings in Rufinus' Account of Frumentius

Although the chronology in the Rufinus narrative is not very precise, independent corroboration of some of its important details exists in another source. This is the letter that Emperor Constantius II (who reigned from 337 to 361 CE) sent to two leading figures in Aksum, Aizanas, and Sazanas. The letter survives in a work by Athanasius (the *Defense to Constantius*), who was then in flight from Constantius. This emperor favored Arianism and had replaced Athanasius as bishop of Alexandria with George of Cappadocia on February 24, 357 CE. The letter could not have been written much after the deposition of Athanasius, so 357 CE is the likely date.[16] Athanasius summarizes the content of the letter and then quotes the text a little later.[17]

In this letter Constantius asks Aizanas and Sazanas to send "your bishop Frumentius" to Bishop George and the other bishops of Egypt. Constantius explains that the reason for this was that Frumentius had been elevated to the episcopacy by Athanasius, a man charged with many crimes. They were to examine Frumentius, and, if he proved satisfactory, he would receive investiture from them. Aksum (Auxoumin) is mentioned as the name of the kingdom. The Aksumite leaders are not explicitly described as Christian, yet the fact that Constantius assumes Christian doctrine is of concern to them may carry this implication. It is not clear, however, whether Christianity is the official religion of Aksum or just firmly implanted there.[18] Since Rufinus does not cite this letter in talking about either Frumentius or Constantius II, he was probably unaware of it. Thus, it represents an independent historical source, and its significance in this respect lies in its agreement with Rufinus that Frumentius was consecrated bishop of Aksum by Athanasius.[19] Yet it is also illuminating on two points that Rufinus does not specify in his account. First, it confirms that the kingdom for which Frumentius was ordained bishop was indeed Aksum; this carries the further consequence that the port where Meropius was killed was probably Adulis.[20] Second, it provides the names "Aizanas and Sazanas" as the leaders of that realm. Is this Aizanas to be identified with Ezana (known from Aksumite coins) and to be none other than the son who had grown to become king while Frumentius was helping the queen manage the kingdom? At no point does Constantius' letter refer to the title or function of the pair, except in the farewell where Constantius describes them as "most honored brothers." Nevertheless, Athanasius refers to them as rulers (*turannoi*) in his summary of the letter and in his brief introduction to it.[21] How is this to be explained?

The account in Rufinus speaks of only one king (that is, at the time Frumentius left Aksum for Alexandria), and he is not named. The letter from Constantius of 357 CE is addressed to two named persons, but as noted above their precise roles are not mentioned. What was the status of Aizanas and Sazanas? Some scholars believe that the throne of Aksum was sometimes shared between two rulers, and, if so, Sazanas was a joint king. In Ethiopian legend there are two figures named Abreha and Asbeha, who are mentioned in king lists as brothers who adopted Christianity under the influence of St. Frumentius around 333 CE. These seem to be a legendary reflection of Aizanas and Sazanas, although Ethiopian histories in Ge'ez do not know the name Aizanas/Ezana.[22]

Robin poses the interesting argument that Edesius (Rufinus' source) returned to Tyre when there was only one king and did not have knowledge of the later period, when there were two kings. Robin further suggests that when Frumentius returned from Alexandria, where he had been made a bishop, he discovered that the king had taken a coruler and that both had embraced Christianity.[23] Although it is possible that the king had a colleague when he returned, it is equally possible that this happened some time later. But Phillipson has warned against the view that Aizanas and Sazanas were brothers and has suggested that Sazanas may have been one of Ezana's military commanders.[24] This view is rather hard to square with the fact that in one of his inscriptions "Aeizanas" names "Saiazanana" and Adefan as his two brothers whom he sent off to fight a rebellious people.[25] However, if any Aksumite coins were issued in the name of Aizanas and Sazanas, none have survived. This is a rather telling absence and suggests that while Ezana did have brothers, one of whom was named Saiazana, he reigned as king on his own.

Yet not much turns on the nature of Aizanas' relationship with Sazanas. What really matters is that Aizanas is almost certainly to be identified with Ezana, since there are extant inscriptions referring to this person (as we know from his possessing the same patronymic and hometown) in which his name is sometimes spelled Ezana and sometimes Aizanas or Azanas.[26] The coins are also decisive, in that we can confidently deduce from Ezana's coin types, with their transition from non-Christian to Christian images (see below), that it was during his kingship that Christianity began its journey to preeminence in Aksum.

Since from a numismatic point of view the king preceding Ezana was Ousanas, we can be reasonably sure that this was Ezana's father and the king to whom Frumentius and Edesius were brought after the murder of their companions. In Ethiopian tradition the king to whom the two boys were brought is called Ella Allada or Ella A'eda, so this figure is to be identified with Ousanas.[27] Scholars have further identified Ousanas with Ella Amida, a patronymic of Ezana known from inscriptions.[28] Furthermore, one of Ezana's coins states that he was the "son of Ella Amida."[29]

Frumentius' Activities in Aksum

But how was Christianity fostered under Frumentius? We need to distinguish two periods, the first being his initial time in Aksum and the second when he returned as its bishop. As for the first period, it is likely that the rapid rise of Frumentius in the king's service was predicated upon his ability to speak and write Greek, the language of trade and of political relations.[30] Greek was regularly used in Aksumite inscriptions, as we saw in chapter 1, and coinage in Greek would have greatly facilitated use of the coinage by traders moving between the Mediterranean and the Red Sea, and even farther afield, to India and Sri Lanka in the East.

Rufinus' account indicates that Frumentius' initial activities were restricted to enabling (probably Greek-speaking) merchants of the Roman Empire, who were no doubt already Christian and living in Aksum to facilitate their trading activities, to practice their religion, especially by constructing churches, certainly in Aksum but probably also in Adulis. It is likely, however, that these congregations of merchants, with the official protection of the state in the guise of young Frumentius, very quickly became the Christian cells from which evangelization began among the local population.[31] At the time that Frumentius and Edesius left Aksum, they stood very high in the regard of the new king and the queen, who earnestly beseeched them to stay, so it is likely that no impediment was imposed on the Christian cells that they had encouraged.

In relation to the second period, Rufinus could not have been indebted to Edesius for the material in his account after the return of Frumentius to Aksum. Instead Rufinus writes an account that depicts Frumentius as a latter-day apostle, working signs and wonders, and making numerous converts.[32] Yet we can make some reasonable assumptions about the return of Frumentius. First, even on a personal level, the king and his mother would have been very happy to see him back. Second, they would have welcomed his return because of his knowledge of the affairs of the kingdom. Even though now a bishop with significant responsibilities, he would have been able to offer them counsel and advice. It is very difficult to envisage him as anything other than a frequent visitor to, even member of, the royal court, just as the *abunas*, Ethiopia's bishops in later centuries, would spend much of their time at court, even in its form as an encampment of tents that moved around the country. Aksum's bishop would have been too important a figure for the king not to have had ready access to him.

But what of Ezana and Christianity? We must first consider evidence that he converted and then assess what role Frumentius may have had in this process.

Evidence for the Conversion of King Ezana to Christianity

A number of inscriptions on coins that King Ezana had minted and inscriptions he ordered to be erected following successful military campaigns afford us an unexpectedly nuanced picture of the process by which, under his rule, Aksum became Christian. The reason these sources are so revealing is that they allow us to compare his views before and after he became Christian and to see what steps he took to make the new religion acceptable to his people. Let us begin with his coinage.

Ezana's Christian Coinage

In chapter 1 I mentioned coinage of Ezana that was essentially the same that of as his non-Christian predecessors. Of utmost importance is that in the period 330–350 CE, during the reign of King Ezana (ca. 330–365), there is a transition on the coinage from pagan symbols such as crescents, disks, and stalks to crosses. Now a Greek cross replaces the crescent and disk symbol and appears at the top and bottom, and on both sides of the coin. This most probably reflects the conversion of the Aksumite dynasty to Christianity.[33] An example of this type of coin from a later king, Ebana, in the fifth century CE (figure 2.1), shows the crosses at the top, bottom, and on both sides of the coin, with the king still enclosed with staffs of wheat.

Figure 2.1. *Gold coin of King Ebana, fifth century CE*

There is a very interesting type of coin, for which the identification of the king(s) is obscure, but where

> conceivably the earliest issues date to his [sc. Ezana's] reign. This has a fairly simple bust of the king on the obverse and is accompanied by a large Greek cross right in the middle of reverse, surrounded by the legend in Greek: *Touto arestē tē chōra*, meaning "May this be pleasing to the country."[34]

This looks very like a recommendation to the Aksumite people, or one part of it (see below), of a faith that was new to it.

Ezana's Inscriptions

Ezana's surviving pre-conversion inscriptions celebrate in detail three different military campaigns. Unlike Greek and Roman inscriptions, none of them contains any indication of the year in which the campaigns took place. His actions against the Agwezat and Tsarane are each recorded in one inscription, and in both cases the language used is Ge'ez.[35] At the start of the Agwezat inscription, the king is described as "the son of the invincible Mahrem," who was a god of war, like Ares and Mars. The beginning of the inscription describing the Tsarane campaign also states that the king is "the son of the invincible Mahrem." At the end of this account, Ezana states that he raised a throne and put it under the protection of three other gods, Astar, Beher, and Meder. As we saw in the previous chapter, Astar was associated with Zeus (for the sky). Beher was the god of the sea (roughly equivalent to Poseidon), and Meder (or Medr) was the god of the earth.[36] The inscription concludes with his making a thank offering to Mahrem. He was a war god, associated with Ares, and viewed as the royal or dynastic god, father of the king, and the god who protected him from danger.[37] His campaign against the Beja is more interesting since inscriptions describing it are extant in Ge'ez and in Greek. Presumably this was to maximize the reach of his communication. Native Aksumites who spoke Ge'ez, Ezana's own people, in other words, could access the version in that language, while Greek-speaking merchants, diplomats, or travelers visiting Aksum could read the Greek account, thus spreading knowledge of the king's triumph far and wide. As Munro-Hay notes, the Greek and Ge'ez versions are more or less the same in content.[38] Ezana again claims sonship of Ares (Greek version) / Mahrem (Ge'ez version) at the outset and at the end notes that they (meaning him and his two brothers, Saiazana and Adefan) have raised statues in his honor.

Very different, however, are the inscriptions relating to Ezana's campaign against the Noba (the Nubians), which must be dated to after he had become a Christian. Here we have some long versions in Ge'ez and a shorter (and it is not fully extant) one in Greek.[39] Here are the opening six lines from a Ge'ez version:

> By the might of the lord of heaven who in the sky and on earth holds power over all beings, I, Ezana, son of Ella Amida, Bisi Halen, king of Aksum, Himyar, Raydan, Saba, Salhin, Tsiyamo, Beja and of Kasu, king of kings, son of Ella Amida, never defeated by the enemy. May the might of the Lord of heaven, who has made me king, who reigns for all eternity, invincible, cause that no enemy can resist me, that no enemy may follow me! By the might of the Lord of All I campaigned against the Noba when the Noba peoples revolted.[40]

After this come another thirty-seven lines, containing a highly detailed account of the campaign. On two occasions in this narrative, he attributes his success to the might of the Lord of the Land (lines 14 and 33) and once mentions what the Lord of Heaven has given him (lines 40–41). The inscription ends as follows:

> And I set up a throne in Shado here by the might of the Lord of Heaven who has helped me and given me kingship. May the Lord of Heaven reinforce my kingship. As he has now defeated my enemies for me, may he continue to do so wherever I go. As he has now conquered for me, and has submitted my enemies to me, I wish to reign in justice and equity, without doing any injustice to my peoples. (lines 44–48)

He then says that he puts "this throne" that he has raised "under the protection of the Lord of Heaven, who has made me king, and that of the Earth [*medr*] which bears it" (lines 48–50). After invoking a curse on anyone who defaces the inscription, he concludes, "and I have raised this throne by the power of the Lord of Heaven" (lines 51–52).[41]

The Greek version, which is only extant for the first thirty-two lines, is remarkably different.[42] It begins:

> With faith in God and by the power of the Father, son and Holy Spirit, who saved the kingdom for me, with the faith in his son Jesus Christ, who has helped me and will always help me, I, Azanas, king of the Aksumites, and Himyarites, and Reeidan and of the Sabaeans and of Sileel and of Khaso and of the Beja and of Tiamo, Bisi Alene, son of Ella Amida, servant of Christ, thank the Lord my God. (lines 1–11; author's translation)

How are we to explain the intriguing differences between the Ge'ez and the Greek versions, especially the sudden appearance of Trinitarian language in the latter? One easy solution would be that there were actually two campaigns against the Noba, with the first occurring before Ezana had become a Christian and the second afterward. But this does not seem likely. Although we lack the balance of the Greek inscription where the details of the campaign would have been inscribed and the extant part does not precisely repeat the actions taken against the Noba, there is one major similarity suggesting that they relate to the same military operation: in both cases mention is made of the Noba oppressing the Mangurto, Hasa, and Barya peoples.[43] It is hard to credit that the Noba, having been crushed by the Aksumite for oppressing these peoples, would have repeated the offense, only to be defeated again.[44]

The solution appears to be that the Ge'ez text is a work of propaganda for internal use, whereas the Greek version presents Ezana in a different light. The Greek version focuses on the cry for help by the peoples being oppressed by the Nubians and the king's response. This is the image that Ezana wants to present to Greek-speaking merchants and to envoys and visitors from Byzantium, an audience that may also explain the lack of the phrase "king of kings" in this version.[45]

Yet it is the religious dimension to the differences between the two versions that matters here, since it opens up interesting vistas on the Christianization of Ethiopia. The critical question is why, in the Ge'ez version, does Ezana refer to "the Lord of Heaven," or "the Lord of the Land," or "the Lord of All," a lord who holds power over all beings in the sky and on earth? One answer, noting that the religious tenor of the Ge'ez inscription is monotheistic, connects its religiosity with a form of monotheism that was widespread in Himyar during the fourth century CE.[46] Himyar was located in the southwestern corner of Arabia, facing Aksum across the Red Sea and frequently claimed by Aksumite kings, such as Ezana himself (as above). Nevertheless, there is good reason to doubt such a connection. If this Himyarite monotheism is what motivated Ezana in the language of the inscription, why did he use different expressions, referring to the specific gods—Mahrem, Astar, Beher, and Meder—in other inscriptions, such as those recording his campaigns against the Agwezat and Tsarane discussed above.

More convincing, therefore, is the suggestion that these expressions in the Noba inscription in Ge'ez are indeed monotheistic and yet stand in relationship with Aksumite paganism. To speak of "the Lord of Heaven" evokes Astar and the "Lord of the Land" evokes Meder, while "the Lord of All" reminds the Ethiopians that these are but manifestations of the power of the one Lord. The strategy is the cautious one of leading them from polytheism to monotheism by reassuring them that the one God whom they must now acknowledge contains all the dimensions of the individual gods that they previously acknowledged. The approach is not entirely unlike that adopted by Paul in his Areopagus speech in Acts 17. It illustrates "how the sacred symbols of traditional culture may be used to facilitate radical innovation."[47]

Ezana's Conversion

The fact that Ezana reigned for a period before converting to Christianity raises the question of what role, if any, Frumentius played in this process and when. The Rufinus account has Frumentius and Edesius leaving Aksum almost as soon as Ezana came of age, that is, on his accession to the kingship. The inscriptions mentioned above of his campaigns against the Agwezat and Tsarane mean that he cannot have been a Christian at the time of Frumentius' departure for Alexandria. Frumentius' assistance of Christian merchants in Aksum cannot have been enough to sway the king. His conversion came later. Perhaps Frumentius had more of an impact on Ezana after his return from Alexandria, with his enhanced status as a bishop. If in later centuries (as we will see in chapter 3) a Jesuit at the imperial court was able to persuade an emperor to become a Roman Catholic, it is not too much a stretch to attribute the same powers of persuasion to Frumentius. But while one can imagine Ezana's immediate family and, perhaps, his courtiers becoming Christians along with the king, the wider population would have needed time and persuasion to reach the same view. This explains the care he takes in the Ge'ez version of the Noba inscription not to parade his newfound Trinitarian belief in Father, Son, and Holy Spirit but to begin talking about God in ways that were not offensive to Christianity but were yet connected with traditional Aksumite religious beliefs. One wonders whether it was Frumentius himself who had the cultural sensitivity to advise the king to adopt this approach. The coin mentioned above carrying an image of the cross and the legend "May this be pleasing to the country" may represent a further sign of Ezana's caution, for the legend is in Greek and not in Ge'ez. Was the message aimed more at a Greek-speaking elite in the country than at the general population? While the subsequent course of history suggests that Aksum became thoroughly Christianized, it is not possible to track its progress in the period of Ezana's reign and that of the kings immediately after him. Nevertheless, from toward the end of the fifth century CE we have signs of a significant effort to spread Christianity throughout the kingdom, and that suggests that the process of its Christianization was not yet complete. That effort involved the Nine Saints, who lead us into the next chapter.

3

Fifth to Seventeenth Centuries

The Period from King Ezana to King Kaleb

The letter of Emperor Constantius II mentioned in chapter 2, written in around 357 CE, proves that Ezana was still on the throne at that date. Yet the date of Ezana's death is unknown, and few sources exist for the history of Aksum in the period between his reign and that of King Kaleb, who reigned in the early sixth century CE. Yet the kings of this period continued to mint coins, so trade was still occurring, no doubt centered on exports to and imports from ports on the Red Sea, like Adulis. The kings whose names appear on these coins between Ezana and Kaleb (and some kings from this period have not left identifiable coinage), in the order in which they reigned (which can be deduced with reasonable certainty from the changing physical characteristics and appearance of the coins), are as follows: Ouazebas, Eon, Mehadeyis, Ebana, Nezana, Nezool, Ousas, and Ousanas.[1] The coinage of all of these kings contains at least one cross, thus demonstrating their Christian faith. One of them, Mehadeyis, issued coins that, most unusually, copied (on the reverse) a statue of Victory holding a

Greek cross modeled on a Byzantine coin (for example, as issued by Theodosius II in ca. 422 CE) with a legend in Ge'ez reading, "By this cross he will conquer" (which is very similar to Constantine's famous motto: *In hoc signo vinces*, "By this sign you will conquer," in that case referring to the Chi-Rho sign for Christ). Mehadeyis was thus a king who took his Christianity very seriously. Yet maybe he had good reason to celebrate the cross in this way, since on the obverse of these coins he is described, in Ge'ez, as "The victorious king Mehadeyis."[2] On some coins minted by King Nezana appear, in Greek, the words "Thanks be to God," sometimes accompanied by a picture of the king and sometimes by a Greek cross.[3] Kings Nezool, Ousas, and Ousanas also issued coins with their image surrounded by the Greek for "Thanks be to God."[4] Ousanas issued coins with the legend, around his image, containing the Greek for "By the grace of God."[5] The devotion to Christianity that would generally typify the emperors of whom we have knowledge later in Ethiopia's history was thus inaugurated and maintained in the very earliest period of the faith.

In the early sixth century Ethiopia produced an impressive king mentioned in inscriptions, coins and some historical sources. His name, according to an inscription in Ge'ez, was "Kaleb, Ella Atsbeha, son of Tazena [or Thezena], a man LZN, king of Aksum, Himyar, Raydan, etc."[6] "Ella Atsbeha," also called "Ella Asbeha," is the thronename, that is—in line with standard Ethiopian royal practice before and after him—the name he took on his accession as king, in this case meaning "the one who brought about the morning," or "the one who collected tribute."[7] In this same inscription Kaleb revealed the strength of his Christian faith when he declared:

> The Lord strong and brave, the Lord mighty in battle. By the power of the Lord and by the grace of Jesus Christ, the son of the Lord, the victorious, in whom I believe, who has given me a strong kingdom by which I dominate my enemies and trample underfoot the head of my adversaries, who has guarded me since infancy and established me on the throne of my fathers . . . I trust myself to Christ so that all my enterprises

succeed, and that I may be saved by him who pleases my soul. With the help of the Trinity, the Father, Son, and Holy Spirit.[8]

Given Kaleb's Christian piety, it is not surprising that Justin I (the Eastern Roman emperor from 518 to 527 CE) turned to him for help in ending the persecution and slaughter of Christians in the town of Najran by Du Nawas, a Jewish convert who was the king of Himyar (in modern-day Yemen) sometime around 524/525 CE. This formed part of the ongoing struggle between the Byzantine Empire and the Sassanians for control of the sea route to India via the Red Sea. The Aksumite army, having crossed the Red Sea with Byzantine help, landed in Yemen, where it defeated and executed Du Nawas. Thereafter, the army Christianized the country. Kaleb rebuilt the churches in the country that Du Nawas had destroyed, then returned to Aksum and abdicated. According to some sources he wanted to end his life next to his monastic mentor, Zonainos, who may well be one and the same as Abba Pantalewon in Ethiopian hagiography, who lived in a cell on a hill to the northeast of Aksum. Ethiopian tradition holds that the Emperor Kaleb had visited Abba Pantalewon before leaving Aksum to take action against the persecution of Christians in Yemen. This cell was to form the kernel of the monastery of Abba Pantalewon established on that site. Kaleb is recognized as a saint by the Ethiopian Orthodox Church. He had two sons, Israel and Gabra Masqal.[9] Kaleb exemplifies what became a dominant feature of Ethiopian kings, namely, their sense of responsibility for the continuance and health of the Christian faith, which we will see at many points in the subsequent history.

Valuable information on Aksum and Aksumite Christianity during Kaleb's reign in the early part of the sixth century CE is found in the *Christian Topography* of Cosmas Indicopleustes. Cosmas flourished in the reign of the Emperor Justinian (527–565), and he must have written the book in about 547 CE. Cosmas was most probably a native of Alexandria. In his earlier life he had been a merchant. His commercial pursuits carried him across seas and into countries far away from his home. Thus he tells us that he had sailed on the Mediterranean, the Red Sea, and the Persian Gulf, as far as India and Ceylon ("Indicopleustes" means "voyager to India").[10] One of the most interesting parts of the book is his description of Ethiopia, especially his account of a biennial expedition by the Aksumite kingdom to exchange oxen, salt, and iron for gold.[11] More importantly, in this work Cosmas also provides evidence that by the beginning of the sixth century CE Christianity had made tremendous progress in Ethiopia. He records that in many places across what we now call the Near East, including Aksum and all its environs, "there are everywhere churches of the Christians, and bishops, martyrs, monks and recluses [sc. hermits], where the Gospel of Christ is proclaimed."[12] Of considerable historical significance is that Cosmas records that he was actually in Adulis for the campaign mentioned above, when Kaleb was preparing his forces for the war against Du Nawas ("the Homerites") and (with the help of another merchant) drafted for the governor of Adulis (on the ultimate instruction of Kaleb) a copy of a Greek inscription then extant there.[13]

The Nine Saints and the Sadeqan

The conversion of King Ezana by Frumentius probably did not entail the Christianization of the whole country. Christianity may have been restricted initially to members of the royal court and foreign merchants and their households. The original clerics were foreign, and Greek was probably the major language used. While there must have been some permeation of Christianity into the wider community, especially given the fact that the kings themselves were Christian, a major impetus for conversion in the kingdom of Aksum came toward the end of the fifth century with the arrival of the missionaries, first, the so-called Nine Saints, and, second, a much less attested group called the Sadeqan (Righteous). At this time Aksum was still a large and powerful state. The arrival of the Nine Saints seems to have corresponded to the reigns of kings such as Ella Amida, Tazena, Kaleb, and Gabra

Masqal. The names of the Nine Saints were Abba Afse, Abba Alef, Abba Aragawi (also known as Za-Mikael), Abba Garima (also known as Isaac), Abba Guba, Abba Liqanos, Abba Pantalewon, Abba Sehma, and Abba Yemata.[14] Of these the most famous were Aragawi, Garima, and Pantalewon. Ethiopian churches frequently contain paintings of the Nine Saints (see figure 3.1).

It is possible that these figures came to Ethiopia to escape the anti-miaphysite persecutions conducted in the Byzantine Empire after the Council of Chalcedon 451 CE.[15] More specifically, they may have been reacting against the promulgation of the Henotikon, that is, the "Edict of unity" aimed at reconciling Chalcedonians and miaphysites and issued by the Byzantine emperor Zeno in 482 CE.[16] At least some of them seem to have come from Syria. Otherwise, it is difficult to explain the presence of so many

Figure 3.1. *Painting of the Nine Saints in the Arbat Ensesa Church in Aksum*
From left to right: (Abba) Yemata, Afes, Guba, Liqanos, Pantalewon, Aragawi, Alef, Garima, and Sehma. Arbat Ensesa means "four animals," and the reference is to the four animals of the Apocalypse.

Syriac loan words for important theological concepts in Ethiopian Orthodoxy. Also much of the church in Syria and Egypt refused to accept the Chalcedonian formulation of Christ's nature.[17] Whereas before their arrival the effective sphere of influence of Christianity was probably restricted to the narrow corridor along the caravan route between Aksum and the port of Adulis, the Nine Saints radically expanded the zone of Christianization by establishing monasteries in a much wider area. Abba Alef founded a monastery at Bi'isa in the North, overlooking the Marab River. Yemata went south and established a monastery at Garalta. Closer to the center of the kingdom, Liqanos and Pantalewon built monasteries near Aksum, Aragawi at Dabra Damo, Garima north of Adwa, and Afse at Yeha.[18]

Aragawi was a disciple of the Coptic abbot Pachomius (ca. 292–348), who had been the first to found monasteries in Egypt.[19] The monastic life had been inaugurated by St. Anthony (251–356 CE), but he had lived alone, as did many of those who were inspired by him, in what is called the "eremitic" lifestyle, that is, the life of a hermit, from the Greek word *eremos*, meaning "desert." The communal lifestyle initiated later by Pachomius is called, by way of contrast, "cenobitic," from Greek words meaning "a common life." Unlike European monasteries of a later period, where large buildings housed the monks and contained rooms for other purposes, Pachomius favored a collection of smaller buildings. Aragawi and the other founders of monasteries in Ethiopia followed this pattern. This arrangement persists today, with Ethiopian monasteries usually being located in a walled compound, with the centerpiece a round church and a collection of smaller buildings, some of them huts, in which the monks sleep and eat and perform other functions (such as copying manuscripts). The monastic compounds usually contain many trees and are characterized by a sense of peace and natural beauty. Often the monasteries are located in very inaccessible places, as with Aragawi's at Dabra Damo, which is still in operation and which can be reached only by rope (figure 3.2). The church Aragawi built there (see figure 6.3) is probably the oldest

Figure 3.2. *The hill (amba) on which is built the monastery of Dabra Damo*

example of Christian architecture in Ethiopia, having survived Muslim invasion and Italian colonization.

Thus were established vital centers of Christian learning and outreach deep in the interior of Ethiopia. It is highly likely that among the first things the Nine Saints did in these places was to translate the Bible and other works into Ge'ez so that the local people could understand them. Soon local people were entering these monastic communities and becoming educated for service in the church. Some established schools for children in parishes, a process encouraged by the Aksumite kings, with royal support strengthening the economic position of the church.[20]

Although many miracles are attributed to the Nine Saints, one attributed to Garima deserves close attention: he copied (or perhaps translated) the Gospels with the help of angels. This is one of a number or indications that one or more of the Nine Saints worked on translating Greek texts (such as the New Testament) from Greek into Ge'ez. The Nine Saints, since they largely came from the Greco-Roman East, would certainly have known Greek.

However, the presence of scriptural citations in Ethiopian inscriptions prior to their time and the fact that Greek was known in Aksum (especially, one imagines, among merchants and traders) suggests that some translation at least must have occurred in the 150 years or so between the episcopate of Frumentius and their arrival. Nevertheless, the monastery of Garima, not far from Adwa in northern Ethiopia, is celebrated as possessing the oldest manuscripts in Ethiopia, notably the three Garima Gospel books, two of which appear to date from the sixth or seventh centuries CE. As such they are the only surviving examples of Christian parchment in Ethiopia from the Aksumite period.[21] I will return to the Garima Gospels in chapters 5 and 6.

The second group, the Sadeqan, was reputed to be a group of Byzantine monks who initially lived for a year in Aksum and then split into smaller groups and scattered around the highlands. Ethiopian tradition identifies these small groups in relation to the places in which they settled: Bakaknaha, Kadih, Hawzen Qahen, and Dagwe.[22]

The Decline of Aksum and the Ethiopian Dark Age

The decline of Aksum appears to have begun with the loss of its possessions in Yemen at the end of the sixth century CE when Persia occupied southern Arabia and brought Christian rule there to an end. The Persians also disrupted the trade routes across the Red Sea that were so central to the prosperity of Aksum. Yet Persian hegemony in this region soon collapsed with the rise of nascent Islam. There are Muslim traditions that relations between Muhammad and the Aksumite king were friendly, with the latter having offered refuge to some early converts to Islam. But this situation could not last. Hostilities may even have commenced between the Muslims and Aksumites before the prophet's death in 632 CE. Initial Aksumite successes in naval encounters fairly quickly gave way to expanding Muslim expertise in maritime warfare. The Muslims had soon conquered all of Arabia and north Africa, thus greatly restricting Ethiopian contacts with its spiritual source in the Patriarchate of Alexandria and with the Byzantine Empire. Indeed in the early 700s the Muslims occupied the Dahlak islands in the Red Sea, which had previously served as a base for Aksumite invasions of southern Arabia. Although Aksum continued to engage in some skirmishes at sea as late as 770 CE, by about the middle of the eighth century, the Muslims had taken control of the Red Sea and its maritime trade. Not surprisingly, it was at about this time that Aksum stopped minting coins. Ethiopia was compelled to retire to its mountainous plateau and turn in upon itself. Its long isolation from the rest of the world had begun.[23]

Yet the Christian kingdom did not disappear. Although documentation is sparse, it is clear that from its heartland in the North, in southern Tigray and Angot, the kingdom began to expand southward, into the central and southern parts of the highlands, toward Amhara, Lasta, and Shoa. This expansion was a feature of the ninth century and continued into the tenth, reaching even into the valleys of the Awash and Omo Rivers. While by the early tenth century the Ethiopians had recaptured part of the coastal strip and the Dahlak islands, the concentration of the kingdom in the extensive mountain massif gave the people a geographical unity and identity that had not characterized the Aksumite empire with its extensions into Yemen. Arab writers of the period paint a picture of the Habasha (who became Abyssinians in European languages) controlling a large and impressive state. This expansion, however, was severely checked toward the end of the tenth century by the actions of a queen of the Bani al-Hamawiyah, in the Agaw region, who led her people against the Christians. She seems to have taken over much of the country. The crisis seems to have been resolved eventually by a strong revival of Christianity, stimulated by the arrival from Alexandria of the new abuna (sc. patriarch), named Danel, and consolidated in the conversion of the peoples of Agaw to miaphysite Christianity. Yet even then the Ethiopians were apparently unable to return its southern dominions to their control.[24]

Around this time another serious threat began to manifest—the tenth to twelfth centuries witnessed serious Muslim encroachment along the coastal plains to the east and southeast (including the Dahlak Archipelago and the Danakil and Somali coasts), but also in the north and in the west. The Fatimid dynasty achieved absolute power in Egypt in 969 CE, making Cairo the capital of the caliphate. The Fatimids became an extremely powerful force with a strong interest in the Red Sea littoral, and this inevitably meant increased Muslim pressure on Ethiopia. In addition, Muslim traders operated freely across the Christian kingdom, eventually replacing Byzantine merchants. In particular, one of the primary means of Muslim expansion was through the slave trade. The traders set up bridgeheads deep in the interior of the country, and these became the basis for the establishment of small states and sultanates. The spread of Islam was aided by the number of people who converted to the faith as a means of avoiding enslavement. Particularly significant as a threat to Ethiopia was the establishment of the sultanate of Ifat under the Walasma dynasty on the southeastern edges of the Shoan plateau.[25] And yet, while the twelfth century witnessed active Muslim proselytization in southern Ethiopia, it was also a time that was notable for a revival of the Christian kingdom in the North.

The Zagwe Dynasty (1137–1270)

The period from 1137 to 1270 is regarded in Orthodox tradition and memory as a period when control of the Christian kingdom was usurped by kings with no legitimate claim to the throne—this was the Zagwe dynasty. Some favor an earlier date for the start of this dynasty, perhaps in the tenth century, but the evidence for this is debatable. Much Ethiopian tradition treats this dynasty as an unfortunate interruption of the legitimate line of succession, represented in Delna'od, the last king before the start of the Zagwe dynasty in 1137 and the commencement of the Solomonic dynasty in the form of Yekunno Amlak in 1270. Much of the hostility toward the Zagwe kings seems to stem largely from the fact that they were culturally different in not speaking a Semitic language. The Zagwe kings were from the Agaw people who spoke a Cushitic language called Agawigna. The name Zagwe means "who (are) of the Agaw" in Ge'ez. The Agaw were concentrated in the regions of Lasta and Wag, from where they derived most of their support. The Zagwe kings came, in particular, from the region of Bugna. However, certain initiatives taken by these kings did much to shape subsequent Orthodox identity in the country. Indeed, their advent led to a revival of the fortunes of the Christian kingdom in the late twelfth century. Three of the Zagwe kings (including Lalibela) were later canonized by the Ethiopian Church.

Very little historical evidence remains of the first two Zagwe kings. More is known of the third king, Yimreha Krestos, who took a step that resulted in this dynasty leaving a priceless architectural legacy to Ethiopian Orthodoxy—he inaugurated the tradition of building churches hewn from living rock. Yimehra was also important in other ways. He appears to have revived strong connections between Ethiopia and Egypt, with the Ethiopian *Life* of this king even recording that he asked the caliph in Egypt to send him the wooden door in his hall made from cedar of Lebanon so that Yimreha could use it in the construction of a church. A number of foreign ecclesiastics came to Ethiopia during his reign and remained there after his death. Even more significantly, the number of Ethiopian pilgrims to the Holy Land also appears to have increased, with Salah ad-Din (Saladin in the West, who took Jerusalem from the crusader kingdom in 1187) alleged to have given Ethiopians many of the sites in the city.[26]

The most famous of the Zagwe kings was Lalibela, who reigned during the late thirteenth and early fourteenth centuries. He had a brother, Harbay, who preceded him on the throne.[27] Lalibela's name has a traditional etymology: one day his mother saw her child surrounded by a swarm of bees, but they did not harm her baby. So she called him Lalibela, in Agaw meaning "the bees obey him."[28] Written sources reveal his role in establishing the collection of churches that now bear his name. There is also a wooden *manbar* (throne) in the church Medhane Alam in Lalibela inscribed with his and his wife's names, clearly demonstrating his link to these churches. According to an Ethiopian source known as the *Acts of Lalibela*, God revealed his plan for the site in a dream and commanded him to build a replica of Jerusalem in the place where he was born. This legend is reflected toponymically in a number of place-names at the site: a watercourse called the Jordan (complete with a spot commemorating the baptism of Christ), a Mount of Olives, and a Golgotha. Ethiopian tradition connects the erection of this New Jerusalem with the fall of Jerusalem in 1187.[29] We will return to the churches in Lalibela in chapter 5. At one point the Zagwe kings had moved their capital to Adafa, in the security of the mountains of Lasta. Later Adafa was renamed Lalibela in honor of this king.

The Zagwe dynasty came to an end in 1270 when their last representative, Yetbarak, was defeated and killed by the forces of Yekunno Amlak, a young Amhara prince claiming descent from the royal house of Aksum. Yetbarak had taken refuge in the Church of St. Qirqos, the patron saint of his dynasty, in Gayant, on the northern shore of the Basalo River. There he was captured and killed.

In Ethiopia it is believed that the "restoration" of the Solomonic dynasty was due in large part to the efforts of the important national saint, Takla Haymanot, who managed to persuade Yetbarak to voluntarily abdicate in favor of Yekunno, and the saint's labors were rewarded by the king granting the church one-third of state revenue.[30] This view, however, depends upon a much later tradition and is unlikely to be historical. Nevertheless, it is certainly true that Takla Haymanot was a central figure in the resurgence of monasticism in the thirteenth and fourteenth centuries (see below).[31]

The Solomonic Dynasty (1270–1974)

Traditional Ethiopian historiography claims that Yekunno Amlak (reigned 1270–1285) was descended from Delna'od, the last Aksumite king and therefore a descendant of Menelik I, son of King

Solomon and the queen of Sheba. This view entailed that Yekunno was thus the "restorer" of the Solomonic line, a claim formulated in the *Kebra Nagast* (The glory of the kings) and in other Ethiopian chronicles. This historiography further claims that the Solomonic lineage was preserved to the time of Emperor Haile Selassie in the twentieth century until his death and the end of the monarchy in 1974. This means that the *Kebra Nagast* provided religious legitimation for a dynasty that survived for just over seven hundred years, and its central story became universally known and widely believed in Ethiopia. It is worth a closer look.

The *Kebra Nagast* (discussed more fully in chapter 5) is a collection of legends and stories that was probably written in Arabic (and maybe in Coptic before that) and then translated into Ge'ez, probably by the early fourteenth century.[32] It makes three central claims.[33] First, the lawful kings of Ethiopia descend from the union of Solomon and the queen of Sheba through their son Menelik I. Second, the original tablets of the law that God gave to Moses were removed from Jerusalem by Azariah, the son of the Jewish high priest, brought to Ethiopia with Menelik's party when he was returning from a visit to Jerusalem, and placed in the shrine at Aksum, Ethiopia's ancient Christian capital. Third, Ethiopia is the legitimate successor to Israel since God has transferred his place of abode from Jerusalem to Aksum, which means that the kings of Ethiopia are therefore of divine origin. At least from the fourteenth century onward, the *Kebra Nagast* was treated as an ultimate and largely uncontested authority for the monarchy's claim to political power and divine kingship, especially among the Tigrinya- and Amharic-speaking people of the Ethiopian highlands. It became, in effect, the Ethiopian national saga and contributed to the development of Ethiopian national ideology in the nineteenth and twentieth centuries.[34] Although a large number of Ethiopians still consider the Aksumite kings to be descended from Solomon and the queen of Sheba and are very proud of this line of descent, there is no evidence that Aksumite rulers ever claimed they enjoyed Solomonic descent or that there was in fact a continuous blood lineage from Solomon and the queen of Sheba, right through to Emperor Haile Selassie.[35] Most scholars, accordingly, regard Yekunno Amlak as the founder of an entirely new dynasty that took over and adopted for its own purposes the Solomonic ideology reflected in the *Kebra Nagast*.[36] Only in the sense that Ethiopia once more had a monarch operating in a Semitic language could the commencement of this dynasty count as a restoration.[37]

Royal descent among the Solomonic dynasty was not always from father to son. Claims to the kingship could be made by almost anyone from the Solomonic family, usually, but not always, by males. This factor meant that struggles over succession were very common. Claimants often consigned rival claimants to prison. The monastery of Dabra Damo (see above) was one such place used for keeping potential royal claimants away from the court. Solomonic descent also had a strong religious as well as political dimension. Members of the dynasty saw themselves as defenders of Ethiopian Orthodoxy and legitimate kings needed to be members of the church.

With the onset of the Solomonic dynasty, we enter a period for which we have fairly abundant historical documentation. Indeed the *Royal Chronicles* provide a continuous account of the kings and the events of their reigns.[38] The dynasty centered itself in Amhara, the heart of the great Ethiopian Plateau. Its initial political imperative was to end the Muslim threat to the province of Shoa represented by the sultanate of Ifat, a project that necessitated a long period of conflict. While this was going on, the Solomonic kingdom began to enjoy an impressive literary renaissance. Just as significantly, the kings of this dynasty oversaw a very close integration of church and state, with a huge number of churches and monasteries being founded and missionary activity intensified.[39]

One aspect of church–state relations, unique to Ethiopia, requires particular comment. From its conversion to Christianity in the fourth century CE, following the preaching of St. Frumentius, the kingdom of Aksum took its senior ecclesiastic from the church in Alexandria, and this arrangement was to persist until

1959. The patriarch of Alexandria (the archbishop and head of the Egyptian Coptic Church) nominated the metropolitan for the Ethiopian Church from among Egyptian monks.[40] This figure was referred to as the abuna in Ethiopia. Upon the death of each abuna, the Ethiopian king had to dispatch ambassadors to Egypt with gifts to encourage the Egyptian Coptic patriarch in Alexandria to elevate a monk to the vacant episcopal see. This became a very complicated process from the seventh century CE onward, after the Muslim conquest of North Africa, since the ambassadors sent by the Ethiopian king had to ensure that the appointment was endorsed by the Muslim authorities in Egypt.[41] Further tensions in this arrangement were generated by the fact that the Ethiopian king also claimed authority in relation to affairs of the church in Ethiopia. Although the king had to be crowned by the abuna, he nevertheless had real authority over both the abuna and the church, since he had a double role as a temporal and a spiritual leader. He even had a say in the doctrine of the church. He convened and presided over councils, which the abuna could not do.[42] The main functions of the abuna were few but vital: to consecrate kings, to ordain priests, and to consecrate tabots (replicas of the tablets of the law of Moses that are kept in every Ethiopian Orthodox church). He was the only person in the country who could do this. He also had the power of excommunication.[43] This meant that the leadership of the church in Ethiopia was split between two figures: the abuna and a veritable priest-king, the king of kings:

> Neither was able to claim to exert full religious authority since, in the eyes of the kingdom's ecclesiastics, the King was always suspected of being involved with political interests and the bishop represented a distant hierarchy subject to Egypt's Islamic authorities. Local responses to this ambiguous situation generated a decentralized organization founded on monastic networks.[44]

The early years of the Solomonic dynasty witnessed a marked revival of monasticism in Ethiopia. Although monasteries were first founded (as noted above) in the late fifth and early sixth centuries CE, their power and influence seem to have been quite limited until the middle of the thirteenth century. The two figures who radically enhanced the role of the monasteries in Ethiopia's religious and political life were Takla Haymanot (ca. 1215–1313) and Ewostatewos (ca. 1273–1352). Prior to their appearance the church seems to have been dominated by the secular clergy (who could marry and have children). After the revival of monasticism, monks competed very successfully for influence with the people and at the royal court. Takla Haymanot founded the monastery of Dabra Libanos (originally called Dabra Asbo) in Shoa 1284, which was to become the most important monastery in the country. But both he and Ewostatewos founded large groups of monasteries, which led to the development of traditions attached, respectively, to the traditions of the "houses" of Takla Haymanot and Ewostatewos. The pattern was for a single monk to travel to a new area and to begin living a pious and ascetic life there. In time he would attract other men and, often with local support, commence the erection of a church and other monastic buildings. The increasing power and influence of resurgent monasticism, not least because the economic resources of the monasteries were dependent on royal handouts, soon brought the monks into conflict with the Solomonic kings.[45] One issue of contention was the personal morality of the kings, with Basalota Mikael, who founded the great monastery at Dabra Gol, rebuking Emperor Amda Seyon for his non-Christian matrimonial and sexual habits.[46]

For present purposes it is unnecessary to mention all the kings of the three centuries after Yekunno or to detail all the major events of their reigns. It will be enough to refer to three kings, especially for their relevance to the subsequent development of Christianity in Ethiopia—namely, Amda Seyon, Yeshaq I, and Zara Yaqob—and the people known as the Falasha. Amda Seyon was Yekunno's grandson and reigned from 1314 to 1344. He consolidated the kingdom and greatly expanded its borders in a series of successful military campaigns, especially against encroaching Muslim powers, during which he increased the size of the army he had at his disposal. Amda Seyon also took control of the trade routes across Ethiopia, and his kingdom became immensely rich in consequence. Some of that wealth, it should be noted, derived from the enslavement of members of the non-Christian peoples his armies had subjugated. He carefully reorganized his court, which lived in tents as it moved around his realm.[47]

The Ethiopian chronicle of the wars of Amda Seyon also records the first reliable reference to the people later known as the Falasha, meaning "wanderers," or "landless people." This source states that he sent a force against people "like Jews" in what is now the region of Gondar. The people called themselves the Beta Israel (House of Israel), and this campaign appears to mark the beginning of almost three hundred years of conflict between the Beta Israel and the Christian leaders of Ethiopia.[48] While more will be said about the Falashas / House of Israel later in this volume, it is worth noting a little about them here. Until the 1970s there was an almost unanimous view among the authorities on the subject that they were the descendants of a group of Jews who had emigrated to Ethiopia at some point in the distant past, perhaps from Egypt or south Arabia. More recently, scholarly opinion has shifted decisively to the view that they began their existence as an ethnic group in Ethiopia around the fourteenth century CE when political, economic, social, and religious factors led to the emergence of a group that called itself Beta Israel but was referred to by others as Falasha.[49] The first Ethiopian emperor to wage war against the Falashas was Yeshaq I (reigned 1414–1429 CE). He inflicted a devastating defeat on them and put pressure upon them either to convert to Orthodox Christianity or to lose their right to own land. Most were unwilling to convert and thereafter held land only as tenants of Christian owners. While this marked the beginning of the deterioration in their socioeconomic position, it also led them to adopt new means to express their group identity, and these mainly involved their surprising adoption of aspects of the surrounding Christian culture to strengthen their specifically Israelite identity. These included the introduction of monasticism and the development of more rigorous laws of ritual purity.[50]

After ninety years of mainly undistinguished kings in the period 1344–1434, the accession of Zara Yaqob (who reigned from 1434 to 1468) marked a dramatic improvement in the fortunes of the Solomonic dynasty and Ethiopia. Zara Yaqob has been described by one eminent authority as perhaps "the greatest ruler Ethiopia had seen since Ezana, during the heyday of Aksumite power."[51] He was born in 1399, the youngest son of King Dawit. At this time a drawn-out conflict between the followers of Ewostatewos and the rest of the Ethiopian church led by their Egyptian patriarch was coming to a head. The followers of Ewostatewos believed that the Sabbath should be celebrated on both Saturday and Sunday. The rest of the church opted for Sunday only and regarded the observation of a Saturday Sabbath an illicit reversion to Judaism. In 1404 Zara Yaqob's father granted the followers of Ewostatewos permission to celebrate the Sabbath on Saturday and Sunday, and the custom then spread among other communities in spite of the protest of the Ethiopian abuna.[52] Yet this still left a nasty schism in Ethiopian Orthodoxy. It was an Ethiopian custom during the Middle Ages that the young princes of the ruling family (at least those closest in line to the throne) be confined on an *amba*, a steep mountaintop, in the charge of an official trusted by the king, to avoid their becoming involved in palace intrigue and disorders. On Zara Yaqob's accession to the throne in 1434, he had long been confined on such a mountain, yet he had developed a keen interest in the role of the Orthodox Church.[53] On his accession in 1434 Zara Yaqob was enthusiastic about reunifying the church. He moved in favor of the position of Ewostatewos, aided by the fact that the two new Egyptian abunas who arrived in 1438 (Mikael and Gabriel) were amenable to this decision. He resolved outstanding issues at a council in 1450 that he himself chaired, a role that allowed him to introduce a series of religious reforms that were the hallmark of his reign.[54] Whereas in Ethiopia church and state have often been closely intertwined, rarely was this more evident than when Zara Yaqob was emperor.

From the last quarter of the thirteenth century onward, the Ethiopian kingdom had greatly expanded its area of control, and churches were established wherever there were military colonies. Yet much of the Kushitic population of the Ethiopian highland that had been brought under Ethiopian political control persisted with animist forms of religious belief. The general religious pattern in these regions appears to have consisted of a belief in a sky god and in numerous good and evil spirits that inhabited mountains, lakes, rivers, and trees. Sorcerers were employed to placate the evil spirits. Christianity was only a thin veneer in these newly conquered areas. On the one hand, some "converts" were Christian in name only, for the political and economic benefits that Christian affiliation would bring, and maintained their loyalties to non-Christian gods and their priests. Some Christians, on the other hand, consulted non-Christian sorcerers and used magical prayers to ward off evil spirits. Zara Yaqob was determined to confront this situation and, in essence, reorganized the Ethiopian Orthodox Church for this task. The most serious problem was the insufficient number of priests and deacons in the kingdom. Priestly ordination was a principal task of the abuna, and Zara Yaqob now had two. So he sent Mikael to Shoa and Gabriel to Amhara. They busily went about their task, and their presence also boosted the morale at the monasteries in their areas. The emperor also divided the country into a number of spheres of influence, which he distributed among the major monasteries. Significant beneficiaries were the Ewostathian monasteries in the North and the monastery founded by Takla Haymanot at Dabra Asbo, which Zara Yaqob renamed Dabra Libanos. The king built new churches in Shoa and Amhara and staffed them with clergy from Dabra Libanos. He also conducted a vigorous offensive against animist forms of worship, officially banning its practice in the kingdom. Consulting witch doctors and offering sacrifice to non-Christian gods was made punishable by death, so too was the use of magical prayers. Christians were required to affix the sign of the cross to their belongings, and fasting and holy days had to be strictly observed. Every Christian was required to have a father confessor (which still remains a characteristic feature of Ethiopian Orthodoxy). The king did much to encourage devotion to Mary among Ethiopia's Christians, by ensuring that readings from the works of Mary's miracles then becoming popular in Ethiopia (as elsewhere in the Christian world) were prescribed in churches during ceremonies in her honor.[55] Zara Yaqob was, however, harsh, even despotic in the way he enforced this new regime. Opponents, Christian as well as non-Christian, were regularly tortured, imprisoned, and executed. There are signs of revolt against the harshness of his rule. And he himself remained polygamous to the end of his life. In spite of this, his reorganization of the church, especially by strengthening the economic and spiritual power of the monasteries, and his encouragement of Ethiopic literature (in which he actively participated) were abiding achievements of his reign.[56]

During the fourteenth and fifteenth centuries, the Falasha seem to have become increasingly well defined politically, and by the late sixteenth and seventeenth centuries the leader of the Falasha was the "political and military leader of an ethnic-religious community."[57]

The Muslim Conquest of Ethiopia in the Sixteenth Century

Ethiopian Christianity in the sixteenth and early seventeenth centuries was dramatically shaped by a combination of three powerful factors: the rise of Portugal as a military, especially naval, power; a devastating Muslim invasion; and the arrival (and departure) of the Jesuits.

Early in the fifteenth century, Portuguese sailors had begun to explore the northwestern coast of Africa. As the decades passed they voyaged farther and farther south. In 1488 they rounded the Cape of Good Hope and thereafter sailed up the eastern coast of Africa. In 1498 a small squadron of boats led by Vasco da Gama crossed the Indian Ocean and reached Calcutta in India, the emporium for the spice trade.[58] Da Gama had turned east from Melinde (now Malindi, on Kenya's Indian Ocean coastline) and later built a pillar there to mark the event and as a navigation guide (figure 3.3). Goa was occupied in 1510 and Ormz, controlling the Persian Gulf, in 1515.[59]

The Portuguese realized that to fend off Arab forces in the Red Sea and Persian Gulf area it would be useful to enter into an alliance with the only significant Christian power in that area, the emperor of Ethiopia, who, through vassal states, exercised power on the east African coast north of Melinde and in the southern reaches of the Red Sea.[60] Another reason for Portuguese interest in Ethiopia was that from the thirteenth century onward a belief had developed in Europe that India was the home of Prester John, a legendary eastern king of fabulous wealth and power.[61] In 1487 an envoy of the Portuguese king, Pero da Covilhã, traveling overland, had reached Ethiopia and the royal court in search of this figure and to seek out a possible sea route to India, but he was forbidden to leave Ethiopia.[62]

Figure 3.3. *The pillar of Vasco da Gama, at Malindi, Kenya*

Lebna Dengel was born in 1501, became emperor of Ethiopia in 1508 (with his mother, Empress Helena, initially acting as regent), and died in 1540 (in the monastery of Dabra Damo). It was his misfortune to reign during a period that witnessed a Muslim invasion that almost brought the long history of the Ethiopian kingdom and Ethiopian Christianity to a violent end.

In her role as regent, Empress Helena shrewdly realized that the peaceful coexistence then prevailing between Ethiopia and the Muslim strongholds on the Red Sea coastline might not last. To that end she sought, at the suggestion of Pero da Covilhã no less, the assistance of Portugal's navy.[63] Her foresight was well judged, although the assistance would be decades in arriving. In 1517 the Ottoman sultan Selim I conquered the Mamluke Sultanate of Egypt and awakened the spirit of a holy war. Around the same time, Muslim armies overran Yemen and, in 1516, began advancing into the foothills and highlands of Ethiopia under the leadership of Emir Mahfuz of Adal, governor of the port of Zeila in Adal (where Djibouti and Somalia exist today).[64] But Lebna Dengel, by then (having reached his majority) emperor, was prepared. In 1517 he trapped the Muslim army in a mountain gorge and achieved a complete victory, with Mahfuz himself slain. He then briefly invaded Adal itself.[65] In the meantime, a Portuguese fleet had reached Zeila at a time when its garrison was off fighting under Mahfuz, with the result that the Portuguese were able to occupy and sack the town. Ethiopians were overjoyed by the result of the campaign and believed the Muslim menace had been removed.[66]

Shortly after these events, in 1520, a Portuguese embassy under Rodrigo de Lima, with Francisco Alvares as its chaplain, arrived in Ethiopia, primarily to discuss a Portuguese occupation of the main Arab ports on the Red Sea. But, after six years of negotiations, no agreement had been reached, and the embassy left Ethiopia in 1526. Alvares later (in 1540) published an account of the embassy containing a full description of the country under the title *True Relation of the Lands of Prester John*,[67] the title reflecting the then-general assumption that Prester John was a designation of the Ethiopian emperor. This work has a particular value as the only detailed account of the country before much of it was destroyed by the Muslims.[68]

Of particular interest are the accounts Alvares provides of the religious practices of the Ethiopians. He observed that the Ethiopians circumcised not only boys but also girls. They baptized boys forty days after birth and girls sixty days. If the baby died in the meantime, he or she went without baptism. They gave the children communion at their baptism, a very small amount with water.[69] The priests' sons were also mostly priests, since, as there were no schools, or lecture halls, or masters to teach, the clergy taught what little they knew to their sons. The priests married one wife, and if she died, the priest did not remarry.[70] But the monks did not marry, and they ate communally. Most of the monasteries were placed on high mountains.[71] The Ethiopians practiced severe fasting. During Lent, which lasted for fifty days (not forty days as in the West), at one point monks, clergy, and laity observed severe fasting for three days, during which some monks ate no more than once and then only herbs. The common food was bread and water.[72] The usual practice of monks and nuns was to eat only every second day and always at night.[73] In general, the people ate only once a day, at night. During Lent all the people refrained from meat, milk, eggs, and butter, eating only vegetables and fruit (in addition to bread). Everyone fasted on Wednesday and Friday throughout the year.[74] The people observed two holy days per week, Saturday for the Old Testament and Sunday for the New Testament.[75] They abstained from pork.[76] Only clergy were entitled to enter the churches. The priests went to the door of the church to read the Epistles and Gospels and to give communion to the people.[77]

Meantime, the sultanate of Adal was torn by internal struggles. In due course there arose a general who took the title of Imam Ahmad ibn Ibrahim al-Ghazi (nicknamed the "Gragn," or "Left-handed"). In 1529 he began an invasion of Ethiopia that almost achieved complete success before he was defeated and killed in a battle against a joint Portuguese-Ethiopian army in 1543. The story is told in great detail in a sixteenth-century account by one Shihab ad-Din based on eyewitness testimony.[78] After training his army, which was composed mainly of Somali and Danakil soldiers, in small raids and expeditions, he inflicted a major defeat on Emperor Lebna Dengel in 1529 at the Battle of Shimbra Kure. Both sides suffered heavy casualties, and the Gragn withdrew to rebuild his forces. He returned with a vengeance in 1531, burning churches and monasteries and forcing large numbers of Christians to become Muslims in Dawaro and the Shoa Province. Two years later he did the same in Amhara and Lasta and in other regions of the country. In 1534 his army reached Tigray, where it suffered some reverses at the hands of the ferocious and courageous Tigrayans fighting in country that was often mountainous and inaccessible. At this point Lebna Dengel saw the wisdom in following his mother's advice to seek help from the Portuguese.

João Bermudes, a physician in the embassy of Rodrigo de Lima, had remained in Ethiopia at the court of Lebna Dengel when the embassy returned to Portugal in 1526. He appears to have persuaded the emperor and the abuna, the (at that time) very elderly head of the Ethiopian church (as always, an appointee of the patriarch of Alexandria), of the need to transfer the allegiance of the church from Alexandria to Rome. In 1538 the abuna went so far as to consecrate Bermudes bishop, handed over to him all his rights and prerogatives, and acknowledged him as head of the Ethiopian Church. Although the pope refused to recognize his consecration and installation as patriarch by the abuna, the Portuguese did, and with this status Bermudes helped organize a military expedition to assist Lebna Dengel. The expedition was led by none other than Cristovão da Gama, the son of Vasco da Gama.[79] He arrived with four hundred men and some artillery pieces at Massawa in 1541, and, aided by the Ethiopian leader Bahr Negash Yeshaq, who had resisted the Muslim army at Debaroa, set off into the interior. There is a near-contemporary account of these events in Pedro Páez's *History of Ethiopia* (1622).[80] The Portuguese captured a steep hill occupied by the Muslims and were then successful in two battles against them but were unable to press their advantage.[81] In the next battle, the Gragn had the benefit of Turkish reinforcements with artillery pieces and won the battle, with Cristovão da Gama being captured and executed shortly afterward.[82] Fortunately, two hundred Portuguese escaped that engagement. They joined up with what remained of the Ethiopian army, defeated the Gragn's army, and killed the Gragn himself at the Battle of Wayna Daga, east of Lake Tana, on February 21, 1543. Although there were some minor engagements between the two sides later, the Muslim menace hanging over Ethiopia was ended. But this result came at a terrible cost. Monasteries and churches had been destroyed across vast swathes of the country, manuscripts and works of art were burned, and much of the population forced to convert to Islam. One commentator describes the situation like this:

> The holocaust enveloped most parts of Ethiopia and brought in its train misery, murder, ruin and devastation. Much of the literary and intellectual heritage of Abyssinia was irretrievably lost, and the barbarism and brutality had an effect far transcending that age. To Ethiopians a good deal of their hard-won civilization was destroyed, while to the historian and *éthiopisant* precious documentation and irreplaceable evidence perished forever.[83]

As the military conflict wound down, however, a religious one was about to start. Shortly after the final battle against the Gragn, in October 1543, Bermudes tried to persuade the new emperor Gelawedros (Claudius) to adopt Roman Catholic practices and submit to the pope. The young emperor was unhappy with this suggestion but, in need of Portuguese military aid, acknowledged the pope as head of the universal church and Bermudes as patriarch. In fact, however, Bermudes had permanently alienated Claudius from Rome.[84] Later emperors, however, would soon prove more receptive to the blandishments of Roman Catholicism.

The Oromo Invasion

Yet although the Muslim invasion was defeated, Ethiopia soon faced another external threat, this time from the Oromo people (formerly called, by outsiders not the Oromo themselves, the Galla). They began invading the Ethiopian Plateau from the south and the east in the 1520s and profited from the destruction that had been wrought in parts of the country by the Muslim onslaught. They moved into territory of Ethiopia itself and also of Muslim-controlled areas such as the Harar region. Huge numbers of Oromo migrated into these regions and occupied vast swathes of land. They took control of most of the Shoa Province, reached Amhara, and found their way into the southern and eastern reaches of Lasta. The only part left untouched was the northern highlands, the location of the old Aksumite kingdom. Emperor Claudius died in 1559 and was followed by the brief reign of Minas, who proved ineffective. But not so his son, Sarsa Dengel (reigned 1563–1597), who was a warrior king in the mold of the Amda Seyon. He battled against the Oromo for much of his reign but in his frequent successes could do little to staunch the advance of the great mass of people pushing into his country.[85]

The Arrival of the Jesuits and Their Expulsion

The Jesuits were interested in Ethiopia right from their foundation as a religious order. The Jesuits, or Society of Jesus to use their formal title, had been formed as a religious organization by the Spaniard Ignatius Loyola, a former soldier, and six followers (including Francis Xavier) in 1534, and they were officially approved by the pope in 1540. By a curious coincidence, this was the same year in which Francisco Alvares published his account of the embassy to Ethiopia of 1520–1526. From the very beginning the Jesuits cultivated deep learning (even in areas such as astronomy and mathematics) and a missionary zeal. In many ways, they were the shock troops of the Counter-Reformation. By the end of the sixteenth century they were actively engaged in mission work in south Asia, in China and Japan. But as early as the period 1546–1554 St. Ignatius of Loyola himself was giving close attention to the situation in

Ethiopia. Ignatius had read Alvares' account and had also discussed the country with an Ethiopian monk named Piedro, who had been in Rome since 1540. With agreement of the king of Portugal and the pope, Ignatius arranged the appointment of a new patriarch, aided by two assistant bishops (one of whom was the Jesuit, Andrew de Orviedo), to replace the irregularly appointed Bermudes.[86] Based on his considerable knowledge of Ethiopia from Alvares' book and Piedro, Ignatius also drew up instructions for all Jesuits traveling from Portugal to that country to respect the distinctive nature of the Ethiopian Church. They were, for example, to permit circumcision and various other "Jewish" customs to continue and to have sermons translated into Amharic, while introducing Western customs, such as Corpus Christi processions, which might appeal to the people.[87] If these instructions had been followed, which (as we will see) they were not, the Jesuits might have brought the Ethiopian church into union with Rome just as they were to achieve with the Maronite Church of Lebanon in 1580.

As events transpired, however, news reached the West that the Emperor Claudius was a resolute defender of the traditional Ethiopian faith, just as a small preliminary group, including two Jesuits, discovered on their arrival in Ethiopia in February 1555.[88] Annoyed by one of the Jesuits writing a treatise on the errors of the Ethiopians, Claudius wrote to the pope in June 1555 stating, inter alia, that his people adhered to Jewish customs not because Jews did so but because this was what the early Christians had done.[89] Around this time, Claudius also obtained a new abuna, named Mark, from Alexandria in the age-old Ethiopian fashion. Mark began to excommunicate anyone discovered reading the Jesuit treatise on Ethiopian errors.[90]

As a result of this difficult situation, the size of the expedition was diplomatically scaled down, and the main Jesuit mission to reach Ethiopia consisted of only Andrew de Orviedo and five other Jesuits. They arrived in March 1557.[91] Claudius himself engaged in theological argument with the Jesuits. Annoyed by his lack of success, Orviedo tactlessly made widely known his disapproval of the Ethiopians' refusal to accept the Roman Church. In 1559 he lost patience with Claudius and the Ethiopians and left the royal court.[92] Later that year Claudius was killed in battle against the Muslims and was replaced by his brother Minas, who was passionately opposed to the Jesuits and their mission. He revoked the liberties Claudius had granted them, confiscated lands that had been granted to the Portuguese, imprisoned Orviedo for six months, and then banished him from court. Eventually, he allowed the Jesuits to settle on the northern frontier, which was at risk of invasion, at a place on a mountain that Orviedo named Fremona, after Frumentius. In 1563 Minas died and was succeeded by Sarsa Dengel, who reigned until 1597.[93] Sarsa tolerated the Jesuits, who ministered to approximately six hundred Portuguese and part-Portuguese people in the country. In 1577 Orviedo died. He had not succeeded, although he might have, had he behaved with greater sensitivity to Ethiopian distinctiveness in the way that St. Ignatius Loyola had recommended.[94] His successor, the Jesuit Pedro Páez, was much more diplomatic.

Pedro Páez, born in Spain in 1564, joined the Jesuits at a young age and was sent as a missionary to Ethiopia. He sailed from Lisbon in a vessel bound for the Portuguese base of Goa in March 1588.[95] The plan was to sail westward from Goa to a port on the southwestern shore of the Red Sea, which meant avoiding Muslim vessels that were a strong presence in the area. Because of various delays, accidents, and opposition from local Muslim leaders, it took fifteen years for Páez to reach Ethiopia! He arrived in Massawa, the principal port of and gateway to the country, on April 26, 1603.[96] Páez proved admirably suited to the task of bringing Ethiopia within the Roman Catholic fold. He was "cautious, tactful, and tolerant."[97] He was also extremely curious and scholarly, visiting the source of the Blue Nile and writing a *History of Ethiopia*.[98] Yet there were problems from the start. So impressed with Páez was Za Dengel, emperor from 1603 to 1604, that he converted to Roman Catholicism, wrote to the pope acknowledging his ecclesiastical supremacy, and proclaimed that thenceforward Sunday and not the Jewish Sabbath should be kept as the weekly holy day in the Roman manner. These steps alarmed the Ethiopian clergy and many members of the country's elite.[99]

After Za Dengel's death in battle in 1604, a civil war followed, culminating in the accession to the throne of Susenyos I, in 1606. He reigned until 1632. At that time there was stiff resistance to embracing Rome among the Ethiopian clergy and people. This was due not so much to differences as to the nature of Christ (whether he had two natures, one divine and one human in hypostatic union, the Roman position, or whether he had one nature, the Ethiopian position), although that was a factor. Rather, the Ethiopian resistance principally arose from their desire to preserve their distinctive religious practices that went back a millennium, many them having a Jewish dimension: abstinence from pork, hare, and non-scaly fish; the uncleanness of women after menstruation and childbirth; circumcision of male and female children; and weekly observance on the Sabbath. Páez was very sensitive to these issues and respectful of Ethiopian traditions, as had been St. Ignatius Loyola himself.[100] When Susenyos, who was so greatly taken with Páez as a person and with the force of his reasoning that he expressed a desire to become a Roman Catholic, Páez urged caution.[101] Susenyos also adopted the two natures view of Christ's identity, a view that attracted strong opposition from the abuna of the time (named Simon), who also argued for the importance of keeping the age-old link between the Coptic Church in Egypt and the Ethiopian Church.[102] In 1614 Abuna Simon fomented a revolution against Susenyos. Although this was suppressed, supporters of the link to Egypt continued to incite the people against the Jesuits.[103] In 1622 Susenyos finally became a Roman Catholic, and Páez died.[104]

The Jesuit replacement for Páez was one Alfonso Mendes, who arrived in Ethiopia as patriarch in 1625. From the start he proved a disastrous appointment and paid little if any attention to the advice St. Ignatius Loyola had given on a culturally sensitive approach to the Ethiopians. Even on his arrival in Goa, he entered in full pontifical vestments, with an escort, in direct contradiction of the advice he had received from other Jesuits to enter the town quietly and without pomp so that the Arabs would not learn of his arrival.[105] In preparation for his arrival, Susenyos went to Aksum, the ancient cradle of Christianity in Ethiopia, and there drafted a letter to his people setting out the reasons why he had become a Roman Catholic and criticizing several abunas for erroneous views and for behavior (much of it involving sexual misconduct) that fell far below that of the Jesuits. Susenyos and Mendes finally met on February 7, 1626, on which occasion Mendes delivered a thirty-thousand-word address to the court! A few days later, on February 11, 1626, the emperor and the great men of the clergy and laity swore allegiance to Rome.[106]

In this period, however, Mendes took a step that undid everything his Jesuit colleagues had done before him and irrevocably doomed the Jesuit mission to failure. He made a proclamation to the effect that the Ethiopian clergy and monks could no longer say Mass or perform any ecclesiastical function unless he had given them faculties, everyone must embrace Roman Catholicism *under pain of death for refusal*, circumcision was prohibited, and the ancient liturgy was to be reformed.[107] With the emperor behind him, Mendes operated on the *cuius regio eius religio* principle then in operation in Europe and saw no reason for not imposing Roman Catholicism on the whole population.[108]

An indicator of the Ethiopian opposition to this measure came in the actions of sixty monks when they first heard of the emperor's edict requiring them to become Roman Catholics: they committed suicide by throwing themselves headlong over a precipice.[109] Between 1628 and 1632 rebellions broke out against the emperor in the name of the established religious order. At one battle in 1632, his men killed eight thousand Ethiopians opposed to him. Faced with so hostile a reaction, he had in 1629 persuaded Mendes to agree to some concessions that consisted of reintroducing the ancient practices in relation to liturgy of the Mass, fasting, and the restoration of feast days in the Ethiopian calendar.[110] In 1632, Susenyos went much further. Over Mendes' objections, he permitted his people to choose to follow the Ethiopian or Roman Catholic version of Christianity. Shortly after, he abdicated in favor of his son Fasilidas (reigned 1632–1667), who allowed complete restoration of the old practices, including circumcision. Fasilidas then began to crack down hard on the Jesuits. He ordered them to Fremona and then expelled them from the country. But the Portuguese settlers in the country were allowed to remain; some of them helped the emperor to build his new capital at Gondar.[111] So ended the Jesuit mission to Ethiopia. But that mission is remembered with real bitterness by Ethiopians to this day.

4

Mid-seventeenth Century to the Present

Recovery and Decline

Ethiopian kings traditionally lived in huge encampments that moved around the country. As early as the beginning of the sixteenth century, European observers had noticed that the encampment was always established on the same design.[1] The life and person of the monarch in this mobile court were the focal point of the Christian empire of medieval and early modern Ethiopia. The core of the encampment consisted of two concentric enclosures that held the private quarters of the king and his family. The inner enclosure was exclusively for the use of the king and was separated from the outer enclosure by curtains or a fence. Ten tents were pitched in the inner enclosure, for the king (and his personal servants) and for his senior officials (the inner court). Thirteen separate exits, each with its own name, led to the outer enclosure. The main exit appears to have opened to the west, meaning there were six entrances on either side, creating a spatial division, as one exited, of right and left that designated those two zones in which the royal wives and other family members and officials were located. In the outer enclosure were situated the king's treasure houses, royal chapels, and royal kitchens. The outer enclosure also contained thirteen exits, lined up with those of the inner enclosure. In the encampment beyond the outer enclosure were found courts of justice, prisons, the cage that housed the royal lions, and at least one church. The religious dimension to the encampment was significant, and usually the abuna resided there, moving with the court as it moved.[2]

In around 1618, however, Emperor Susenyos asked the Jesuit missionary Pedro Páez to help find a suitable location for him to build the first permanent capital of the empire. In the end Susenyos made his own decision, but Páez surveyed the site. This was almost certainly Gondar,[3] although the emperor's son, Fasilidas (reigned 1632–1667), who (as we have seen in chapter 3) terminated the presence of the Jesuits in Ethiopia and prevented the spread of Roman Catholicism, was ultimately responsible for building the city.

Fasilidas began the building of the royal compound in Gondar, many of the monuments of which survive to this day (in spite of exigencies since, such as British bombing of the Italians using the buildings in 1941). The first and most imposing edifice constructed by Fasilidas was his five-towered royal palace (figure 4.1), "a massive solid-looking building constructed of unsquared dark stone and mortar, with cut stone arches of red tufa from Qwesqwam above the windows and doors."[4] As well as building Gondar, Fasilidas rebuilt the cathedral in Aksum that had been destroyed by the army of the Gragn.

Fasilidas's predecessor, Susenyos, had taken further action in waging a major campaign against the Falasha, which involved ending their autonomy, confiscating their land, selling many of them as slaves, and forcibly converting many others. While his abdication after this victory may have somewhat diminished the long-term impact of Susenyos' policies against them, Fasilidas would not have decided to situate his capital in Gondar if the surrounding region had not been pacified in relation to the Falasha.[5] Nevertheless, as early as the sixteenth century the Falasha had begun to develop skills as craftsmen, masons, and carpenters, and

Mid-seventeenth Century to the Present 77

Figure 4.1. *The Palace of Fasilidas in Gondar*

Fasilidas and other emperors after him utilized these capabilities in the building of Gondar. By 1668 they were a recognizable group living in the city.[6]

There was a downside to the choice of Gondar as the site of the capital: it embodied aspects of Ethiopia that would persist for two centuries, namely, its comparative isolation, xenophobia, and relative lack of material or intellectual progress. Gondar is in the North of the country, beyond Lake Tana. This was a site that seemed to protect the court from invasion by Muslims and the Oromo, it was also a long way north of the geographical center of Ethiopia. Its situation thus reduced the reach of royal control over the kingdom and fostered the growth of regionalism and the independence of local feudal lords. The Oromo, now settled in the central areas of the country, while beginning to assimilate into its social and political organization, also contributed to the country's decentralization and diminished cohesion.

Fasilidas' son, Yohannes (John) I, had a comparatively peaceful reign (1667–1682). He tried to segregate Muslims but mainly succeeded in driving them into commerce.[7] Substantial remains of the library and chancellery he built at Gondar survive to this day (figure 4.2).

The period from the end of the seventeenth to the middle of the nineteenth century requires only brief consideration here. Yohannes was succeeded by his son Iyasus I (the Great), who reigned, very effectively, from 1682 to 1706. He was a warrior king who pushed the power of the kingdom southward, introduced tax reforms, and did much to improve the lot of the princes who were exiled for life at Amba Wahni, a setting that inspired Samuel Johnson's work *The History of Rasselas, Prince of Abissinia*. From 1699 to 1700 he was attended by a French physician, Charles Jacques Poncet, who published an account of his visit, which included a description of the emperor, in 1704. But Iyasus was deposed by his

Figure 4.2. *The Library and Chancellery of Yohannes I at Gondar*

own son and assassinated in 1706, and these events ushered in a cycle of royal murders and palace revolts. Political affairs in the country reached such a pass that the period from 1769 to 1855, when Tewodros (Theodore) II came to the throne, are referred to in Ethiopia as the time of the *masafent* (judges), for the reason that it so closely resembled the era of the Old Testament recounted in the book of Judges when "there was no king in Israel; every man did what was right in his own eyes" (17:6 RSV). Throughout this period, however, there was one unifying agent in Ethiopia, and that was Orthodox Christianity and its powerful institutions and traditions.[8] The church "functioned as the repository of the national culture and thus embodied a strong sense of historical continuity."[9] During this period, however, the Falasha lost most of the economic advantages they had enjoyed under the Gondarine kings. Local rulers could exploit them, and the lack of large imperial building projects meant less scope for the application of their construction skills, which led to their focusing on lower-status activities such as smithing, pottery, and weaving.[10]

From a religious point of view, Roman Catholicism continued to be viewed very negatively, while the religious controversies that had been stimulated by the Jesuit presence were now transformed into increasingly bitter disputes among Orthodox clerics on theological matters, especially as to the nature of Christ and the Trinity. But the seventeenth century witnessed the arrival of the first Protestant missionaries, and their numbers expanded in the eighteenth and especially the nineteenth century, in ways to be explained in chapter 8. In 1859 and 1860 the Falasha began to be targeted by Protestant missionaries from England (the London Society for Promoting Christianity) and Scotland (the Church of Scotland). Since the missionaries criticized the Falashas' religious practices in relation to normative Judaism elsewhere, they thus became the first outsiders to treat them as Jews in the universal sense of the word.[11] From 1867, by contrast, representatives of Jewish organizations began visiting the Falasha to assist them, especially in resisting the efforts of the Christian missionaries. The situation soon became well known to Jews outside Ethiopia.[12]

Ethiopia in the Modern Period: 1855 to the Present

The Reign of Tewodros II

The situation in Ethiopia took a decisive turn for the better in 1855, with the accession of Tewodros II to the throne. Tewodros was his throne name, his natal name being Wassa (figure 4.3).

An important feature of the reigns of Tewodros and the emperors after him was a desire to centralize power over all of Ethiopia in the person of the king. These sovereigns generally took the view that the church had a vital role to play in unifying the kingdom around a common Christian identity, with the clergy acting as agents of the state through the monasteries and parishes scattered across the land. It became evident, however, that the existence of an abuna in the form of an Egyptian monk appointed by the Coptic patriarch of Alexandria was incompatible with the total submission of the church to royal power that was necessary for it to be used as the agent of the king. Tensions between kings

Figure 4.3. *Tewodros (Theodore) II*

and abunas and the Egyptian patriarchs who appointed them were to become commonplace from the mid-nineteenth century until their resolution in the mid-twentieth century.[13]

Tewodros was born in 1818, at which point the so-called emperor, *negusa nagast* (king of kings) in Gondar had little wealth or power while the great princes of Tigray, Shoa, and Amhara were engaged in continual strife and bloodshed. His father died when he was a boy, and he was sent to a monastery to be educated in the traditional way as a deacon. During this period he developed a deep attachment to Ethiopian Orthodoxy and a mystical form of faith, while also becoming interested in Ethiopian literature. He escaped when his monastery was destroyed and rose to be the head of a company of bandits who revered him as brave, skillful, and fiery. His fame allowed him to marry the daughter of Ras Ali, the lord of Begember, whom he then set about supplanting, together with another lord who had sided with Ras Ali. In due course he also defeated the lords of Tigray and Shoa and was anointed king of kings in 1855 by Abuna Salama (who was abuna from 1841 to 1867). He had thus defeated the main feudal lords and united a fragmented country in the space of a few years. Among his first actions as emperor were the attempted abolition of the slave trade and polygamy, although he achieved only limited success with each. He had a strongly developed sense of justice and defended the weak against the depredations of the powerful, allowing everyone access to him for judgment. He also transferred the capital from Gondar to Magdala, which was more centrally located in the kingdom. In the long tradition of Ethiopian emperors who embodied monarchy and Orthodox faith, he regarded Ethiopia and Orthodox Christianity as identical. One aspect of this belief was the strong support he gave to the hostile policy that Abuna Salama implemented against heterodox movements that challenged his authority. Yet this alliance of king and abuna did not last. When Tewodros sought to reform the kingdom by using part of the lands owned by the church to finance better administration, Abuna Salama excommunicated him, in 1864. This presaged the eventual decline of his reign.[14]

And trouble was quick to arrive. Tewodros brutally repressed the numerous revolts he faced, and gradually traits of cruelty and megalomania in his character became more and more dominant. But it was his falling out with the British that led to his downfall. After unsuccessfully reaching out to Queen Victoria (the British failed to reply to his letter) and after a string of misunderstandings on both sides, he became disillusioned with Britain and imprisoned a group of British missionaries. This led to a powerful British military intervention led by Sir John Napier. Magdala was captured on Easter Monday 1868, and Tewodros committed suicide by shooting himself. The British ransacked his possessions, including his crown, his queen's dress, numerous manuscripts, and several tabots (miniature arks of the covenant), one of which is central to every Ethiopian Orthodox church, and took them back to the UK. Some of these objects ended up in public collections, including several tabots in a locked room in the British Museum. The British also took his son back to England, but he died soon after. In 2018–2019, to mark the 150th anniversary of the capture of Magdala, there was an exhibition of some of the Ethiopian possessions removed from Magdala in the Victoria and Albert Museum.[15]

The Reign of Yohannes IV

After the defeat and death of Tewodros, three rivals contended for the imperial throne: Menelik, king of Shoa; Kassa, the ras of the Tigray; and Gobazye, ruler of Lasta. The first stage was settled when Kassa defeated Gobazye in battle and had himself crowned Yohannes (John) IV in the ancient capital of Aksum. Yohannes, an ardent Christian, reigned for eighteen years (1871–1889), and he was constantly at war with threatening Muslim powers and also resisted European penetration. Menelik recognized him as king of kings and, in return, was largely left to rule in the South while Yohannes ruled in the North. They also agreed that Menelik would succeed Yohannes as emperor. An attempt by Egypt in 1875–1876 to conquer the country ended in the comprehensive defeat of the Egyptian army. During this period the king accused Abuna

Atnatewos II (abuna from 1868 to 1876) of maintaining relations with the authorities in Egypt and entirely excluded him from the affairs of the kingdom.[16] Yohannes and Menelik led a joint campaign against the Oromo in 1878, but Yohannes' fanatical insistence on their becoming Christian was disavowed by Menelik when he assumed power.[17]

The last few years of Yohannes' reign witnessed the beginnings of Italy's colonial aspirations in Ethiopia. After earlier tentative steps, their landing at Massawa in 1885 signaled the seriousness of their intentions. In 1887 the Ethiopian ruler of Eritrea trounced a much smaller though well-armed Italian army in a battle at Dogali in Eritrea, and this prompted the Italians to send out a more powerful force. Yohannes was prevented from attacking this new Italian army by his need to cope with a major threat on his western flank, an invasion of Mahdists from Sudan. He defeated them in the Battle of Metemma in 1889 but was fatally wounded in the process.[18]

The Mahdists had also done considerable damage to Ethiopian towns. Gondar especially suffered at the hands of the Mahdi's army, but its wonderfully illuminated church of Dabra Berhan Selassie (figure 4.4) was saved by a swarm of bees that attacked the Mahdists as they were entering the courtyard of the church, forcing them to withdraw.[19]

The Reign of Menelik II

On the death of Yohannes, Menelik became emperor, being consecrated by Abuna Matewos (abuna from 1889–1926) at Entoto Maryam, in the Entoto mountains, and the center of power in the country moved to the south. He reigned from 1889 to 1913. After several years in which Menelik sought to reach an accommodation with the Italians, including permitting them to have a colony of limited extent in the North (covering Eritrea especially), relations soured, and an Italian army led by General Baratieri moved into Tigray and occupied Adwa. One component of the Italian army advanced as far south as Makalle, where it was annihilated by the

Figure 4.4. *Dabra Berhan Selassie Church, Gondar*

Ethiopians in the Battle of Amba Alagi. Menelik issued a call to arms, and a large army of Ethiopians converged to meet the Italians at Adwa. Some eighteen thousand Italian troops were opposed by more than a hundred thousand Ethiopians and decisively defeated, with seven thousand Italians killed. Their victory in the Battle of Adwa remains a cause of great pride for Ethiopians, and paintings of the battle are commonplace across the country, showing the emperor's wife, Empress Taytu, a battalion commander, taking part in the fighting with a pistol in her hand (figure 4.5).[20]

There is an unprepossessing yet moving memorial to the Italian dead in Adwa, which records the simple message "Ai Caduti: Adua 1896: Non dobbiamo dimenticarti" (To the fallen: Adwa 1896: We must not forget you; figure 4.6).

The Treaty of Addis Ababa of 1896 provided that the Italians could retain Eritrea. In retrospect, this provision in the treaty meant that Eritrea would thereafter continue to have an identity separate

Figure 4.5. *Ethiopian Painting of the Battle of Adwa*

Figure 4.6. *Memorial to the Italian dead at Adwa*

from Ethiopia, and the treaty thus contributed to a process that would ultimately see Eritrea emerge as an independent nation. As well as seeking to defend the external integrity of the kingdom (with the exception of Eritrea), Menelik also sought to assume sovereignty over territory controlled by Muslims and peoples with animist religions in the South. He took control of the southern Awash Valley and the Sidamo and Janjero regions. In 1897 he conquered the Kingdom of Kaffa and around this time took over Harar in the east.

Menelik also undertook significant internal administrative reforms. In 1882 he had left Ankober, a town in central Ethiopia (and formerly the capital of Shoa), and built a new palace at Mount Entoto in the south of the country. In 1886 the emperor, at the urging of the empress, decided to build a town in a valley south of the mountain with better supplies of water and firewood, which they called Addis Ababa, or "New Flower." Around this time, Menelik decided to bring in fast-growing eucalyptus trees from Australia, to provide firewood and building material. They were well suited to the Ethiopian climate and topography and were soon planted and flourished right across the country. Addis Ababa became the capital when Menelik succeeded to the throne in 1889.[21]

On Menelik's death in 1913, his grandson, Lidj Iyasu, then only seventeen years old, was designated emperor. He disclaimed his Solomonic ancestry, fabricating instead a descent from Muhammad, took Muslim wives, and spoke of a Muslim empire in Ethiopia. Not surprisingly, all of this outraged Christians in Ethiopia, and in 1916 he was deposed. He was replaced in 1917 by Zawditu, daughter of Menelik, who was consecrated empress (queen of queens) by Abuna Matewos, with her son, Ras Tafari, as regent and heir. During the regency, Ras Tafari proved an able and progressive ruler. He gained experience in government and traveled extensively in Europe. On Zawditu's death in 1930, Ras Tafari became emperor, taking the regnal name Haile Selassie (Might of the Trinity).[22] In due course his original name would be taken up by the Rasta movement in Jamaica and elsewhere.[23]

The Reign of Haile Selassie

Haile Selassie was a forward-looking ruler who sought to push the empire in the direction of a modern bureaucratic state, to which end he promoted education, took steps to abolish slavery, and introduced land reforms, while also implementing reforms in the army, transport, and communications. At the level of government, a constitution was approved, and ministries were set up. At the same time, however, he sought to consolidate power in his hands as emperor and to control the pace of reform. While Addis Ababa developed greatly, most of the rest of the country did not.

The issue of slavery requires a closer look. Slavery in Ethiopia has a depressingly long history. An inscription of Queen Hatshepsut at Thebes from around 1495 BCE suggests that the land of Punt (covering at least part of modern-day Ethiopia) was already a source of children and adult slaves. Pliny the Elder, the first-century CE work the *Periplus of the Erythrean Sea*, and Cosmas Indicopleustes all mention the export of slaves from this area. By the time of the Muhammad there was a significant number of Ethiopian slaves living in Arabia. More germane to this volume is that the *Fetha Nagast*—the thirteenth-century code of Ethiopian law that remained immensely influential until well into the twentieth century (see chapter 5)—accepted on the basis of biblical statements that slaves could be captured in war or inherited from generation to generation, while nevertheless prohibiting the sale of Christians to nonbelievers. Here is a sample of its provisions on slavery (from chapter 31):

> Mosaic law shows that unbelievers and their children must be held as slaves since it is written there: "Those whom you take from the people who dwell around you and the aliens who dwell among you, let them, men and women, be your slaves. You shall [buy] slaves from among them and from among their offspring born in your land and they shall be for you and your children after you, as an inheritance."[24]

This part of the text continues a little further below: "The sale of a believing slave to an unbeliever is not allowed." This meant

Christians could sell Christian or non-Christian slaves to other Christians, and Muslims were also able to sell slaves and were very active in doing so.[25] In the nineteenth century there was a very extensive trade in slaves across the Red Sea, with perhaps as many as five hundred thousand in that century. A significant number appear to have come from the Sudan, captured in the course of "brutally violent slave-raiding and trafficking."[26] Yet an additional occasion of slavery was the expansion of the Ethiopian kingdom during the nineteenth century into the southwest. People captured in war were frequently reduced to slavery by Ethiopians and even by the Ethiopian rulers.[27] In 1918 Ras Tafari, as he then was known, issued an edict banning the slave trade. But he made it plain to Europeans who were enthusiastic to see slavery abolished speedily that this was only the beginning of a long and difficult process, since it meant the government destroying an institution with an extensive history in the country that was thought to be of benefit to both slave and owner.[28] The Ethiopian Orthodox Church, at least until the early part of the twentieth century, did not take a stand against slavery. Indeed, the *Fetha Nagast*, as just noted, legitimated the practice with respect to scripture. The *Fetha Nagast* even envisaged that there could be monks who were slaves (at least to people outside the monastery), since at one point (in chapter 10) it provides in relation to a man seeking to join a monastery, "If he is the slave of a member of the faithful, he shall not be accepted without the approval of his master."[29]

Haile Selassie's efforts to move his country forward were interrupted by the invasion of the Italians in 1935 under Mussolini's government. This meant six very difficult years for Ethiopia, with a large number of people killed by the Italians. After a number of military defeats, Haile Selassie left the country in May 1936. The Italians sought to promote Roman Catholicism and, correspondingly, to weaken the position of the Orthodox Church, which became a focus of resistance to them. They viewed the Protestant missions as dangerous foes and, as a result, dismantled Protestant institutions, expelled foreign missionaries, and discouraged gatherings of local converts. In spite of all this, the South of the country witnessed a remarkable growth in Protestant Christianity during the Italian occupation (see chapter 8). At the same time, the Italians projected themselves as liberators of the Muslims and encouraged them in the practice of Islam.[30] The Italians also took steps to abolish slavery, with a proclamation to this effect in Tigray in October 1935 and a wider decree to the same effect in April 1936. Italy actually claimed to have liberated 420,000 slaves, some of whom were placed in communal settlements.[31] The country was liberated from the Italians by British and Ethiopian forces in 1941.[32] Haile Selassie returned to the country at that time.

On his return, Haile Selassie began to rebuild war-torn Ethiopia. On the religious front, Protestant missionaries who had been expelled by the Italians were allowed to return. Later, in 1944, he formulated a policy that divided the country into "closed" areas where Orthodoxy was strong and "open" areas where it was weak; missions could operate in the closed areas if they were promoting social services and did not seek to convert Orthodox Christians, while in the open areas they could operate freely. Addis Ababa was opened up to all missions, a major development since it was the center of national life.[33] In 1942 Selassie abolished slavery and the slave trade,[34] a clear indication that his 1923 decree had not been effective, nor had the actions taken by the Italians.

In 1950, pursuant to a United Nations resolution, Ethiopia and Eritrea were joined in a federation. In 1962 Haile Selassie, in consequence of the activities of the Eritrean Liberation Movement, "unified" the two countries by the device of dissolving the Eritrean Parliament and annexing Eritrea. This resulted in a war of independence by the Eritreans that ended with their victory in 1991. Eritrea declared its independence and gained international recognition in 1993. Between 1998 and 2000 the two nations fought a war. A boundary commission suggested a border in April 2002, but, since it held that much of the contested western border region belonged to Eritrea, its findings were rejected by the Ethiopians, resulting in a state of unresolved conflict between the two countries. Only in June 2018 did the appointment of a new prime minister in Ethiopia lead to friendly discussions to settle the border issue. On July 9, 2018, the leaders of the two nations, after peace talks, announced that peace had now been restored.

It was only in the mid-twentieth century that the old arrangement whereby the patriarch of Ethiopia (the abuna) had to be an Egyptian Coptic monk appointed by the Coptic patriarch in Alexandria came to an end. When Haile Selassie returned to Ethiopia in 1941, attempts were made to have an Ethiopian appointed as patriarch. Agreement on this point was reached with the Coptic Church in 1948 and put into effect in 1950 when the last Coptic abuna died and the Ethiopian Basilios was chosen as archbishop.[35] He was elevated to the status of patriarch in 1959.

In December 1960 a coup led by the commander of Haile Selassie's Imperial Bodyguard was launched against his rule when he was visiting Brazil. But the coup leaders failed to arrest senior officers in the Ethiopian army (who then deployed forces against them), Abuna Basilios actively denounced it, and the provinces stayed loyal to the emperor. Within a fortnight the coup had failed.[36]

Toward the end of Haile Selassie's reign, in 1972, the Orthodox Church introduced a critical reform, namely, the creation of parish councils. The parish council was established as a body under the local diocesan administration and had to cooperate with government and private organizations to achieve its aims. The aims were to provide spiritual services, establish schools, expand the Christian faith, render social services, improve the administration of the parish churches, and maintain and develop church property. Each council was to be composed of clergy and laity (including women).

The Derg (1974–1991)

The end of the imperial regime, and of the Solomonic dynasty, came with a revolution in 1974, the radical nature of which has invited comparisons with the French, Russian, and Chinese Revolutions. Although Haile Selassie had been an avowed reformer, in the 1960s and 1970s, while he continued to encourage higher education, his reforming zeal faded away, and he failed to respond adequately to the increasing demands for reform and modernization of Ethiopian society. The intellectual setting for the revolt came from university students imbued with radical Marxist ideology and the rising elite who strongly opposed the way that Haile Selassie (then an octogenarian), his family, and a social elite controlled most of the country's wealth. In these quarters it was commonplace to bemoan Ethiopia as a "feudal" society, even if that term applied more to certain sectors and regions of the country than to the nation as a whole.[37] Those parts of rural land that operated under the *gult* system (which persisted till 1966) where land grants were made by the emperor or provincial governors to farmers who then had to pay tribute to the grantor did look rather like feudalism in Europe. Land that the emperor granted to the church was called *samon*, and the peasants who worked such land paid tribute (called *samon gult*) to an individual church or monastery.[38] It seems possible that the Ethiopian Orthodox Church was not very effective in developing approaches to engage with the youth of Ethiopia in the radically modernizing 1960s, and this left an intellectual and ideological void that, for many, Marxism was able to fill.[39] Much of the dissatisfaction with this state of affairs grew with an economic downturn in the 1960s and 1970s and a disastrous famine in 1972–1974 that the regime initially tried to hide and that caused one hundred thousand deaths. The fuse for the revolt was lit by an army mutiny in the remote town of Neghele in January 1974. Power soon passed to a military junta calling itself the Derg (the Committee), initially of about one hundred junior and mid-rank army officers. Haile Selassie died in August 1975, under uncertain circumstances. In February 1977 the Derg had shrunk in numbers as a result of a series of murderous purges, and Major Mengistu Haile Mariam (usually called Mengistu) emerged as its leader, enjoying almost autocratic power.[40] Mengistu consolidated power during 1977 and 1978 in a process called the Red Terror, which led to hundreds of thousands of people being killed. The Derg would remain in power until 1991.

The Derg (1974–1991) described its ideology of governance as a "revolutionary dictatorship of the working classes."[41] This ideology found early expression in the nationalization of most of the economy in December 1974. One aspect of this was the "land to the tiller" process, whereby in March 1975 land was declared state property, seized, and then allocated to the farmers who worked the land on the basis of ten hectares per family. No specific mention was made of the church, and it was taken for granted that this action finally deprived it of its ancient landholding privileges.[42] In fact, church properties, land, and buildings were confiscated.[43] The government provided the church with a meagre annual budget to compensate for the loss of the land, but that measure actually brought the church more under its control.[44] This was a momentous step. The church had been a very large landowner. Some suggest it owned perhaps one-third of the land in the country, while a more realistic view is that it owned no more than 5 percent of the total land mass of Ethiopia and up to 20 percent of all arable land, still a huge amount.[45] Haile Selassie had encouraged provincial governors to allocate large stretches of land to the church, since he saw the clergy as allies in his imperial rule.[46]

Another slogan of the Derg was "equality for all." As far as ex-slaves were concerned (and the Italians had acted to abolish slavery in 1935 and 1936, while Haile Selassie had only finally prohibited slavery thirty years earlier), this proved particularly advantageous, since the Derg opened up many lower administrative positions for them, with some even becoming church leaders. Some ex-slaves, however, used the opportunity to take revenge on their former oppressors.[47]

While farming families in areas where they had been often badly treated, notably the tenant farmers of wealthy landlords, welcomed the "land to the tiller" process, there was less enthusiasm in the North where smallholdings were the dominant form of land use. But enthusiasm paled on all sides when the government set up a purchasing monopoly on all agricultural produce, allowing it to buy crops at low prices.⁴⁸ Compulsorily moving farming families out of their houses scattered across the countryside into centralized villages ("villagization") also proved immensely unpopular.

At the start of the revolution, there were passionate calls for religious freedom. "The Revolution made it possible for Islam to emerge from the shadows of the past, and for its adherents to attain equal citizenship status with Christians."⁴⁹ Three Islamic festivals, together with five Christian, were declared public holidays. Muslims began to appear among the new officialdom, even as members of the Derg.⁵⁰ The Ethiopian Islamic Affairs Supreme Council was established. As far as the Protestant churches were concerned, permission was granted to Pentecostals to congregate in public.⁵¹

These actions meant the decline of Orthodox Christianity as the state religion. Not only, as just noted, was the Ethiopian Orthodox Church dispossessed as a large landowner but, through the official separation of church and state, it was pushed out of its privileged place as the religious legitimator of the regime and as the source of normative political imagery for the nation. It has not had a formal political role since.⁵² In addition, the dedication of the regime to scientific socialism soon led to polemical campaigns against religion and an onslaught on the Ethiopian Orthodox Church, culminating in the execution of Abuna Theophilos in 1976.⁵³ He was the second indigenous patriarch of the Ethiopian Orthodox Church. The Derg then oversaw the election of a new abuna, Takla Haymanot, previously a monk of extreme asceticism who it thought would be biddable to its will; he proved increasingly not to be but died of natural causes in 1988. In his place Abuna Merkorios was appointed; he had previously been the archbishop of Gondar. The Coptic Church in Egypt never recognized the two Ethiopian patriarchs appointed under the Derg, on the argument that unless the death of Theophilus was confirmed, a new appointment would be uncanonical.⁵⁴ It should be noted, however, that many Ethiopian clergy considered (and still consider) the appointment of Takla Haymanot and Merkorios to be canonically valid.⁵⁵

In addition, as part of its anti-religious actions, the Derg closed all Pentecostal and many Protestant churches, with many turned into schools. Clerics were imprisoned and sometimes murdered, church elders were harassed, and people were discouraged from taking part in religious activities. By the start of 1984, nearly all congregations of the Mekane Yesus Church had been closed, while another major Protestant church, Kale Heywet, suffered a similar fate (see chapter 8 for these churches).[56] The Muslims in eastern Ethiopia, accused of siding with the Somalis in the Ogaden War (1977–1978), were harshly treated.[57]

The period of the Derg was also not a happy one for the Falasha. Their modes of communal life and religious ceremonies were disrupted, their contacts with outside Jewish groups viewed with suspicion, their young men conscripted, and emigration strictly prohibited. In spite of the prohibition, from 1980 Falasha began to migrate to refugee camps in the Sudan, and from there the Israeli government, recognizing them as Jews entitled to *aliyah* (the right of return to the land), began flying them to a new home in Israel. By the end of 1983 four thousand had been taken to Israel. When the Derg collapsed in May 1991, fourteen thousand of the twenty thousand Falasha who had moved to Addis Ababa were flown to Israel over a period of thirty-six hours. Villages in which the Falasha once lived, especially in the Gondar region, are still to be seen in Ethiopia (figure 4.7).

The EPRDF (1991–)

The Ethiopian People's Revolutionary Democratic Front (EPRDF), a ruling coalition of four political parties whose dominant member was and is the Tigrayan People's Liberation Front, came to power in 1991, with the collapse of the Derg, in part occasioned by the decline of the Soviet Union on whom it had been dependent for support, as Mikhail Gorbachev cut off military aid. The EPRDF moved quickly to fill the political vacuum thus created.[58]

The EPRDF, while advocating "revolutionary democracy," effected the greatest change to Ethiopia by adopting a system of

Figure 4.7. *A beta salot (house of prayer, or synagogue) in an ex-Falasha village outside Gondar*

ethno-regional federalism. As stated in article 13 of the new Constitution of 1995: "The national emblem on the flag shall reflect the hope of the Nations, Nationalities, Peoples as well as religious communities to live together in equality and unity."[59] The religious plurality of Ethiopia dovetailed nicely with the country's rich ethnic plurality. From 1991 onward, again as specified in the Constitution of 1995, the EPRDF recognized religious freedom, while making clear that Ethiopia was to be a secular state with no state religion.[60] In so doing, it reinforced the legal status and public role of the Protestant churches and of Islam. They were able to develop organizations, receive foreign funding for educational and building activities, and expand their media presence, both print and digital.[61] Yet the government also required registration of all religious organizations (except the Ethiopian Orthodox Church), and this was one means of control. But all land is owned by the state pursuant to the Constitution and must be leased to the churches, and this allows for governmental interventions rather at odds with the commitment to religious freedom.[62] Some of the church properties (other than land) were given back to the church.[63] The EPRDF regime effectively "domesticated" the church. It also sought to do the same with the Muslims.[64]

Yet the entire political situation in Ethiopia was upended in 2018 with the appointment of a new prime minister. On March 28, 2018, the country's ruling coalition elected as its new leader a former Muslim who had become a Pentecostal Protestant from the large Oromo ethnic group, Abiy Ahmed. He took office on April 2, 2018. He has a PhD from Addis Ababa University with a thesis on the resolution of interreligious conflict. Its focus was on the reconciliation of Muslims and Orthodox Christians after a violent incident in a village outside Jimma that threatened to provoke a much wider Muslim-Orthodox conflict.[65] In the months following his appointment, he proved to be a remarkably dynamic reformer, ending an unpopular state of emergency that had been declared by his predecessor, ordering the release of thousands of political prisoners, and establishing peace with Eritrea after decades of warfare and tension between the two countries. One aspect of the peace deal with Eritrea is to reunite the Orthodox Churches in the two countries and also the two Catholic Churches. He even managed to reconcile the two branches of Ethiopian Orthodoxy that were sundered in 1991 in circumstances now described.

Two Abunas

One aspect of the takeover by the EPRDF in 1991 was the departure of Abuna Merkorios. The circumstances of his demitting office are debated, with some observers favoring his resignation, while others view it as a result of action by the EPRDF.[66] Some written and oral evidence has recently emerged supporting the latter view.[67] In June 1992 the Holy Synod of the Ethiopian Orthodox Church elected Abuna Paulos as its new patriarch. He was a former protégé of Abuna Theophilos, had been imprisoned with him, and had then earned a PhD at Princeton Theological Seminary in 1988.[68] It is reported that while in the United States Paulos clashed with Abba Yishaq (1933–2005), the archbishop of the Western Hemisphere (as the diocese for Ethiopian Orthodox Churches in Europe and the United States is called). It has been claimed by two academic authors that Yishaq was viewed by Paulos as too closely aligned with bishops appointed under the Derg and as having supported the appointment of Theophilus' successor. Paulos ran a church in New York that appears to have attracted Ethiopians who opposed the Derg and not to have accepted Yishaq's authority. Paulos was an obvious choice for the Ethiopian Church to replace Theophilus since he was a significant figure in exile and well known internationally.[69] The fact that Theophilus' remains were buried the day before Paulos was installed signals the Ethiopian Church's attempt to restore canonicity that had arguably been threatened and to secure the recognition of the Coptic Church.[70]

In 1992 Abuna Merkorios left Ethiopia for Kenya, claiming he had not abdicated willingly. This led to Abba Yishaq leading a secession of the Western Hemisphere Diocese. He declared on September 22, 1992, in New York City that his group was independent of the mother church in Addis Ababa.[71] It should be noted that in the past thirty years some one million people have emigrated from Ethiopia and Eritrea, and many have settled in the United States.[72] This meant a synod in exile had come into existence, which attracted Ethiopian clergy disaffected with the appointment of Paulos. In 1997 Abuna Merkorios moved to the United States and in 2007 appointed thirteen bishops for the church in exile, which led to the factions excommunicating one another.[73] The church in exile took the view that the appointment of Paulos was engineered by the EPRDF, a view contested by the hierarchy in Ethiopia.[74] Abuna Paulos died on August 16, 2012, and he was replaced by Abuna Mathias, previously the archbishop of the Ethiopian Orthodox Church in Jerusalem and the Holy Land, on February 28, 2013.

Yet on August 1, 2018, the innovative approach to old problems being implemented by Ethiopia's new prime minister, Abiy Ahmed, led to a resolution of this rupture between the two branches of Ethiopian Orthodoxy. In a truly remarkable feat of reconciliation of religious conflict, Ahmed returned to Addis Ababa from an unofficial visit to the United States with Abuna Merkorios on his plane. Not surprisingly, they were met at the airport by an enthusiastic crowd of dignitaries and musicians. The prime minister had brokered a reconciliation in Washington, DC, between the branches of Ethiopian Orthodoxy. The two Synods had agreed to reunite and had rescinded their mutual excommunications. As part of the agreement, Abuna Matthias was to serve as the administrative patriarch, while Abuna Merkorios was to serve the church's spiritual functions on an equal authoritative footing.[75] They were both to share the patriarchal compound in Addis Ababa. In relation to these events, the new prime minister of Ethiopia expressed the wish that the church would receive more autonomy but also focus on the causes of the poor and of justice.[76]

PART THREE

ETHIOPIAN ORTHODOXY

5

Intellectual and Literary Traditions

Writing existed in Ethiopia from about the seventh century BCE (see chapter 1). The use of writing continued in Ethiopia with the arrival of Frumentius and the Nine Saints. Writing has perdured in Christian circles in the country in an unbroken line for some 1,700 years. In spite of the introduction of modern processes of printing on paper, the writing and copying of manuscripts on vellum, with the parchment balanced on the knee of the author or copyist just as in ancient Greece and Rome, continues to this day. Sometime around the fourth century CE, when Frumentius was promoting Christianity in Ethiopia, a new way to write Ge'ez, a Semitic language spoken in Aksum, was invented. This entailed modifying the shape of each of the twenty-six consonants used in the language to form an additional six versions of each letter that indicated which vowel followed the consonant. Of all the Semitic languages, only in Ge'ez was such a modification of the consonants ever introduced. Possibly under the influence of Christian scribes familiar with Greek, the convention of writing the language from left to right was introduced (rather than, for example, from right to left).[1] Ge'ez, written in this form, became and remained the dominant language of the Ethiopian Church. Across fifteen centuries ancient texts from the Mediterranean world have been preserved in Ethiopia (normally by translation into Geʻez from sources written in Greek, Coptic, or Arabic), even though some disappeared elsewhere in the Christian world, and a vast new corpus of literature was composed in Geʻez. Unfortunately, very few people, "outside the circle of scholars of ancient languages truly realize the importance of this body of literature found in Ethiopia and written in Geʻez."[2] This chapter is devoted to answering this need by giving some indication of the nature and extent of this literature and the intellectual and literary traditions it embodies.

The Aksumite Period (ca. 350–750 CE)

Manuscripts began entering Ethiopia probably as early as Frumentius but certainly with the arrival of the Nine Saints. Aksum's importance in the Mediterranean and Red Sea trade until the seventh century CE encouraged relatively easy movement of people and manuscripts from various parts of the Christian world, Egypt and Syria especially, to Ethiopia. The construction of monasteries from the time of arrival of the Nine Saints onward inevitably meant the establishment of an infrastructure for the composition, copying, illuminating, and preservation of manuscripts and the intellectual activity and theological reflection that the availability of such texts enabled and fostered.

The most important texts for the early Christians were those of the Bible, the New Testament especially, but also the Old Testament. At an early point, probably in the fifth or sixth centuries CE, these were translated from Greek into Geʻez. In Ethiopia a number of other texts were regarded as part of the Old Testament and were copied and have survived to this day. Chief among them are the ancient Jewish apocalyptic text, 1 Enoch, and the book of Jubilees, which retells traditions relating to the patriarchs and Moses, assigning them to chronological periods. While 1 Enoch became particularly important among the extra-biblical texts in Ethiopia, the process whereby it acquired that status was quite complex.³ Jubilees and 1 Enoch, both highly significant texts in themselves and for understanding certain biblical works, have been preserved in their entirety only in Ethiopia in Ge'ez. The Ethiopian Orthodox Church today regards the Bible as composed of eighty-one texts, forty-six in the Old Testament (as opposed to thirty-nine in the Protestant Bible) and thirty-five in the New Testament (as opposed to twenty-seven in the Protestant and Roman Catholic Bible). Apart from biblical texts, another work that has been preserved only in Ethiopia is the *Ascension of Isaiah*. Recent research has illuminated a significant aspect of the interest of the Ethiopian Church in the New Testament during the period while Aksum was still a powerful kingdom. This research concerns the Garima Gospels.

The Abba Garima Monastery, established by Abba Garima (one of the Nine Saints) in the sixth century CE, is located in hilly country in the northern Ethiopian region of Tigray. It has long been known to possess three ancient illuminated Gospel books (now known as Garima I, II, and III), written in Ge'ez, which had previously been dated to between the eighth and thirteenth centuries. At a conference held in Oxford in November 2013 to discuss these Gospels came the exciting news that a fragment of Garima III had been radiocarbon dated to 330–650 CE, which made it the oldest surviving illuminated Gospel book in the world. In addition, Garima I had been radiocarbon dated to 530–660 CE. Garima II is more recent than these but still older than any other Ethiopian Gospel book.⁴ The age of Garima III remarkably meant that not Europe (for all its libraries and universities) nor the ancient monasteries in the Middle East and Armenia but Ethiopia, long on the fringe of the Christian world and with a turbulent history including its almost total destruction by a Muslim army in the early sixteenth century, had preserved the oldest illuminated Gospels. They constitute powerful testimony to the longevity and magnificence of the intellectual and aesthetic traditions of Ethiopian Orthodoxy, with the former the subject of this chapter and the latter covered in chapter 6.

The illuminations of the Garima Gospels contain details (including Ethiopian birds and aspects of Aksumite architecture) demonstrating that they were executed in Ethiopia, and this strongly suggests the texts of the Gospels, in Ge'ez, were inscribed on vellum pages there as well. It is highly likely that Garima I and III were produced in a monastery (perhaps, but not necessarily, Garima itself) in the Kingdom of Aksum. Garima I and III therefore have the honor of being the only written outputs of Aksumite civilization to have survived on parchment. Their particular relevance for this chapter, however, is that they do not just contain the Ge'ez translations of the Gospels of Matthew, Mark, Luke, and John but also another feature that incontrovertibly points to a high level of intellectual and theological reflection by the monks for whom these Gospels were produced. The monks on this extreme southern flank of Christianity shared this feature with others like them across the Christian world. The feature in question is the "canon tables" that these Gospels contain.

The canon tables were an invention of St. Eusebius (ca. 260–ca. 340 CE). Although our system of chapters and verses to identify different parts of the Gospels and other texts of the New Testament had not yet been invented, in the Greek-speaking Christian East a standardized system had developed in which the Gospels were divided into sections identified by numbers in their margins. Eusebius had the bright idea of formulating ten "canons," or tables, distributed across eight pages, which identified how the Gospels agreed with or differed from each other. Thus canon 1 identified which sections appeared in all four Gospels, canon 2 identified which appeared in Matthew, Mark, and Luke, canon 5 those in Matthew and Luke and so on. As Francis Watson, in a brilliant discussion of the Garima canon tables, has pointed out, this system shows the real order and harmony underlying what might appear to be a fairly chaotic situation caused by having four Gospels.[5] "The primary function of these tables is to make parallel passages available for consultation, but they also serve to *display* the harmonious order underlying the apparent chaos of gospel interrelations."[6] In time the tables came to be depicted in the context of decorative schemes.

Intellectual and Literary Traditions 105

They became framed in elaborate imagery from architecture and the natural world (figure 5.1). Alongside this development came decreasing emphasis on their function.[7] This process is very evident in the numerous errors and omissions that are to be found in the tables of the Garima Gospel books, coupled with

Figure 5.1. *Colored reproduction of the canon table from Garima Gospel book I, from a wall poster in the Abba Garima Monastery*
Garima Gospel book I, page 5, in an enlarged wall poster on display in a manuscripts room in the Abba Garima Monastery, Tigray, northern Ethiopia

their powerful and complex visual imagery that tends to underline the links between Old and New Testaments, so that these Ethiopian examples now become "objects of contemplation, an end not a means."[8] Nevertheless, even in this form the tables disclose significant intellectual and theological energies being deployed in Ethiopia, as in the rest of the Christian world, to understand and utilize the scriptural diversity occasioned by the existence of the four Gospels. Accordingly, in the very earliest stratum of Ethiopian Orthodoxy, we discover the beginnings of potent intellectual and visual traditions that will persist through time and in the face of extreme adversity.

While never forgetting, in particular, the enormous destruction wrought by the Gragn and his Muslim army in the sixteenth century, the fact that the Abba Garima Monastery in the North still possesses Gospel books probably written in the fourth to sixth centuries CE illustrates the remarkable reality of scholarly continuity in Ethiopia.

The Ethiopian Orthodox Church was closely connected with the (Coptic) Orthodox Church in Egypt. Athanasius, the patriarch of the latter, had ordained Frumentius bishop over Ethiopia (around 335 CE), and, as noted in chapter 3, this tradition continued, with some interruptions, until 1959. "This position has determined the dogmatic choices of the Ethiopian Church, which is miaphysite just like its mother Church."[9] The Egyptian Church and others, such as the Armenian Apostolic Church, the Syriac Orthodox (Jacobite) Church, and the Malankara Orthodox Church (of India) all rejected the teaching of the Council of Chalcedon in 451 CE that Christ had two natures, one human and one divine, joined in a hypostatic union. These churches insisted that Christ had only one nature, and in this respect they diverged from the theology of other Eastern Orthodox Churches, such as those of Constantinople, Antioch, and Jerusalem. In the official name of the church in Ethiopia, the Tewahedo Orthodox Church of Ethiopia, the word Tewahedo means "made one" or "unified" and refers to this single nature of Christ.

Given that the Ethiopian Church followed its Egyptian mother church in relation to this central question of Christology, we would expect it to have maintained close links in other ways. Remarkable evidence for that connection, and for the intellectual activity of the Ethiopian Church that is evident in the Garima Gospel books during the Aksumite period, emerged with the discovery of a manuscript in Geʻez at Ura Masqal, in Tigray, northern Ethiopia, in 1999, by Jacques Mercier, and its speedy analysis in the same year by Alessandro Bausi. The manuscript is dated no later than the thirteenth century, but its text proved to be much older. It is a translation of a work from Greek into Geʻez undertaken in the Aksumite period (fourth to seventh century CE). The Greek work was a collection of documents written from the fourth to the second half of the fifth century CE that emanated from the Coptic Patriarchate in Alexandria. It includes a history of that patriarchate, numerous canons from ecumenical councils, liturgical texts, passages from Patristic authors, several letters of historical importance, theological texts, prayers, and some other material.[10] This recently discovered work is evidence, therefore, of someone in Aksum, probably a monk and connected with Egypt in such a way as to allow him to have possession of a Greek document originating from there, translating it into Geʻez for use among other Ethiopians, presumably those who did not know Greek. One text in the collection deserves special mention: *The Refutation of the Council of Chalcedon*.[11] The theological distinctiveness of the Ethiopian Orthodox Church lies especially in its rejection of the Chalcedonian formulation of Christ's nature, and here we find a work along these lines being translated into Geʻez during the Aksumite period. This confirms the antiquity of opposition to Chalcedon among Ethiopian Christians.

The establishment of the monasteries in the fifth and sixth centuries CE necessitated the translation into Geʻez of monastic manuals from the foundation of monasticism in Egypt in the fourth century CE. This explains the very early translation of the *Life of St Anthony*, the founder of eremitic monasticism (written by

Athanasius), the *Life of St Paul the Hermit*, and the *Rule of St Pachomius*,[12] who founded cenobitic monasticism.[13] The monasteries in Ethiopia followed the Pachomian pattern, of a walled compound in which was built a church and a number of other buildings, including a refectory and small huts for the monks, and, by and large, they do so to this day.

Other patristic texts were translated into Geʻez for the purposes of doctrinal teaching in religious settings. The oldest such manual in Ethiopia is the *Qirillos*. It contains some of the writings of St. Cyril (Qirillos) of Alexandria, patriarch of Alexandria from 412 to 444 (and hence an authoritative figure in Ethiopia), and a collection of homilies and extracts from the writings of early church fathers, such as Theodotus of Ancyra, Severus of Sinnada, and Juvenal of Jerusalem. St. Cyril of Alexandria was also a source for the theological idea that the divine and human represented one nature in Christ, not two. Cyril was thus one of the foundations for the miaphysite theology of Ethiopian Orthodoxy. Less exalted theologically, but very popular, was *The Physiologus*. This text, composed in Syria in the third or fourth century CE, was a collection of observations about animals, plants, and minerals that concluded with a spiritual moral and was translated from Greek into many languages, including Geʻez.

The Zagwe Period (ca. Twelfth to Thirteenth Centuries CE)

Literary remains from the Zagwe period are virtually nonexistent. This does not mean that texts were not being copied or even composed but that little evidence of them survives. This was a time when Ethiopia had a settled royal capital and some patronage of literature—to match the efforts put into the construction of the superlative stone churches at Lalibela (see chapter 6)—seems likely. There are, moreover, references to the Ethiopia of this period in Arab works of a historical or geographical nature, and while none of their authors appear to have visited the country, some, such as

Al Yaqubi and Al Masudi, had access to accurate information. There is also useful material in Coptic in the biographies of the patriarchs of the Coptic Church in Alexandria, which occasionally mention Ethiopian affairs, especially since the patriarch in Alexandria appointed the head of the Ethiopian Church, who had to be an Egyptian. These sources sometimes lend credibility to documentation in Ethiopia itself, which dates from the fourteenth century.[14]

The fact that Lalibela was earlier known as Roha, the Syriac name of Edessa, suggests the possible diffusion throughout the country during the Zagwe period of the legend of Abgar, king of Edessa, and his correspondence with Jesus Christ. Although the *Ethiopic Legend of Abgar* is only extant in manuscripts of the seventeenth century, they could well be based on manuscripts from the Zagwe period.[15] Similarly, although the earliest known version of the *Gadla Lalibela*, the text venerating the deeds of King Lalibela, dates back to the fourteenth century,[16] it may have antecedents in the Zagwe period.

The Solomonic Period (1270–1974 CE)

Fourteenth-Century Literature

With the beginning of the Solomonic period, Ethiopian literature, much of it on religious subjects or written by monks or priests, becomes much more common. The earliest Solomonic text is the *Zena Amda Seyon* (The chronicle of Amda Seyon), which describes the various successful wars waged by Amda Seyon I, the ninth king of this dynasty, who reigned from 1314 to 1344. This work was written between 1331 and 1344. An English translation of part of the text (a campaign against Muslim rebels in 1329) was published in 1965.[17] The work has a vividness that suggests it was written very close to the events it describes but in a smooth and unadorned style. It is not simply an account of events but also includes discourses by its heroes. The text draws upon biblical passages at numerous points. The author was most likely a chaplain to the royal court of Amda Seyon who was close to the king and had witnessed the wars about which he writes.[18]

The fourteenth century not only witnessed songs celebrating Amda Seyon as a great warrior and written in Amharic, which are not relevant to this volume, but also sacred poetry of considerable artistic value, most of it still unpublished. The subject is usually the heroic deeds of martyrs, told in dialogue. One hymn concerns St. Mercurius (224–250 CE), one of four military saints revered in Ethiopia, and describes how, when Mercurius had been burned to death, St. Michael the archangel descended to put out the fire and his body was then stolen away and buried. Another hymn concerns the martyrs of Najran (in northeast Yemen) who in 523 CE had been killed by a Yemenite prince. These events are connected with the expedition of Kaleb to conquer Yemen (see chapter 3), with Kaleb being celebrated in the hymn. A third hymn, "For the Crucifixion," is a dramatic poem on Christ's death.[19]

The Kebra Nagast

From the fourteenth century also comes a work that is so significant as to require more detailed attention—the *Kebra Nagast* (The glory of the kings). This is not merely a literary work but "one of the most powerful and influential national sagas anywhere in the world" and "the repository of Ethiopian national and religious feelings."[20] This Ge'ez version, which many scholars date to the years 1314–1322 CE (the early years of the reign of Amda Seyon), may have been a translation, at least in part, of an Arabic original. Parts of the text may have been circulating in Ethiopia in earlier centuries. The point of the book, however, is crystal clear. It is to describe the origin of the ruling Solomonic dynasty and to legitimate its authority by tracing it back to King Solomon and the queen of Sheba.

The text mentions the tabernacle (*tabot*) in its first chapter as one of the glorious things that God gave to the children of Adam, whose creation it also describes (chapter 1).[21] It then reformulates its purpose as stating "which of the kings of the earth, from the first event unto the last, in respect of the Law and Ordinances and honour and greatness, we should magnify or decry" (chapter 2).[22] After an account of the patriarchs and Moses and Aaron (chapters 3–17), the story turns to its central narrative, concerning the queen of the South (Matt 12:42; Luke 11:31) and Solomon and their son, Menelik I (chapters 21–39). In this narrative the queen of the South is described as the queen of Ethiopia (chapter 21) but is also called Queen Makeda. Encouraged by a merchant who has been supplying goods to Solomon for the construction of the temple and is very impressed by the king and his wisdom, the queen travels to Jerusalem, where she and Solomon are greatly taken with one another as they engage in protracted conversation (chapters 22–27). After six months of this, the queen sends word to Solomon that she must return to Ethiopia. This induces the following thought on Solomon's part: "A woman of such splendid beauty hath come to me from the ends of the earth! What do I know? Will God give me seed in her?" The narrator then comments that "Solomon the King was a lover of women," with four hundred queens and six hundred concubines, not for the sake of fornication "but as a result of the wise intent that God had given unto him, and his remembering what God had said unto Abraham, 'I will make thy seed like the stars of heaven for number, and like the sand of the sea.'" Eventually Solomon tricks the queen into sleeping with him. He swears not to take her by force so long as she swears not to take by force anything of his in the palace. But he has made sure she was fed very spicy food beforehand, and, when she surreptitiously tries to drink some water during the night, he reminds her of her oath. And so she lets him sleep with her (chapters 29–30). She sets out for Ethiopia richly laden with gifts Solomon has given her (chapter 31). Nine months into the journey she gives birth to a son, who grows to be very much like Solomon in appearance. Having turned twenty-two, the young man resolves to visit his father (chapter 32). He receives a very warm welcome in Israel, and Solomon wants him, his firstborn son, to become king of Israel (chapters 33–37). But the young man insists on returning to Ethiopia. So Solomon resolves to make him king of Ethiopia and to send him home with the firstborn children of the Israelite nobility (chapter 38). Once the young man has been invested with kingship, Zadok the priest gives him careful instruction in central aspects of the law of Moses (chapters 40–42). Solomon ordains that the young men who are to be sent back to Ethiopia with his son should have high functions in government matching those of his court: so Solomon is sending back not just a king but a collection of the major courtiers who will be needed to manage the royal administration (chapter 43). The young men traveling to Ethiopia, advised by one of their number, a son of the High Priest, resolve to take the ark of the covenant with them and, to that end and with God's help, remove it from the Temple, leaving a dummy structure covered in purple cloths in its place (chapters 44–48). Solomon blesses his son, and the group departs, leaving Jerusalem sorrowful and bereft, even though its inhabitants do not realize the ark is leaving with them (chapters 49–50). Eventually their procession reaches Ethiopia, to universal joy (chapter 55). A sorrowful Solomon recounts to Zadok a dream he had during the queen of Ethiopia's visit in which the sun moved from illuminating the country of Judah to the country of Ethiopia. This leads to Zadok's discovering the ark has been stolen and his immediate death (chapters 56–57). A furious Solomon sets off in pursuit, intending to kill the young Israelites with his son but to no avail (chapters 58–62). There is then a break in the story, until it resumes with Menelik's arrival in Ethiopia, his mother's abdication and her extracting an oath from the nobles that the kingdom of Ethiopia should never again be ruled by a queen (but only by male descendants of her son), and his first wars (chapters 84–94).

The dominant purpose of the *Kebra Nagast* was to provide legitimation for the new Solomonic dynasty vis-à-vis the Zagwe dynasty. Yet it also seems to reflect the bias of the local clergy who supported the glorified northern kingdom against a kingdom increasingly based in the Amharic-speaking South. At the same time, the text must be understood within the wider tendency to stress Judaic influences on Ethiopian Orthodoxy. The notion of the Ethiopians as the new chosen people, who had taken the place of Israel as symbolized in the movement of the ark of the covenant to their country, provided a powerful national myth that shaped their cultural identity. Even today the story of the queen of Ethiopia, Solomon, and Menelik I is widely regarded as historical fact among Orthodox Christians, and the ark of the covenant is actually thought to exist in a small building next to the Cathedral of St. Mary of Zion in Aksum (figure 5.2).[23]

Other Fourteenth-Century Works

A number of works from the fourteenth century reflect a curious tradition concerning Mary. According to the *Kebra Nagast* (chapter 68), a pearl was created in Adam's stomach before the creation of Eve. This pearl, a symbol of the Virgin Mary and the salvation that would come from her, did not go into Cain or Abel but into Seth

Figure 5.2. *Chapel of the Ark of the Covenant (in foreground), adjacent to the Cathedral of St. Mary of Zion, Aksum*

and thence into Abraham, Isaac, Jacob, Perez, and Jesse, and then it skipped six generations before lodging in David. Finally, it reached Anna, Mary's mother (and hence Mary herself). Sometimes it was carried by men and sometimes by women, and any who carried it would be saved. The symbol of the pearl, identified with Mary and the redemption of the soul, is also found in another work from this period, the *Book of Mysteries of Heaven and Earth*. It contains revelations sent by the archangel to the author's teacher. Some of it covers material akin to that in 1 Enoch and the Apocalypse of John.[24] Another work mentioning the pearl is the *Life of St Ann*, which probably dates back to the fourteenth century, even though the oldest manuscript is from the fifteenth. The story of the initial childlessness of Mary's parents, Joachim and Anna, dates back to the early Christian work, the *Protoevangelium of James* (images from which were painted by Giotto in the Scrovegni Chapel in Padua). In this development of the tradition, God appears as a white bird descending from heaven and lands on Anna's head. Thereupon the pearl grows within her and becomes the body of the Virgin Mary.[25]

A fourteenth-century work of surprising importance and probably a translation from Arabic or Syriac is the *Zena Eskender* (The chronicle of Alexander). This is based on legends, increasingly fantastical, concerning Alexander the Great that appeared after this death, some of them in a work by pseudo-Callisthenes. In this story Alexander, carried by griffins or eagles, crosses the land of darkness and reaches the land of the living. There he meets Enoch and Elijah and finds the water of life wherein dwell huge fish that no one is able to kill.[26] He learns of half-human, half-animal creatures who are subjects of the kings Gog and Magog, and he employs a bronze door to stop them invading the human world.[27] This story gained wide currency in Ethiopia, not least because Alexander's success against evil forces made this a popular visual motif on Ethiopian prayer scrolls (see chapter 6).

The final fourteenth-century text worthy of mention is the *Synaxarium* (Collection), a large work concerning Christian saints and their lives for reading on each day of the thirteen months of the Ethiopian liturgy. It is probably a translation from an Arabic version but with Ethiopian additions. Over the centuries it was reworked to reflect local traditions and the new saints who were added to the list.[28]

Fifteenth-Century Literature

The fifteenth century witnessed a major uplift in literary activity on religious topics that was associated with the reforming efforts and energies of Emperor Zara Yaqob (see chapter 3). A popular literary form during this period were the acts of holy monks who challenged royal authority, especially that of Amda Seyon (reigned 1314–1344). In these works we see not the king celebrated in the *Zena Amda Seyon* (see above) but an autocrat who is idolized by the complacent clergy at his court and who attacks the monks who call him to account, especially for his marital misconduct. The works reflecting this conflict were the *gadls*, the "struggles," or "contests," of individual saints and monks who were the heroes of particular texts. Over the course of time, new incidents tended to be added to individual *gadls*, which can make it difficult to distinguish the layers of tradition they contain. Major examples include *The Acts of Philip* (third abbot of the monastery of Dabra Libanos in Shoa), *The Acts of Ba-Salota Michael* (abbot of Dabra Gol in Amhara), *The Acts of Samuel* (abbot of Dabra Wagag in southeast Shoa), *The Acts of Honorius* (abbot of the monastery of Segajia in Shoa), and *The Acts of Aaron Taumaturg* (abbot of Dabra Daret). The growth of this literature probably reflects the rising power, influence, and confidence of the monasteries under the patronage of Emperor Zara Yaqob.[29]

Several other types of literature from this period deserve comment. Rather surprisingly, kings from the Zagwe dynasty, replaced by the Solomonic line two centuries before, come to be celebrated as saints. "It is obvious that a long interval, nearly 200 years, had to elapse before it was safe to write with appreciation of members of a dynasty of 'usurpers.'"[30] Not least of these was King Lalibela himself, in whose honor their capital city of Roha later came to be called Lalibela. Another literary type was cycles of acts by founders of important monasteries in the South.[31] These included *The Acts of Iyasus Moa*, the founder of the monastery of St Stephen of (Lake) Hayq, and *The Acts of Takla Haymanot*, founder of the monastery of Dabra Libanos (originally called Dabra Asbo).[32] Many legends collected around Takla Haymanot. One that is recorded in his *Acts* is particularly well known in Ethiopia and often appears in paintings of this saint. Toward the end of his life, he entered his cell, blocking the entry of the cave with a rock, and stood there for seven years, so that his legs swelled from the great torment of this position and one of them dropped off. But he continued standing on just the other leg![33] Another legend recounts that as he was descending a rope from the mountain of a monastery Satan cut it, but God gave him six wings to fly safely to the floor of the valley below.

The fifteenth century also witnessed the composition of acts celebrating the monks of the Nine Saints from the fifth and sixth centuries CE in the mountains of Tigray in the North, but it is unclear whether these are largely fanciful or may depend, at least in part, on the preservation of sources across the intervening period that have not survived from the early centuries (as so little has).[34] One work relating to one of the Nine Saints is the *Homily on Garima*.[35] This saint was the reputed founder of the Garima monastery, home of the Garima Gospel books, two of which are now dated to the Aksumite period (see above). A third type of text from this period was religious poetry. Much of this took the form of hymns composed at the direction of the emperor, many of them on Marian themes. But at this time we observe the first examples of *qene* poetry, which is subject to special treatment below.

A fifteenth-century work that was to have an enormous impact on Ethiopian popular devotion, continuously reinforced in the liturgy and the pictorial traditions of the country, was the *Ta'amera Maryam* (The miracles of Mary). The *Ta'amera* genre has become "perhaps the most characteristic aspect of Abyssinian literature."[36] *The Miracles of Mary*, which largely records miracles that various people had experienced at Mary's intercession, began to develop in France in the mid-twelfth century CE. There was, however, a tradition attributing its composition to St. Ildephonsus of Toledo (who died in 667 CE) to demonstrate his great love for her. To honor him for this devotion, Mary appeared to him and gave him a divine robe and a throne. Soon the text spread across the Christian world. It was translated into Arabic in the thirteenth century and from Arabic into Ethiopic in the fourteenth. By the fifteenth century Ethiopian versions had been embellished with various local history and traditions. As mentioned in chapter 3, Emperor Zara Yaqob prescribed readings for it in the liturgy on Marian feast days. In due course there were thirty-three miracles that formed a kind of canonical set, but in Ethiopia other stories were added.[37] The Ethiopian versions of the text open with the story of St. Ildephonsus.

For the last examples of works from the fifteenth century, we turn to Emperor Zara Yaqob himself. Of him Ullendorff has written:

> The great reformer of the organization of the state and of the religious life of the country stimulated fresh translations from Arabic of all such writings as would lend force to his own endeavours; and he inspired and encouraged polemical tracts that would justify his own political and religious innovations.[38]

Two important works, although more theological than literary in nature, are attributed to Emperor Zara Yaqob himself (it being uncertain whether he wrote them or whether they were ghostwritten for him). These are the *Mashafa Berhan* (The book of light) and the *Mashafa Milad* (The book of the nativity). In the former, the king provides admonitions and regulations, supplies an exposition of his ecclesiastical reforms, refutes heresies, attacks magical practices, and reinstates the equal observance of Sabbath and Sunday. Some of the material in the *Mashafa Milad* is similar; its preface appears to contain the punishments the king had inflicted on traitors who were planning to burn some volumes of these two texts.[39]

The Sixteenth Century

The dominant political event in the sixteenth century was the Muslim invasion led by Imam Ahmad ibn Ibrahim al-Ghazi (see chapter 3). While his army wrought immense devastation on the country, this did not mean that all Ethiopian literature was irretrievably lost, even though much was. Although many monasteries and churches were burned and important collections were destroyed, large numbers of works existed in copies that were distributed in various places so that stocks could be rebuilt once the invasion was over. Accordingly, while it is possible that some works did disappear entirely, there was no irrevocable break in the transmission of literary texts.[40] The survival of so many manuscripts from the fifteenth century, for example, testifies to significant continuity in the tradition. In addition, some significant works were composed in response to the invasion. *The Acts of Takla Alfa* is a work by the abbot of a monastery in Gojjam during the invasion. The work reveals the troubles suffered by religious communities forced to flee to various places during those years. The *Anqasa Amin* (The gate of faith) was written by a certain Enbaqom (ca. 1470–ca. 1565), who was a Muslim from the Yemen who emigrated to Ethiopia, where he converted to Christianity and took that name. He became a monk and, in due course, the abbot of the great monastery of Dabra Libanos, meaning he was the *echege*, the leading figure in Ethiopian monasticism.[41] His *Anqasa Amin* was composed in Arabic but translated into Ethiopic. It is an apology for Christianity against Islam and uses passages from the Qur'an to demonstrate the truth of the Christian faith.[42]

A notable work from the period of the Oromo migrations, published in 1593, is Abba Bahrey's *History of the Galla*.[43] The book is a short treatise on the ethnic and political situation of the Oromo, and it describes people and events otherwise largely unknown. The author argues that the Oromo were militarily successful against a well-armed Christian people because their social organization and customs were more suited to warfare.[44] Although this work has long been regarded as an important historical source, more recent scholarship regards it as pseudo-anthropology rather than history and based not on the wider Oromo population but on only a local branch of this people, and therefore scholars argue for its controversial and even superficial nature.[45]

The arrival of the Jesuits later in the century (Imam Ahmad ibn Ibrahim al-Ghazi having been defeated and killed in 1543) and the animosity that they eventually stirred up led to the lively production of texts by champions of traditional Ethiopian Orthodoxy. One of these was a defense of the faith by Emperor Gelawedros (Claudius) himself, who reigned from 1540 to 1559, known as the *Confession of Claudius*. The first part of the text is a formal defense of the miaphysite Christology characteristic of Ethiopian Orthodoxy, and the second part provides a defense of Ethiopian customs, such as circumcision, Sabbath observance, and the ban on pork.[46] Other works reasserting traditional Ethiopian beliefs from this period included the *Sawana Nafs* (Refuge of the soul) and *Fekkare Malakot* (Exposition of the divinity) that set out what would become classic statements of miaphysite doctrine. Also from this period, based on an Arabic original, was *Haymanota Abaw* (Faith of the fathers) containing homilies from the fathers, pastoral letters, and theological discussions on topics such as the nature of the Trinity, the incarnation, and the meaning of miaphysitism. In similar vein, but more polemical in tone, was the *Mazgaba Haymanot* (Treasure of the faith), which stirred up a strong response from the Jesuits in defense of Roman Catholicism.[47]

There are some other sixteenth-century works that deserve mention. *The Book of Barlaam and Josaphat* is a Christianized story of one of the legends of Buddha. It originated in India and then spread westward to the wider Christian world, where it became widely popular. It was translated into Ethiopic by Enbaqom, the abbot of Dabra Libanos (see above), about 1553 CE. The story relates how astrologers prophesied that King Abener's son, Josaphat, would one day become a Christian. The king tried to prevent this, but the prince met a hermit called Barlaam and converted to Christianity. He became king in due course but eventually abdicated from the throne and retired to an ascetic life with Barlaam.

A very important text, especially for its influence on Ethiopian art, was the *Gadla Giyorgis* (The struggle [or acts] and miracles of St. George). This consists of the juxtaposition of two works that had a Greek Christian origin. One is the *Miracles of St George*, written by Theodosius, bishop of Jerusalem, describing twelve miracles, and the second is *The Encomium of St George*, written by Theodotus, bishop of Ancyra. In Egypt, and then in Ethiopia, extra miracles were added. In the fifteenth or early sixteenth century *The Acts of St Sebastian*, written around 1424, was translated into Ethiopic.[48]

Mid-seventeenth to Mid-nineteenth Centuries

There was also some literary activity in the two centuries of isolation and fragmentation of central power, from the mid-seventeenth to the mid-nineteenth centuries. Some of this was stimulated by the heated debates with the Jesuits, including *The Treasury of Faith*, a summary of decisions of church councils in the fourth and fifth centuries CE and of debate on Christology held in the presence of Emperor Claudius, who had reigned from 1540 to 1559. At the same time, the fact that the Catholic-Orthodox disputes had been conducted in Amharic (spoken in central and southern Ethiopia) legitimated wider use of this language. Religious literature and commentaries began to be written in Amharic. This language proved particularly suitable for the *qene* form, discussed below.

The *Gadla Walatta Petros* (Struggle [acts] of the daughter of Petros) was written in 1673–1674 by a monk from the Afaf-Faras community that had been founded by Walatta Petros, who had died in 1644. She had been an energetic champion of Ethiopian Orthodoxy against Roman Catholicism during the reign of Emperor Susenyos. After the restoration of Orthodoxy, she stoutly opposed any deviation from what she regarded as correct Christian discipline (figure 5.3).

Another work from this period is the *Chronicle of John, Bishop of Nikiu* (in Egypt), which runs from the creation of the world to the Arab conquest of Egypt (for which it is a source of the utmost

Intellectual and Literary Traditions 121

Figure 5.3. *St. Walatta Petros, from a manuscript dated 1721*

importance), that appeared in an Ethiopic translation from the Arabic in 1602. The manuscript was brought back from Magdala by a member of the British expedition under Sir John Napier of 1868.[49]

The last work to be considered is the *Fetha Nagast* (The laws of the kings).[50] This was not an original Ethiopian composition but was rather derived from a work written in 1238 in Arabic by an Egyptian Christian jurist. According to Ethiopian tradition it was probably translated into Ge'ez during the reign of Emperor Zara Yaqob (1434–1468), although that date is disputed. For centuries this work, along with the Bible, provided Ethiopia with a wide-ranging legal code. Only in the twentieth century was it replaced by civil law enacted by the state. It came strongly to represent the Ethiopian Christian heritage.[51] The laws derive from the Bible with some commentary, the writings of early church fathers including

St. Basil and St. Hippolytus, and possibly also Byzantine legal codes. It has been suggested that the *Fetha Nagast* contributed to the Ethiopian respect for the rule of law. It was the main source for the national law that was taught in Ethiopian schools and remained in force until the time of Haile Selassie.[52] The work is divided into two parts. The first part contains twenty-two chapters dealing largely with issues relating to the Orthodox Church in Ethiopia, for example, laws relating to the appointment, ordination, and status of bishops, priests, deacons and subdeacons, and monks and nuns; the Mass; prayer; fasts; alms; tithes; the sick; and the dead. The second part contains twenty-nine chapters covering the most important issues in civil and criminal law, such as marriage, loans and pledges, slavery and manumission, guardianship, sale, partnership, leases, wills and succession, personnel and procedure at judicial proceedings, blasphemy, homicide, fornication, theft, and drunkenness.

An incident that Aida Edemariam recounts in her absorbing 2018 memoire of her Ethiopian grandmother, *The Wife's Tale*, well illustrates the central role of the *Fetha Nagast* in Ethiopian life until very recently and the close interconnections between the church and the Solomonic dynasty that it enabled. The grandmother was married to a very learned cleric who became a person of some influence and position in Gondar. Before the Italians arrived he had previously served as (a comparatively minor) judge in the Saturday market. When Emperor Haile Selassie, after his return from exile in 1941, heard that this cleric had learned all of the *Fetha Nagast* by heart, he appointed him as a judge in the provincial criminal court.[53]

Qene

The penultimate section of this chapter focuses on an aspect of the literary traditions of Ethiopian Orthodoxy that made its appearance some seven centuries ago and is still part of Orthodox culture—the form of poetic composition known as *qene*. Qene, derived from *qenaya*, which means "to sing, or make music," is an improvised, allegorized form of poetry that follows strict rules, used in the liturgy and on other occasions and seldom written down. Although documentation is lacking, it appears that qene made its appearance in the literary renaissance that occurred during the centuries after the rise of the Solomonic dynasty (from 1270 CE onward). Invention of qene is attributed to Tawanay of Gojjam in the fourteenth century. The two earliest-recorded examples of qene date from the reign of Emperor Eskender (1478–1494). They are not very elaborate. The first refers to the punishment to which the king had condemned certain Stephanite heretics and the second to the punishment impending on a rebel who had tried to seize the throne during Eskender's reign.[54] The important schools of qene have always been located in Amhara country. While the churchmen of Tigray have also mastered qene, the use of "wax and gold," which will now be explained, occurs much more often in the vernacular in Amharic than in Tigrinya.[55]

Each instance of qene is created and delivered orally for a particular occasion and used only once.[56] "There is nothing like qene in any other part of the Christian world."[57] It springs from and is closely linked to the culture of the Amhara people of northern Ethiopia, the largest group within Christian Ethiopia, who love verbal ambiguity and complexity.[58] The crux of qene is to say one thing while implying a different thing at the same time and in the same sentence. In Ethiopia these two parts, the obvious meaning and the implied meaning, are referred to as "wax" (*sem*) and "gold" (*warq*). This analogy derives from the craft of the goldsmith in making jewelery. The goldsmith first forms a copy of the desired object in wax, which is soft and easy to mold, and then covers the wax with a cast of clay or plaster and allows it to harden. When molten gold is poured into the cast, the wax melts, leaving the gold in the desired shape. Applied to qene, this means that the first meaning gives way to the second, richer one.[59] It is not a perfect analogy, since in qene the two meanings coexist at the same time, whereas the wax and gold are consecutive, but it is a very vivid one.[60] There are nine basic forms of qene, which begin with a simple two-line verse called a *gubae kwana*, and become progressively more complex until they culminate in the eleven-line *etanemoger*.

The point of qene is to reveal a truth that is hidden, not to conceal a truth that is plain. Theologically speaking, it parallels the conundrum of faith, namely, that we must speak of God, yet God is so far removed from our own experience that our words cannot reach him.[61]

Prior to a *balaqene*, or qene master, creating and reciting a qene, he will reflect, pray, and think, as his qene slowly takes shape. He will then recite it without writing it down, and once the performance is over the qene is gone. Nevertheless, occasionally some outstanding examples of qene are remembered by their appreciative audiences and are written down.

Here is an example of qene:

Since Adam your lip did eat of that Tree
The Savior my heart has been hung up for me.

In this instance the qene has its "wax," or surface meaning, a statement about sin and redemption, roughly meaning:

Because Adam ate of the apple from the Tree of Knowledge
The Savior of the world has been crucified for thee.

To comprehend the "gold" or deeper meaning, however, one needs to know that the Ge'ez word *tasaqala* not only means "was crucified" but also "is anxious to be near." This produces the following "gold" meaning:

Because of your (tempting) lips
My heart is anxious to be near thee.

Thus an overtly theological meaning is actually concealing a message of love.[62]

More elaborate is the following example:

The son of a hermit, high rank to display,
Made love with Christ's wife yesterday;
When she fed him leaves he wasted away.

Intellectual and Literary Traditions

The "wax" meaning is that a man had relations with a woman of higher status than him ("Christ's wife") to gain prestige and further his position. But he lost all his power when she fed him (medicinal) leaves. The "gold" meaning refers to the experience of the hermit (a not uncommon feature of Ethiopian Orthodoxy). His "son" is the hermit's hunger and "Christ's wife" symbolizes fasting. Thus the meaning is that a hermit's hunger is heightened by his embrace of fasting but diminishes when he is fed leaves, the diet of a hermit.[63]

The mastery of qene revealed in examples such as these requires a very deep knowledge of Ge'ez, a meticulous use of language, a prayerful meditation on the subject, and creativity that is based on long-term ascetic discipline and learning. Yet the genre continues because of a large and appreciative audience for this form of poetic creation. Taking these two factors together justifies the conclusion that qene is emblematic of the potent intellectual and literary traditions that have characterized Ethiopian Orthodoxy since the foundations of Christianity in the country during the Aksumite period.

Maintaining the Traditions: Educating the Clergy and Quasi-Clergy

As we have seen, the intellectual and literary tradition of Ethiopian Orthodoxy has, in spite of severe threats at times, been maintained without interruption since the fourth century CE. Striking features of this continuity include the fact that clergy and quasi-clergy know large amounts of scripture by heart, that manuscripts are still handwritten on vellum in a manner essentially the same as in the Greco-Roman world of late antiquity, and that the musical traditions inaugurated by St. Yared in the sixth century CE (see chapter 6) flourish still. The explanation for this continuity lies in the highly distinctive character of clerical education, coupled with the failure of modernity to make much of an inroad into Ethiopia until the second half of the twentieth century. To the Ethiopian system of traditional education we now turn.

Right up until the end of the nineteenth century, education in Ethiopia was the province of the church alone. It appears that the system of church education in Ethiopia was devised in the seventeenth century in the city of Gondar, then the newly built capital of the dynasty of kings founded by the Emperor Fasilidas (reigned 1632–1667).[64] This traditional style of church education is still being practiced in parishes and monasteries.

Even today, although modern schools and universities have been established across the country, modern education is widespread, but it is not universal. As recently as 2005 only around 40 percent of boys and 20 percent of girls attended government schools or mission schools where they obtained a modern education, and these were mainly in the cities.[65] A sample of pupils at a church school in Gondar in 2003 revealed that 70 percent were from farming families, and 70 percent were the youngest in the family.[66] These statistics suggested that church education is rural rather than urban and that farmers encourage the elder sons to stay on the family farm and help with the agriculture, while sending some younger sons to church schools. At a meeting in London in 2003 Liqa Ma'imran (Reverend Professor) Abebau Yigzau expressed the view that church education is still going strong in Ethiopia, particularly in the rural setting. There are, he claimed, more students, more schools than ever before. Moreover, they enjoy better conditions than ever, financially supported at last by parish councils. "Our system of education is excellent," he said. "We don't confuse chemistry with geography. When you study zema, you study zema. Our students know the 150 Psalms of David by heart."[67]

The primary role of church schools was and continues to be to instruct children in Christian religion and literature and to recruit and train suitable candidates to become Orthodox priests or the quasi-clerical (that is, unordained) functionaries known as *dabtarat* (singular: *dabtara*), roughly, unordained clerics who perform hymns and sacred dances in the liturgy and often have considerable literary skills. The church schools also assist the development and propagation of national culture and the creation of a national literature.⁶⁸ The values instilled in a traditional education like this are rather different from those aimed for in modern, Western styles of pedagogy. As a general rule, curiosity, creativity, and critical analysis are not particularly valued, whereas memorization of huge amounts of text and obedience are. The teacher acts as a father figure to students, promoting their growth.⁶⁹ Yet we must recognize the real value in the Ethiopian approach. Learning has an almost physical quality as the student "absorbs or takes the learning and scholarship into the heart and mind. The culture is incorporated into the student and the student is incorporated into the culture."⁷⁰

Let us follow the course of typical students in the traditional route. The first, or elementary, level of education occurs in the so-called school of reading (*nebab bet*) that is located in the compound of a parish church or monastery or in or near the house of one of the teachers. In 1971 it was estimated that some 14,500 of these establishments were operating in Ethiopia.⁷¹ Pupils (boys and some girls) attend from about five to twelve years of age. To begin with, they repeat loudly and in groups the letters of the Ge'ez and Amharic alphabets, with the changes that occur to each form when a vowel is added, until they are memorized (meaning 182 signs for Ge'ez and an extra 49 for Amharic). Most of the lessons are oral. Once the alphabets are mastered, the students then learn to read. They begin with reading and memorizing 1 John in Ge'ez. Next they must memorize the Apostles' Creed and another part of the New Testament. The final stage is to read and to memorize all 150 Psalms in Ge'ez and to master the proper intonation to recite them. This is a very demanding task, and a feast accompanies its completion. Yet while graduates of the school of reading can read and recite fluently, their writing skills are not nearly so advanced. Today, however, this stage of education can serve as preparation for entry to modern state education.⁷²

After completing the school of reading, there are three more levels of education, which are far more advanced. These can take as many as three years each to complete. There is the school of liturgical music (*zema bet*, with *zema* being the word for "chanting"); the school of poetry (*qene bet*), where grammar and poetry are taught; and the school of interpretation (*tergum bet*), where students study scripture, the church fathers, ecclesiastical law, and other subjects. Before considering these three levels, it is worth noting the extraordinarily tough regime that the students, at least at the first two levels, experience.

Students usually leave home and travel to a teacher with whom they wish to continue their studies. John Binns, a Cambridge academic, spent three months at a qene bet at a church in Gondar in 2003 and has provided a vivid account of the students' lives there. The course takes place in the tranquil church compound, filled with trees and with a superb view across a valley. There are two long buildings with bare earth floors, concrete walls, and corrugated iron roofs, with rooms that are used for storage, priests' sleeping areas, and a Sunday school. Below these buildings on the hillside are round *tukul* huts, with grass roofs, about five feet in diameter and unfurnished. In each one of them live four to five students. Cooking is done on a patch of land near these huts. Clothes are washed in the river. Except on special occasions, the school does not provide food to the students. To get food they have to beg, and they arrive at the school with a begging bowl for this purpose. The students have one meal a day, in the afternoon. This usually consists of *injera*, the traditional flatbread of Ethiopia made with fermented teff that is cooked with chili pepper and, sometimes, with chick pea flour. The teaching begins at sunset, when the students go to the space in front of the teacher's room and sit in rows on the rocky ground, sometimes on simple cushions. The teacher teaches them orally, and they repeat and memorize what he has said. Nobody takes notes; indeed, it is too dark to do so. After a couple of hours of teaching, the students go off to mull over what has been said and to memorize the lessons. Around midnight they go to sleep but arise at four in the morning and soon resume where they had left off. The days are filled with private study, begging for food, washing clothes, or having their afternoon meal.[73]

But students are exposed to various other challenges, not least from the dogs in the town where they are studying, which nearly all Ethiopian students undertaking traditional education ruefully recall. Aida Edemariam has described the experience of her own grandfather, Tsega, who became an eminent ecclesiastic in Gondar in the early twentieth century, at this stage of his life:

> During the day the students scattered across the countryside, composing their own poetry and begging, as the church provided no food. Tsega hated this aspect of his calling. He was proud, afraid of dogs, and quickly resorted to tall heart-tugging tales.[74]

Let us return then to the three levels of education. To become a deacon or a priest it is necessary to continue study in the school of liturgical music, where one learns how to chant church services.[75] Most Ethiopian religious poetry and prose is meant to be sung. So, whereas in the West a person wanting to become a priest goes to a seminary and studies philosophy and theology as the indispensable curriculum, in Ethiopia one goes to a musical school.

The music school has four separate disciplines.[76] First comes the study of the chant book (*degwa*), which contains all the songs and hymns sung in church during the year. Degwa is taught in Bethlehem, near Gondar, tradition having it that, after the invasion of the Gragn (see chapter 3), no text of the degwa could be found except in the monastery at Bethlehem, so it became the center of such studies. The teacher sings the chants, and the pupils have to memorize both music and the words. Traditionally, they were also required to prepare animal skin as vellum and to copy onto it the whole of the chant book, together with the musical notation (*meleket*). This is a prerequisite for becoming a teacher (*marigeta*). To become a degwa expert, it is necessary to pass the final exams in Bethlehem, which in part involves the capacity to repeat all the degwas. The second discipline is the study of the hymns sung after the communion (*zemmare*) by the choir of chanters (the dabtarat) and the hymns that are sung at funerals and memorial services (*mawasit*). These lessons are delivered in Zuramba, in South Gondar, in the same way as the degwas. The third discipline is the study of the art of singing and dancing in a choir of dabtarat, known as *aqwaqwam* (literally, "how to stand") accompanied by *sistra* (handheld metal instruments with loose pieces that are shaken to produce sounds), prayer sticks, and drums. There are two traditional types of aqwaqwam: the one that is taught in Gondar that is characterized by the use of sistra and one, taught in Gojam and Wollo, that features the use of prayer sticks. A common feature of the Ethiopian liturgy is for a verse to be sung by one of the chanters and then to be taken up and adapted to the aqwaqwam music and dancing. Considering that, in certain reaches of Western Christianity, liturgical dancing is a recent innovation and is still regarded with suspicion, it is a remarkable feature of Ethiopian Orthodoxy that it has for centuries played a central role in the daily liturgy. The fourth and final discipline is the study of the liturgy (*qeddase*), covering features such as anaphoras, litanies, absolutions, and prayers for the sacraments, and the *Horologion*, or *Prayers of the Hours* (*se'atat*). These areas are taught in Serekula, Wollo Province, and in Dabra Abbay Monastery, in Tigray.

The next level of education is the school of poetry (qene bet), where qene, the very distinctive type of Ethiopian religious poetry that was discussed above, is taught. Students are around seventeen years old when they start the qene school. They require around two to four years to complete the course.[77] Outstanding students, however, can complete the course in one year.[78] At the qene school they acquire a thorough understanding of the Ge'ez vocabulary, grammar, syntax, and sentence construction that are indispensable for the acquisition of the main task, to compose qene.[79] As noted above, this type of poetry (although sometimes it is prose) generally combines a biblical, theological, or hagiographical dimension with some contemporary issue, such as ceremonies like weddings or funerals or events in the wider social or national life.[80] Each day the qene lesson begins at about 6:00 p.m. and is conducted orally.

The teacher will begin by composing a qene that students must repeat three or four times, until they are able to say it by heart. There will then be discussion of the various possible meanings and the grammatical function of the words in the qene. The teacher will explain the "wax" and "gold" levels. In due course the students must then create their own qene.[81]

The dabtarat, mentioned above, are graduates of the qene school. The word *dabtara* (singular) does not mean "scribe," as some suggest[82] but is actually the Ge'ez word for "tent, tabernacle, or sanctuary" and comes, by extension, to mean someone with a role in the church and its services who is well versed in traditional ecclesiastical learning,[83] including qene, singing, and dancing. The dabtara "is a very interesting figure in the Ethiopian intellectual and religious hierarchy. He is at once a singer, dancer, poet, scribe, and sometimes, a diviner."[84] He is necessary for the singing and dancing that accompany ecclesiastical services, especially at the big festivals. He is capable of copying manuscripts but also of composing his own poetry and other works. One other function of the dabtara, which is diminishing as Western medicine becomes more common throughout Ethiopia, is to compose prayer scrolls for people who are ill or bewitched (see chapter 6 for details). As these sometimes have magical or astrological dimensions, they tend to attract opposition from many Orthodox churchmen and believers. Aida Edemariam records that her grandfather, Tsega, when he was still in the school of reading, was discovered with a young male relative, whom she calls a chorister (presumably a dabtara), working together on a long medicinal scroll emblazoned with archangels, demons, horned women, and written spells. His father was so shocked that he twisted Tsega's ear fiercely and forbade him ever to pick up pen and write again, except for his own name.[85]

Graduation from the qene school is necessary for progression to the final and highest level of education, the "school of books" (*meshafa bet*). This level is for mature students, either young men who have completed the other levels or elderly monks who wish to study the literature of the church.[86] It involves traditional exegesis, analysis, and interpretation (*tergwāmē*) of the religious books and is taught by commentaries (*andemta*) in four disciplines: Old Testament, New Testament, church fathers, and works on the monastic and ascetic life. Although the andemta commentaries have attracted unfortunately only limited interest from Western scholarship in the past, there has recently been renewed interest in the subject as providing a valuable contribution to biblical interpretation that offers a fresh vision of many texts.[87] Also studied are theology, church history, and canon law. Someone who masters four subjects is called one with four eyes or "four-eyed" (*arat ayna*).[88] The course takes about ten years to complete. Anyone who completes it, whether a priest, a dabtara, or a monk, is regarded with great esteem and referred to as a *liq* (an exalted elder).[89]

Such then is the unique mode of education by which the Ethiopian intellectual and literary tradition has been maintained for centuries. It looks likely to continue, albeit in a context where modern styles of education are becoming more widely available, especially in view of considerable efforts currently being undertaken by organizations of the Ethiopian Orthodox Church to preserve its ideas, culture, and spirituality (see chapter 7).

6

Art, Architecture, and Music

Visitors to Orthodox churches in Ethiopia encounter religious paintings, architecture, and music in forms that are unique in the Christian world. Indeed one's first acquaintance with these features—whether, for example, in a church interior entirely covered in paintings or in the architectural miracle that is the World Heritage Collection of rock-hewn churches in Lalibela, or in a stately dance by hundreds of white-clad priests at a big festival—is likely to be quite overwhelming. Considered together the art, architecture, and music of Ethiopia point to a profound artistic sensibility among the Ethiopian people that, within their own ecological and historical setting, has found expression in highly distinctive ways. The aim of this chapter is to introduce Ethiopian Orthodox art, architecture, and music. While a broad outline of these subjects is presented here, firsthand acquaintance with these riches in Ethiopia is strongly recommended.

Art

What Makes Ethiopian Painting Distinctive?

What is it about Ethiopian paintings that makes them so distinctive, at least before the arrival of European influences with the

Jesuits in the early seventeenth century? For a sample of this art, see figure 6.1.

To begin with, we notice the renunciation of depth, volume, and perspective in their mode of representation. The painting appears "flat," or two dimensional, with the figures and other aspects of the composition pushed up against the picture pane. In this it reveals its lineage from late antique and early Byzantine art, often mediated through Coptic Christianity in Egypt. In addition, there tends to be a naïveté in the representation of human figures: the dimensions of the head are usually enlarged, and the eyes are large and almond shaped, portrayed front-on for virtuous characters (although often with the pupils to one side in a sideward glance) and side-on for evil ones. They tend to be arranged in static poses, with the notable and common exception of St. George killing the dragon. Perhaps most characteristic of this art, however, is its coloration. Flat areas of paint are common, often overlaid with geometric and floral patterns. The pigments of the paintings tend to be heavily saturated; that is, they exhibit a marked intensity of color. The paint used is of the tempura type, that is, the pigments

Figure 6.1. *Two leaves from the Gunde Gospels, ca. 1540*

are combined with a protein or vegetal binder for application to the surface. The sources of the pigments are largely found in Ethiopia itself. Gypsum is used for white. Various kinds of ochre (iron oxide) and cinnabar (mercuric sulfide) produce red. Orpiment (arsenic sulfide) is used for yellow. Indigo (sometimes mixed with white lead) provides blue. A combination of orpiment and indigo, or certain plant materials, is used for green. Black is produced from soot and a mixture of burned plants.[1] Many of these colors remind one of the natural coloration of the Ethiopian landscape. Gold is not used in Ethiopian art (except in some miniatures), and this radically differentiates it from Greek and Russian Orthodox painting, where gold forms the field on which the painting is laid, so that gold is always visible in the background of the painting and even pushing up through the colors. This difference has the effect of making Ethiopian Orthodox painting far less hieratic and more accessible than that of Greece and Russia.

Periods in Ethiopian Art

It is possible to identify eight periods in the development of Ethiopian art:[2]

The Christian Aksumite Period (ca. Fourth through Seventh Centuries CE)

As noted in chapter 2, it is from the beginning of this period, in the reign of King Ezana, that material expressions of Christian belief begin to appear, especially in inscriptions and on coins. In particular, we have seen in chapter 2 how the image of the disk and crescent gave way to the Greek cross. Aksum has a characteristic type of cross (used by priests) that is quite close to this classical form (figure 6.2).

Some churches probably date from the sixth century, including that in the monastery of Dabra Damo, featuring the alternating rows of stones and wood typical of Aksumite architecture (figure 6.3), which is perched on a high cliff and even today is only accessible by rope.

Figure 6.2. *Ethiopian handcrafted crosses used by priests on staffs*
From right to left: the crosses of Aksum, Lalibela (which has a small cross at the top with twelve points, for the twelve apostles), and Gondar.

Figure 6.3. *Church of the monastery of Dabra Damo*

Art, Architecture, and Music 137

One of the most distinctive features of Ethiopian Orthodoxy, indeed one of its crowning glories, is its pictorial tradition, expressed in paintings (especially on church walls) and in the illumination of manuscripts, but not, interestingly, in sculpture.

We now have evidence for that tradition from the Aksumite period (ending in the seventh century CE) in the illustrated Garima Gospel books I and III (see chapter 5). The main illuminations in the Garima Gospels are portraits of Matthew, Mark, Luke, and John, another figure who is probably Eusebius, and the frames for the canon tables that were discussed in chapter 5, with figure 5.1 being one of those frames and another complex illustration of a building. Figure 6.4 is a painting of Mark the Evangelist from the Garima Gospel book III.

Mark is shown side-on, facing right (actually to a page containing the chapter headings of his Gospel). He is seated on a leopard-shaped chair, and in front of him is a lectern shaped like a dolphin. He holds a book on his lap, partially covered in cloth. This is an

Figure 6.4. *Mark the Evangelist from Garima Gospel book III*

image of him, remarkably, as a reader, not as a writer.[3] While the leopard-shaped and decorated chair gives the portrait an African dimension, the style is broadly that of the Mediterranean world in the late antique period. At this early period the manner of representation is not recognizably Ethiopian. Recent research suggests that more than one artist was responsible for the illumination of the Garima Gospels and that they worked closely with the scribes who would be inserting the text onto the vellum.[4] A close partnership between the visual and textual dimensions of these Gospel books is particularly clear in relation to the symbolism present in many of the frames for the canon tables. This is very evident in a complex image in Garima III that shows a building probably meant to represent the temple in Jerusalem, having an imposing door between two pillars, with streams flowing out of it and dear-like creatures emerging from doors in its lower levels.[5]

The Post-Aksumite Period (ca. Seventh to Twelfth Centuries CE)

As we have seen in chapter 3, this was a period of decline in the power and fortunes of the northern Ethiopian kingdom, and very little is known about it. It seems likely some churches were built and some cut from stone, with others being converted from rock-cut underground chambers, for example, the churches of Abreha-we-Atsbeha and Tcherqos Wukro. While little survives of the art from this period, a notable exception exists within the Church of Dabra Selam, near Zarema, in Tigray, which is situated in a cave in a cliff face and is partially built and partially hewn out of rock. In its finely carved chancel, it contains painted scenes from the life of Jesus, including the entry into Jerusalem and Christ in majesty. These are from the eleventh to twelfth centuries and are probably the oldest church paintings in the country.[6]

The Zagwe Period (ca. 1140–1270 CE)

During this period members of the Zagwe dynasty ruled from their capital in the mountains of Lasta. It was one of the Zagwe kings, Lalibela, who, around 1200 CE, initiated the construction of twelve churches and connecting corridors and chambers cut from the living rock in the place now called Lalibela in his honor. Their architecture is discussed later in this chapter. A characteristic aesthetic and religious form from this period is found in the Lalibela crosses (see the middle cross in figure 6.2). The core of the design is two elongated circles entwined with one another. Within each circle there is usually a modified Greek cross (although such a cross does not appear in the lower circle in the Lalibela cross in figure 6.2). From the outer edge of the top circle protrude triangles with circles on top. From the lower half of the cross emerge two or three pairs of wings. A stunning twelfth-century example exists, in the Church of Medhane Alem (Redeemer of the World) in Lalibela. It was stolen by a priest in March 1996 but returned to Lalibela in 2001.[7] There is an enormous amount of religious symbolism concentrated in a Lalibela cross.

The Early Solomonic Period (1270–1527)

This was the period dating from the overthrow of the last Zagwe emperor by Yekunno Amlak (reigned 1270–1285), who legitimated his dynasty by developing the tradition that it dated back to the union of Solomon and the queen of Sheba (see the discussion of the *Kebra Nagast* in chapter 5). This so-called Solomonic dynasty lasted until the deposition of Haile Selassie in 1974. The Solomonics were active patrons of the arts, including the important emperor Zara Yaqob. New churches were built, and numerous illuminated manuscripts were created, with paintings of the saints and illustrations of Old and New Testament scenes. Icons and painted panels were also produced. Jacques Mercier offers a more detailed account of the years 1270–1527, dividing them into three eras: (1) the era of Amda Seyon (1270–1382), (2) the era of Dawit (1382–1478), and (3) the era of opposites: Stephanite and Venetian art (1480–1530). I will now consider these in turn.

The first emperor of the Solomonic dynasty, Yekunno Amlak, constructed new churches, of which two rock-hewn examples survive. One, the rock-cut church of Gannata Maryam (Garden of Mary), near Lalibela, contains murals from this period and a portrait of Yekunno Amlak. More significant, however, in artistic terms, was Amda Seyon, the emperor from 1314 to 1344, who considerably expanded the boundaries of his kingdom and thus assured stability for subsequent generations. Characteristic of this period was the production of Gospel books containing, after the canon tables and the image of a temple (which we have seen goes back to the Garima Gospel books of the Aksumite period), three images of Christ's passion and exaltation: the crucifixion, the holy women at the tomb, and the ascension. These three images all derive from Palestinian prototypes of the fifth to sixth centuries and relate to the holy sites of Golgotha and the Holy Sepulcher. The appearance of these places was known from various sources, including pilgrims' flasks. About ten Gospel books of this type survive from the fourteenth century.[8]

The most significant artistic event in the era of Dawit (1382–1478) occurred during the reign of Dawit himself (1382–1413). During the early fifteenth century, this emperor commissioned a translation of an Arabic version of the *Miracles of Mary* for his personal use. It has survived and is kept today in the Church of Gershan. Its execution is superlative, with tempera, ink, and real gold on parchment. Ten of its twelve images have Dawit at the foot of Mary, flanked by the archangels Michael and Gabriel. This royal style of painting has a geometrical quality, with the figures exhibiting enlarged eyes and hands. It is also characterized by an absence of scenery and an intricate relation of the bands and patterned planes in the clothing. This style of painting remained fashionable to the period of Zara Yaqob (reigned 1434–1468). When Zara Yaqob, who had a very strong devotion to Mary, later wished to promote her cult, he had copies of Dawit's *Miracles of Mary* distributed throughout the country. Zara Yaqob went even further than this, by requiring that there be a portrait of Mary on display in every church during Mass. During his reign some Western artists came to Ethiopia. One of them introduced certain aspects of European iconography as well as the technique of using tempera on gesso-coated wood. This same artist, not particularly distinguished himself, founded a studio that attracted many talented Ethiopian painters, including a certain Fre Seyon, who soon became one of Ethiopia's greatest artists.[9] Fre Seyon's style was widely adopted. During this period painting on wood panels became popular, and dozens survive in the style of Fre Seyon (figure 6.5).

Another characteristic of this period was the practice of engraving figures on broad-armed crosses, with scenes including the crucifixion, the Virgin and the Child, God the Father (the Ancient of Days), angels, and saints.[10] See figure 6.6 for such a cross, although from a later period.

To explain the era of Stephanite and Venetian art, we need a little history. Around 1480 a monk named Ezra returned from Egypt and Jerusalem, where he had gone to be ordained since his order had been excommunicated in Ethiopia. He was a second-generation follower of Estifanos (Stephen), a monk who had been executed by Zara Yaqob for refusing to recognize, let alone honor,

Figure 6.5. *Diptych with Mary and her son, flanked by archangels, apostles, and a saint, likely by a follower of fifteenth-century painter Fre Seyon, late fifteenth century*

Figure 6.6. *Ethiopian engraved processional cross from the late eighteenth century*

royal authority. His martyrdom had actually encouraged the formation of a Stephanite movement. Ezra had completed his training as a craftsman in Egypt and on his return to his monastery continued to perfect his skills, such as in carving wooden crosses, while his brother monks copied and illustrated sacred books. His fame spread, and Ezra was called to court in the reign of the emperor Naod (reigned 1494–1508) and had the prohibition on his order lifted. Under Ezra's influence the Stephanites became the greatest carvers of wooden crosses and illuminators of manuscripts in Ethiopia. Hard on the heels of Ezra, a Venetian artist named Niccolò Brancaleon arrived in Ethiopia and had great influence during the reign of Emperor Eskender (1478–1494). He practiced the international Gothic style. For some forty years he worked on icon painting, book illustration, and church painting. He set up a studio in the royal court and introduced new iconographic elements, such as scenes of St. George and the dragon and the miracles of the Virgin.[11] Yet Brancaleon was also influenced by Ethiopian traditions in art. This is quite evident from a painting of his in the Walters Art Museum in Baltimore (figure 6.7). Here his debt to the Italian Renaissance is visible in the naturalistic facial features and (a rather limited) use of three-dimensional space, while the addition of the two archangels and his use of flat bands of bright colors in the frame and background, executed in colors of the earth and of vegetation, indicate the strong influence of Ethiopian artistic traditions.

The Mid-Solomonic Period (1527–1632)

This was a period of great political instability (with Jacques Mercier referring to it as the era of Muslim and Jesuit turmoil),[12] first with the invasion of Ahmad ibn Ibrahim al-Ghazi (1531–1543) and then the arrival of the Jesuits, who managed to convert Emperor Susenyos to Roman Catholicism in 1622, leading to ten years civil war.

By the time al-Ghazi had been defeated in 1543, most of churches and monasteries in Ethiopia had been pillaged and destroyed. His soldiers even resorted to lighting fires in rock churches to destroy the murals. Only a few places, in Lasta and Tigray, were preserved,

Figure 6.7. *Right half of a diptych with the virgin and child, by Niccolò Brancaleon, ca. 1500*

but blessedly the churches of Lalibela (although not their contents) were among them. From 1543 a major project of rebuilding of monasteries and churches was undertaken, and texts were copied from those that survived and distributed. Most of the new books were not illustrated, but the production of icons for churches flourished. This was not a period of artistic innovation, and resources for artistic production were very limited. Painting developed with a slow fusion of various styles, especially involving a blend of the geometric traditions of monastic art with different influences from the West. Many small icons were produced, notably in Amhara, and they often reveal the influence of Brancaleon. There was some reversion to older decorative conventions, as in the creation of ornamental metal plates for book covers. Because of the pillaging by al-Ghazi's soldiers, objects like crosses that had previously been made from bronze or precious metals were cast in iron.

As discussed in chapter 3, the Jesuits, who arrived in the mid-1550s, brought considerable architectural skills with them, even to the extent of their building a royal palace and churches. Their primary contribution to the development of Ethiopian religious art came in the introduction of some new iconographic variations on the Virgin. The main one was their dissemination of the image of the Virgin and child in an ancient Byzantine icon known as *Salus Populi Romani* (The salvation of the Roman people) in the Basilica of Santa Maria Maggiore in Rome, which was part of a worldwide Jesuit effort to popularize this image. In the image Mary wears a blue shawl draped with folds, with a cross in her hair and a star on her shoulder. She holds Jesus in her arms with her hands crossed. Jesus sits, looking up toward his mother and pointing with his right hand, while he holds a book in his left hand.

Figure 6.8. *Marian icon, known as* Salus Populi Romani, *Basilica di Santa Maria Maggiore, Rome, perhaps sixth century CE*

This image became extremely popular in Ethiopia and tended to supplant earlier ways of depicting the Virgin and child;[13] for an example, see figure 6.9.

The Gondarine Period (1632–1769)

The accession of Emperor Fasilidas in 1632 brought political stability and the construction of a fixed capital in Gondar. Palaces and churches were built, the latter in the circular pattern that thereafter became standard after centuries of basilica-shaped structures. Furthermore, he commissioned profusely illustrated books, especially the Gospels and the *Miracles of Mary*, some of them having as many as two hundred paintings. Before his time no book had contained more than fifty paintings. To assist with the *Miracles of Mary*, the Ethiopian artists drew inspiration from paintings by Brancaleon, and for the Gospels they used the *Arabic Gospels*, printed in Rome in 1591, containing illustrations by Antonio Tempesta. Figure 6.10 is an engraving by Tempesta of Christ curing a leper.

Figure 6.9. *Detail of a Great Triptych, ca. 1700*

Art, Architecture, and Music   147

Figure 6.10. *Engraving by Antonio Tempesta of Christ curing a leper, ca. 1591*

Two styles of painting have been identified in this period. The first Gondarine style (1632–1730) favored bright colors and the absence of shading. Clothing is often embellished with decorative aspects and usually painted red, blue, or yellow. Folds are shown by fluid parallel lines. Faces are modeled using plain coral red highlights on pink faces, which can produce a somewhat unnatural effect. Warm tones predominate. In manuscripts blank backgrounds become common, although, in painting on wood, colored grounds tend to persist. During the late seventeenth and early eighteenth centuries, painters begin to abandon their centuries-old use of geometric patterns and contrasting colors and adopt fluid forms, which aim at a realist expression of gradations of color and tone, although often the older and this newer style can be found in the same book or the same studio, as different artists contributed paintings on different subjects.[14] In the final years of the seventeenth century, Ethiopian artists became innovative in their selection of subjects. A number of works were illustrated for the first time. These included the *Lamentations of Mary* (a poem about the flight of the Holy Family into Egypt), the *Miracles of Jesus*, and, above all, the *Homiliary of the Archangel Michael*.[15] The Walters Art Museum in Baltimore possesses a magnificent example of such a homiliary (figure 6.11).

Figure 6.11. *The archangels Michael and Gabriel, from a* Homiliary of the Archangel Michael, *late seventeenth century*

The second (or neo) Gondarine style (to be dated roughly to the reign of Iyasu II, from 1730 to 1755, although with antecedents as early as the reign of Iyasu I, from 1682 to 1706), is characterized by darker shades of red, lighter contour lines, and a more delicate use of shading, which gives volume to the bodies and faces of the figures. In particular, the red, mask-like patches on the face are abandoned in favor of a delicate modeling. The representation of clothing becomes more realistic and more sumptuous.[16] Nevertheless, paintings executed in this style maintain "a stylized otherworldly monumentality" that has come to be associated by many Ethiopians with notions of spiritual beauty.[17] A very dramatic change in the iconography of Christ becomes evident during the first half of the eighteenth century. The crucifixion, resurrection, and the Last Supper are depicted differently, and new subjects are introduced, such as the healing at the pool of Bethesda (John 5), which had not been depicted previously. It now seems that many of these new subjects were based on engravings by the (Flemish) Wierix brothers appearing in a book entitled *Synopsis of the Life and Passion of Our Savior Jesus Christ* that was brought to Ethiopia and was deposited in the royal library (where it could be consulted by artists) in 1706.[18] The second Gondarine style came to dominate all media, including wood panels, murals, and manuscripts, which had not been the case in the fifteenth century when different styles were used in relation to different media.[19] During this period donors and patrons begin to be depicted, also under the influence of European practice.

Zamana Masafent (Era of the Judges) Period (1769–1855)

This period begins with the deposition of Emperor Iyoas in 1769, an event that inaugurated a fall in the power and prestige of the Solomonic dynasty, as rival warlords fought for supremacy. There were fewer resources available for the commissioning of works of art, and art went into decline, with the exception of mural painting, for which demand remained high.[20] The work that was produced during this period was influenced by the second Gondarine style but in a palette dominated by bright, plain colors. In the mid-nineteenth century artists began to expand their range of subjects, for example, by the addition of philosophical themes.[21]

The Late Solomonic Period (1855–1974)

This period begins with the accession of Tewodros II and ends with the deposition of Haile Selassie, in 1974, thus terminating Solomonic rule in Ethiopia. The second Gondarine style continues to be influential, but contemporary figures and events are increasingly depicted in addition to religious themes. The Battle of Adwa in 1896, in which Emperor Menelik II defeated a large Italian army, was a particularly popular subject (see figure 4.5).

After the Second World War, traditional painting continued, while other artists moved to styles influenced by trends in European art. Synthetic colors became increasingly common.

The Main Subjects of Orthodox Painting

Although imagery in Ethiopia has been influenced by that of other Oriental Orthodox countries, local conditions affected which subjects were portrayed.[22] If the positioning of imagery was determined by theology or the liturgy, the selection was more likely to reflect the general interests of Oriental Orthodoxy. But when popular devotion was the driving force, saints and religious themes favored in Ethiopia were preferred. Since Ethiopian spirituality had a strong interest in protection against malign powers (see the section on prayer scrolls below), a favorite subject comprised holy figures known to bring benefits to believers, expressed in their images and in scenes from their lives. The traditionalism characteristic of Ethiopian art meant that, once certain figures and scenes had come to be represented in the pictorial tradition, they retained their popularity. The most popular patterns for church wall painting were largely established by the second half of the seventeenth century (that is, in the beginning of the Gondarine period) and settled by the eighteenth.

Manuscript illuminations were also important. As noted above, these date back to the Garima Gospel books of the Aksumite period. By the fourteenth and fifteenth centuries gospel books retained the canon tables and portrayals of the evangelists that had been there from the beginning but had added a christological cycle, with short ones of the passion and longer ones covering the life of Christ. By the end of the seventeenth century, deluxe manuscripts were being created that drew on European models and introduced features such as the miracles of Christ. On wooden panels (single panels, diptychs, and triptychs) the most popular imagery was of central theological messages, such as the nativity, the crucifixion, ascension, and resurrection.

Narrative scenes from the Old Testament appeared in church murals from the thirteenth and fourteenth centuries, with the focus being the subject of divine deliverance—as with Abraham sacrificing Isaac, the three youths in the furnace, and Daniel in the lions' den, for example. Although these scenes became less popular in the fifteenth and sixteenth centuries, they began to reappear in the seventeenth century. Larger narrative cycles on subjects such as Genesis and Exodus became popular in the nineteenth century. One important means of dissemination of religious imagery was through illuminated manuscripts that were employed in liturgy and in private devotion. As far as the Old Testament was concerned, narratives were not depicted. Instead, single or grouped figures (such as David and Solomon or enthroned kings) were introduced into the text at the appropriate place.

The most popular apocryphal stories concerned Mary. Some manuscripts (like British Library Orient. 607) contain up to 250 miniatures. The collection the *Miracles of Mary*, illustrated in the second half of the seventeenth century with some thirty-five miniatures, became particularly popular. Other saints who were frequently depicted included the equestrian saints, especially St. George killing the dragon, and martyrs (like St. Stephen and St. Alexis), as well as five Ethiopian saints who were regularly featured: Takla Haymanot, Gabra Manfas Qeddus, Samuel of Waldabba, and Ewostatewos.

In the second half of the seventeenth century, Abba Za-Mikael Aragawi was added. The Nine Saints were also a popular subject. In the eighteenth century St. Yared, singing in front of the king, Gabra Masqal, began to appear (see figure 6.19 below). Archangels and angels were also immensely popular and are now to be seen in gathered ranks on many church walls and ceilings.

Painting Arrangements in Churches[23]

Although the arrangement of mural paintings is the same in no two churches, there are some features that do tend to recur. Inside a round church, the inner face of the outside wall and walls of the sanctuary are usually covered in paintings. West of the sanctuary, on top of the door of the sanctuary, there is the Trinity (which in Ethiopia is nearly always portrayed as three old men with white hair and beards of identical appearance, which avoids the Western pictorial feature of painting the Holy Spirit as a rather diminutive dove—figure 6.12). Underneath are the life and passion of Christ. To the right of the sanctuary entrance are the Virgin and Child (sometimes with donors painted at their feet). On the left there is St. George. On both sides appear other saints, including the saint to whom the church is dedicated. Archangels are often painted on the door to the sanctuary or on the ceiling (figure 6.13, "one of the most famous graphic images of Ethiopia"[24]). The south wall, where the women stand, contains scenes from the life and miracles of the Virgin. The north wall, where the men stand, is illustrated with the lives of saints (often warrior saints) and martyrs. On the eastern wall there are scenes from Christ's life and miracles, martyrs, and saints. Representations of the Virgin presenting Christ commonly portray an angel on each side of her.

Prayer Scrolls

It is not only on the walls of their churches that the faith of Ethiopian Orthodox believers comes into contact with art. Although the practice of having icons in the home never caught on as it did

Art, Architecture, and Music 153

Figure 6.12. *Painting of the Trinity in the Arbat Ensesa Church in Aksum* Arbat Ensesa means "four animals," and the reference is to the four animals of the Apocalypse (Rev 4:7). The four animals—a lion, an ox, a human being, and an eagle—appear at the corners of the painting.

Figure 6.13. *A detail of the ceiling of the Dabra Berhan Selassie Church in Gondar, illuminated with angels, who protect the faithful worshiping there*

in other parts of the Orthodox world, another site of lively intersection between the two exists in the phenomenon of prayer or healing scrolls.[25] These are long, narrow strips of vellum, between three and ten inches wide and five to six feet long, divided into segments containing text (in the form of prayers and spells in Ge'ez) and others with drawn and painted images and designs (figure 6.14). Their production goes back for many centuries in Ethiopia and continues today, although with declining popularity as modern medicine becomes more widespread and accepted.

Prayer scrolls were, and to an extent still are, one way of dealing with illness and misfortune. Each of these scrolls was created for a particular person affected by a specific sickness, usually one that is thought to be the result of demon possession.

Someone, more likely a woman than a man (and it is a woman in the case of figure 6.14), who is sick or troubled might decide to visit a *dabtara*, one of the unordained clerics who sing and dance at religious ceremonies but also fulfil a scribal role, for help. For women the problem often concerns issues of maternity (such as sterility, miscarriage, the death of a child), while for men they are usually aimed at pains attributed to curses.[26] The problem is very likely to be regarded as the product of evil spirits or even human sorcerers. The process begins with the dabtara sacrificing an animal, typically a sheep or a goat. The dabtara then washes the client in the animal's blood as a sign of purification. From the skin of the animal are made three long strips of parchment that are stitched together to produce a scroll equal to the length of the client.[27] Figure 6.14 is 13 centimeters wide and 183 centimeters long—this was for a quite tall woman. The fact that the scroll was as long as the client was tall meant that there was a direct and physical connection with the client, which was no doubt thought to strengthen its curative power. The scroll was then covered in figures of saints, other illustrations (for example, of eyes), and text. At the beginning of the scroll, the words "In the name of the Father and the Son and the Holy Spirit" are in red, as is the anonymized reference to the client, while the rest of the text is in black.

Art, Architecture, and Music 155

Figure 6.14. *Ethiopian prayer scroll*

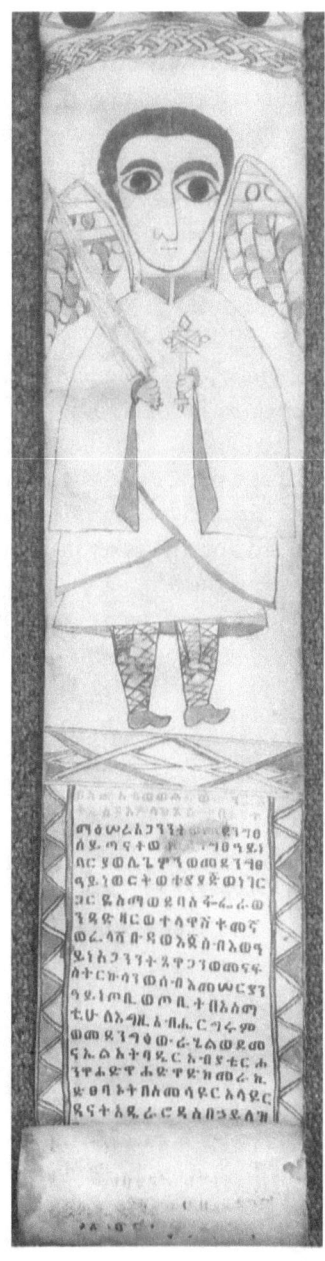

The words and talismanic images are regarded as possessing magical protective power. Not surprisingly, the use of scrolls has often attracted criticism within the church for what were perceived to be their heterodox aspects (sometimes including an astrological dimension). Sometimes the political authorities with a religious bent, such as Emperor Zara Yaqob in the fifteenth century, were actively opposed to them.[28]

In Ethiopian tradition the origin of talismans lies, at least in part, in the world of the book of Enoch, which describes how the angel Azazel led a group of angels to abandon heaven and take human wives (thus producing giant progeny) and to reveal hidden knowledge to human beings, acts that led to chaos on earth and divine retribution. But the spirits of the giants continue to roam the earth and show hostility to human beings (1 En. 15:8–16:1). The result is that today "communication between the two species (i.e., human and angelic) takes place in the negative—in the register of sickness. But the scholar who draws talismans for his patients sees spirits. He moves in the world before the Flood, when spirits revealed themselves to humans and showed them the secrets of the heavens."[29] The scrolls typically invoke the secret names of God, so that the power of God can be activated against the cause of the illness. Prayers protect against the evil eye or demons. As is the practice with Ethiopian manuscripts, the names of God and headings are written in red ink, and the other text in black. The client's name does not appear on the scroll. In figure 6.14 the client is repeatedly referred to, in red ink, as *walatta kidan* (daughter of the covenant). The male equivalent is *walda kidan*.

Particular prayers appearing in the scrolls are associated with particular images. One prayer that commonly appears on the scrolls, called The Net of Solomon, recalls how King Solomon compelled the king of the demon-blacksmiths to reveal his evil skills by pronouncing a name of God.[30] The archangel Michael is also said to have given Solomon a ring bearing a seal that Solomon used to force the demons to build him a palace. This seal is represented as an eight-pointed star with a face at its center. In third century CE Alexandria legends developed concerning Alexander the Great's expedition to the Orient (see chapter 5). These legends were widely disseminated and in Ethiopia were developed with respect to 1 Enoch, by describing how Alexander explores the bounds of the world. Reaching the Land of Darkness he finds enormous birds he rides to the Country of the Living, where he meets Elijah and Enoch (the two biblical figures who had been taken to heaven while still alive). He learns of half-human, half-animal creatures who are subjects of the kings Gog and Magog and employs a bronze door to stop them invading the human world.[31] Saints on horseback often make their appearance, especially St. Susenyos, who destroys the child-killing demon Werzelya. Apart from allusions to such stories, other motifs that appear in the scrolls include frequent depictions of the archangels (including Phanuel, the "expeller of demons"),[32] crosses, and pairs of eyes. The power of the gaze of the afflicted person is crucial, with his or her reciprocal gaze at the painted eyes being needed to defeat the demon.[33] One common talisman is of God in the center of a cross with four eyes around him. It seems probable that the imagery on the scrolls is more archaic than in paintings on church walls and in illuminated manuscripts. Images of Mary and the crucifixion, for example, which have been common in other forms of religious painting since the fifteenth and sixteenth centuries, respectively, are exceedingly rare in the scrolls.[34]

Religious Art in Ethiopia Today

In any religious context in Ethiopia, both inside and outside of churches, one comes across religious paintings. They are an integral and highly prominent feature of Ethiopian Orthodoxy. Some of these paintings are old, and some quite new. Indeed, the large-scale production of religious art continues in Ethiopia today, although in a manner significantly different from that of the past.[35] The big difference is that, whereas religious painting was once largely the preserve of priests who had received a thorough theological education and who led ascetic lives (especially those living in monasteries), today, especially in Addis Ababa, there are far more lay artists involved. Most of these artists, however, come from religious families heavily involved in ecclesiastical affairs. This is not to say that priest-painters have disappeared; they still exist. Moreover, one painter, Qes Adamu Tesfaw,[36] who is regarded by many as Ethiopia's finest living artist, began as a priest, although he later left the priesthood. Yet, even if ecclesiastic figures are no longer producing the paintings, the church still maintains great control over the character of the art. This is because no painting can be hung in a church without the blessing of a priest. "Theologically, the blessing transforms an ordinary painting into a portal leading to the divine."[37] Most Ethiopian priests have knowledge of sacred imagery, even if they have no formal training in the area nor the benefit of formal guidelines, and are concerned to ensure that the paintings to be hung in a church are theologically and aesthetically appropriate.

In most cases, an artist will need a patron for a particular work, with the paintings to be hung in churches or homes. Addis Ababa is the city in Ethiopia where most patrons are to be found and has accordingly attracted artists from all over the country. Patrons produce demand for paintings but also help to raise the profile of individual artists. Patrons both instigate a commission and also finance it. Patrons can be either individuals or groups and range from senior ecclesiastics to ordinary Orthodox churchgoers. Where the patron is a bishop or priest, the artist is likely to be considerably more deferential to him in relation to the theology expressed in the painting. These days modern, factory-made paint is used for commissioned works, rather than paint made by hand from natural materials, as in the past.[38] Perhaps it is for this reason that modern paintings tend to be executed in gaudier colors than in centuries past.

Architecture[39]

Types of Church Architecture: A Historical Perspective

Ethiopian churches come in a variety of shapes. Some, including the Holy Trinity Cathedral in Addis Ababa, follow the standard rectangular shape of the basilica. This form probably dates back to the late Aksumite period and preserves the style that was common in the Eastern Mediterranean at that time, inspired ultimately by Constantine's first church, St. John Lateran in Rome, which was modeled on the Roman basilica.

During the Aksumite period a large church, which soon came to be called Maryam Seyon (Mary of Zion), was built in a central area of the city. It no longer exists, but later sources describe it as a basilica with a central nave and two aisles on each side. Whether it was built by Ezana in the fourth century or by Kaleb in the sixth is uncertain. The Muslim army of the Gragn destroyed it in about 1535. The site on which it was erected is now occupied by the Old Cathedral of Aksum, which dates largely from the seventeenth century and is built on a podium (possibly Aksumite in origin) designed for a larger structure, presumably the Aksumite Maryam Seyon (Cathedral of St. Mary of Zion). This seventeenth-century edifice is regarded as Ethiopia's mother church and of unparalleled holiness.[40]

One of the characteristic features of Aksumite architecture was the insertion of wooden beams between stone blocks to lock the whole structure together. Many of the steles in Aksum have been carved in imitation of this pattern, with the protruding round ends of the wooden beams clearly visible, as well as the cross-shaped, recessed windows also typical of Aksumite architecture (figure 6.15).

A later source on the original Cathedral of St. Mary of Zion mentions numerous "monkey-heads," a reference to the carved protruding ends of wooden beams, which leaves little doubt that the church itself was built in the timber-and-stone Aksumite style.[41]

That style is also visible in what is perhaps the oldest church in Ethiopia, in the Dabra Damo monastery, about 60 kilometers north east of Aksum and accessible only by rope. The large church there (see figure 6.3) was originally built as a rectangular structure, probably (although the evidence is far from conclusive) in the sixth or seventh centuries, that is, during the Aksumite period.[42] This

Figure 6.15. *Stele at Aksum carved to imitate wooden beam and stone block Aksumite construction style*

early date, if correct, would provide some confirmation for the tradition connecting the establishment of the monastery to one of the Nine Saints, Abba Za-Mikael Aragawi.

Lalibela is a collection of churches carved from living rock, a World Heritage Site, which deserves special note. Lalibela as a regular toponym for this place dates only from the nineteenth century, after the king who reigned about 1200 to whom tradition attributes the building of the churches. Ethiopian legend holds that the actual building was undertaken by men during the daytime and by angels at night. The place is located in the old Lasta District of Wollo Province (now subsumed into the Amhara region) and was originally called Roha. There are two complexes of churches and one detached church, making eleven in all.[43] It is possible that construction, although secular and not ecclesial in character, began at the site as early as the eighth or even seventh centuries, possibly in response to the decline of Aksum. Demonstrably Christian construction appears to begin in the tenth century. One of the earlier churches, Beta Madhane Alam, may replicate the original Maryam Seyon cathedral in Aksum. If the building were to be dated between the late tenth and early twelfth centuries, that would match the transfer of political authority south to Lasta as presented in traditions of the Zagwe "usurpation." Emperor Lalibela would be a little later than this, with his early years coinciding with the fall of Jerusalem to Salah ad-Din in 1187 CE. The traditions that claim Lalibela was built as a kind of New Jerusalem cohere with the loss of the actual city to the Muslims.[44] Many features in Lalibela are named after sites in the Holy Land, for example, the Jordan, Bethlehem, Golgotha and the tomb of Adam, Mount of Olives, and Bethany.

The churches at Lalibela were the first truly monolithic structures, inasmuch as they stood completely free from the rock from which they were cut, and when seen from the outside they formed perfect copies of built structures.[45] The Lalibela churches have some architectural features inspired by the Aksumite period. The interior decorations, both carved from rock and paintings from this early period, blend Aksumite and Copto-Arabic influences. Some of the rock-cut churches of Lalibela (see below) are rectangular.[46] A good example is Beta Maryam (figure 6.16), which is roughly rectangular in plan, with small protruding porches on three sides. Its interior has a basilica form and is richly decorated. All four walls are pierced by windows in the Aksumite style.[47]

The largest and most famous of the churches at Lalibela, however, the church of Beta Giyorgis (St. George) is cruciform (figure 6.17).

Contemporary Church Architecture and the Liturgy

Yet most churches today are circular or octagonal in shape. In the countryside, especially, the churches tend to be round, with their shape and material similar to that of traditional village houses.

Figure 6.16. *Beta Maryam in Lalibela (under protective roofing)*

Figure 6.17. *The cruciform church of Saint George (Beta Giyorgis) in Lalibela*

Wooden frames and thatched roofs are common (figure 6.18). Often an ostrich egg (a symbol of life and of the resurrection of Christ) will appear on the cross that tops the roof.

Usually the church is built on a hill or elevated place in a compound, with a wall and gates. The church itself is constructed in concentric rings. In the center is the sanctuary (*maqdash*), or holy of holies (*qeddesta qeddusan*), which is usually square. It has three entrances, but these have doors and curtains to ensure the privacy of the interior. The sanctuary is reserved for the clergy (the priests and deacons). It contains an altar-like structure, topped with a canopy, which is called the *manbara tabot*, meaning "the seat of the tabot." In Ge'ez *tabot* means "ark," and the reference is to the ark of the covenant in the Old Testament. The tabot is a large tablet of wood carved with a cruciform design, the Ten Commandments, and a dedication to the saint after whom the church is named. The tabot is supposed to be a representation of the original kept in an outbuilding of the Church of Maryam Seyon in Aksum that (according to the *Kebra Nagast*, chapters 48 et seq.) was abducted

Figure 6.18. *Round church of a monastery, near Gorgora, on Lake Tana*

from Jerusalem. Without its tabot a church would not exist. Indeed, in Ethiopia "it is not church buildings that are considered consecrated, but the tabot, which is dedicated to the saint whose name the church bears."[48] The tabot, indeed, gives sanctity to the church in which it is located. During feast days and in times of emergency, the tabots are brought out of the church, wrapped in precious cloth, and held on the tops of their heads by priests while they proceed around the church, accompanied by other officiants, some bearing crosses, icons, and censers. Deacons carry colorful liturgical umbrellas (*telas*) above the tabots and other precious items in the procession. The presence of at least one tabot in every Ethiopian church is the physical embodiment of a powerful theology of covenant that permeates Ethiopian Orthodoxy.[49] It has been suggested that the veneration accorded to the tabot in Ethiopia, its carriage in processions to the accompaniment of singing and dancing, the beating of staffs and prayer sticks, the rattling of sistra, and the sounding of musical instruments forcefully reminds one of the scene in 2 Samuel 6 where David and the people danced around the ark:

And they carried the ark of God upon a new cart, . . .
 And David and all the house of Israel were making merry before the Lord with all their might, with songs and lyres and harps and tambourines and castanets and cymbals. . . . So David and all the house of Israel brought up the ark of the LORD with shouting, and with the sound of the horn. (vv. 3, 5, and 15, RSV)

For this reason, Edward Ullendorff says of the tabot procession that "the entire spectacle, its substance and its atmosphere, has caused all who have witnessed it to feel transported into the times of the Old Testament."[50] The exterior walls of the sanctuary are often decorated with paintings, and the doors are frequently adorned with representation of angels.[51]

Moving out from the sanctuary, we find the middle ring that is called the *qeddest*, roughly equivalent to the nave, which is where communion is given to the faithful. Beyond the qeddest is the next ring, or ambulatory, the *qene mahlet*, roughly equivalent to a vestibule. The choir (*dabtarat*) stand in the qene mahlet on the western side, with men on the north and women on the south (that is, in segregated groups) on either side of them. The priests and deacons enter from the eastern side. On the outside there is often a covered area around the whole building. The rectangular churches are also divided into three areas with these same functions.

In addition, the compound usually has a small building to the east of the church called the "house of bread" (*beta lahm*),[52] where wine is prepared and unleavened bread is baked for the Eucharist. There is also likely to be an *eqa bet*, or treasury, in which to safely store precious objects such as liturgical vestments, manuscripts, icons, and crosses. Anyone entering the church from the compound is required to remove their shoes or sandals.

Music

St. Yared

Ethiopian tradition attributes the invention of its music to St. Yared. According to this tradition, Yared was born in Aksum in 505 CE and became a priest. Ethiopian legend has it that Yared disliked study and habitually played truant. While he was sitting under a tree during one such absence, he noticed how a caterpillar kept climbing up a tree to find food and, although it fell many times, eventually succeeded in its task through sheer perseverance.[53] Yared understood the lesson from the caterpillar and returned to his studies, which he thereafter pursued conscientiously. Yared developed a strong interest in music that led to him creating the *zema*, or music and chant of Ethiopian Orthodoxy.

Another legend about Yared concerns an occasion when he was singing with his choir before the king and his court in Aksum in the new style he had invented. The king was so engrossed with the performance that he accidentally pushed his spear into Yared's foot. There are numerous paintings in public places throughout Ethiopia that illustrate this famous incident (figure 6.19). Neither Yared nor the king noticed at the time, but when the song was finished the king (Gabra Masqal, son of Kaleb) apologized and offered to grant him any wish. Yared replied with a request that he be allowed to retire to a monastery to live out the rest of his life in peace.[54]

Yared also composed a system of musical notation, called *meleket*, that utilizes ten symbols used for hymn singing. The names and functions of these symbols are as follows:

1. *Yizet*, a detached and accented tone, equivalent to *staccato*.
2. *Deret*, sung in a low, deep voice, with chest registers, also applied to humming at the lowest range of the male voice.
3. *Kinat*, upward *glissando*.
4. *Chiret*, start high and proceed with downward *glissando*, often connected with a cadence.
5. *Difat*, drop the voice, skip to a lower range (often an octave lower).
6. *Kurt*, a cadential formula that often ends on the home tone.
7. *Rute*, throbbing, warm, and expressive singing style with rapid but narrow pitch variations, equivalent to *vibrato*.
8. *Rikrik*, rapid repetition of a single syllabic tone; it creates a sense of tension at the high range and is equivalent to *tremolo*.

Art, Architecture, and Music

Figure 6.19. *St. Yared stabbed in the foot by the emperor while performing. Painting in the Remhai Hotel in Aksum.*

9. *Hidet*, gradually getting louder and faster, equivalent to *accelerando*, *crescendo*, and *portamento* at the same time.
10. *Serez*, light pause.[55]

Yared is also attributed with inventing three different modes of melodies for *zema*: *ge'ez*, probably the most common and oldest mode and used for ordinary weekday services; *ezel*, a more measured beat that is used for Lent, days of fasting, and funeral processions; and *araray*, which is a lighter and freer form used for feasts and days of joy.[56] He is said to have been inspired to develop these three modes by the singing of three different types of birds.[57] There are several categories of hymns: *degwa* means a book of hymns; *soma degwa* are the hymns sung in fasting seasons; *me'eraf* are sections of psalms set to music and hymns for particular seasons; *zemmare* is a set of communion anthems; and *zik* is the music used at specific festivals.[58]

Ethiopian religious music is easily accessible on YouTube, as in two recent examples referenced below, the first featuring the traditional lines and circles of Ethiopian singers in a slow tempo, and the second a song with a faster beat performed by various singers and musicians led by a female vocalist.[59] A person trained in the Western musical tradition will hear in these songs a single melodic line sung by a soloist or a group accompanied especially by rhythmical and percussion instruments (like drums, sistra, and also prayer staffs); that is, the accompaniment is similar to the melody. In the second example there are also melodic instruments based on strings or a pipe. The accompaniment tends to follow the vocal line, and the music is quite repetitive. The singers use vocal ornamentation and vibrato for expression. This is present in the first chant in particular and is an example of that aspect of musical notation called *rute* that was mentioned above: throbbing, warm, and expressive singing style with rapid but narrow pitch variations.

Aqwaqwam

Although hymns are sung in every Eastern Orthodox church, only in Ethiopia is the singing of hymns found in combination with a tradition of stately liturgical movement. This is called *aqwaqwam* and is derived from Ge'ez word meaning "to stand." Ethiopian oral traditions and iconography present dance as part of Ethiopian liturgy from the earliest times, and Jesuit missionaries commented on the practice in the early seventeenth century.[60] That part of the liturgy or the celebration on big feast days in which aqwaqwam occurs is called *mahalet*. Although aqwaqwam is often called dancing, it is really more a form of solemn movement while standing that accompanies and expresses the meaning of the hymn or other work that those taking part are chanting. The movement is coordinated by the sweeping movements of the prayer staffs carried by the clergy, and rhythm is provided by the shaking of sistra (a form of metal rattle) and by the beating of one or two drums. The whole process is carried out in a dignified way and at a slow pace. The singers stand either in two lines facing one another or in a semicircle holding their sistra and staffs:

> The movements are measured, stately and rhythmical, and gradually build up from a hymn sung by one singer, and then repeated several times with growing levels of rhythm and movement, until with a burst of clapping and ululation from participants and watchers it comes to a sudden end.[61]

The main practitioners of aqwaqwam are the dabtarat, who are non-ordained clergy (whereas members of the other three clerical orders, namely, deacons, priests, and bishops, are ordained). The procedure is for important chants to be initially sung without accompaniment, by two solo singers performing antiphonally, and then to be repeated several times by the choir using different arrangements of instruments and dance. Usually there are twenty-four dabtarat taking part, and they each hold a sistrum and prayer staff. There are three dominant styles of aqwaqwam that have persisted into the present, two of which originated in Gondar and the third in Dabra Tabor.[62]

7

Theology

Chapter 1 of this book began with an Ethiopian Orthodox woman praying intensely before an icon outside the church of Dabra Sahay Maryam in the Qwesqwam Abbey in Gondar during Lent. In many ways she represented something that lies at the heart of this faith: the extent, almost unparalleled elsewhere in contemporary Christianity, to which the everyday life of the believers is integrated into the liturgical life and the theological and hagiographic traditions of their religion. Their daily experience is caught up in the omnipresent dynamics of sacred space, sacred time and memory, and sacred action. As we explore the character of Ethiopian Orthodoxy in the present chapter, this will be the recurring motif.

Sacred Space

Since the time of the Armenian writer, Abu Salih, who compiled a treatise on the Coptic Church in about 1200 CE that included information on Ethiopia,[1] and even more with the arrival of Jesuit missionaries in Ethiopia in the sixteenth century (see chapter 4), a prominent feature of Ethiopian Orthodoxy that has attracted attention has been its notably Jewish features. One aspect of that phenomenon is the extent to which Orthodox Ethiopians regard their country as a new holy land, in many ways similar to the Holy Land itself. As previously discussed (chapters 4 and 5), a feature of Ethiopian Orthodoxy that still retains a great hold on the people is the descent of emperors from King David, via Menelik I, the alleged son of Solomon and the queen of Sheba. This belief became part of the official theology of Ethiopian emperors with the accession of the first Solomonic ruler in 1270 CE. From then until 1974 there was a line of emperors who styled themselves "Conquering Line of the Tribe of Judah, Elect of God, King of Kings of Ethiopia" and "successors of the House of Judah."[2] The story is told in the *Kebra Nagast*, which also makes the claim, also regarded as historically true by many Orthodox Ethiopians, that Menelik I brought the ark of the covenant to Aksum and that it is there today, in a chapel next to the Cathedral of Maryam Seyon in Aksum, which only one monk is allowed to enter, a monk who devotes his whole life to this task.[3] This means that Ethiopia is sacralized in the same way that Israel was when the ark was located within its borders.

Yet just as the land is sacred in a manner very like that of the Holy Land, so too the churches are sacred in a way that largely replicates the holiness of the temple in Jerusalem. The temple was constructed within a courtyard, and the edifice itself had a threefold structure: a vestibule, then a nave, and then the innermost chamber, the holy of holies (Hebrew: *Qodesh Ha-Qodashim*), which contained the ark of the covenant and which only the High Priest could enter, and then only on the Day of Atonement. Every church in Ethiopia (usually erected within a compound) must contain a replica of one of the tablets of the ark of the covenant,[4] called a *tabot*, which is kept in a box, or it is not a church. Associated with the presence of the tabot in each church is the variety of ways in which the churches are constructed and the manner in which access to them is granted for priests and laypeople. These phenomena bear a remarkable resemblance to Solomon's Temple in Jerusalem. Like the temple, each church in Ethiopia is tripartite in form, with a vestibule (*qene mahlet*); a nave (*qeddest*), where communion is given; and a sanctuary (*maqdas*) or holy of holies (*qeddesta qeddusan*), in which the tabot is located and on which the priest prepares communion.[5] Also similar to the temple in Jerusalem is the inaccessibility of the holy of holies to nonclerical believers. In Ethiopia only priests, deacons, and kings can enter the holy of holies of a church.[6] Certain rules governing when people can enter a church appear to replicate or echo rules relating to entry to the Jerusalem temple. Thus, boys must be baptized after forty days and girls after eighty days, and until that time a mother may not enter the church because of her bleeding.[7] The notion of covenant is central to many other Ethiopian Orthodox practices and beliefs.[8]

It is useful to move on from this description of these features (i.e., their phenomenology), which anyone encountering Ethiopian Orthodoxy will soon come across, to the question of how they are to be explained. This involves investigating the underlying social dynamics of the replication of purity in spatial and architectural arrangements. The way the Jerusalem temple was configured reflected an overwhelming concern among ancient Israelites with questions of purity. The British anthropologist Mary Douglas famously explained in *Purity and Danger* (1966) that purity and holiness are really concerned with keeping things within their proper boundaries. One aspect of this issue surfaced in the food laws in Leviticus, and she argued that the Israelite interest in maintaining the purity of the body by controlling the food that went into it reflected a concern with maintaining the external boundaries between Israelites and the outside world, especially when the powerful peoples surrounding Israel often represented a threat to its national security or even existence. But the same type of argument applies to questions of space and architecture, especially as to who might or might not enter particular space, as well as to the body. Mircea Eliade argued in *The Sacred and the Profane* (1959) that for religious people space is not homogeneous. It is divided into space that has been sacralized by some manifestation of divinity and secular space, the profane and ordinary space lying outside this zone of sanctification. "Every sacred space," he wrote, "implies a hierophany, an irruption of the sacred that results in detaching a territory from the surrounding cosmic milieu and making it qualitatively different."[9] So, when in Genesis 28:10-19 Jacob had his dream in Haran of a ladder with angels ascending and descending it and heard God speaking from above, he said, "How awesome is this place! This is none other than the house of God, and this is the gate of heaven." In antiquity temples were preeminent sacred places in this sense because they were regarded as the locus of a god's presence on earth. Many of them, such as the temple in Jerusalem, were located on mountains since this put them in a position closest to heaven.[10] The temple was often seen as the center or navel of the cosmos, and there were Israelite traditions that described the rock on which the Jerusalem temple was built in this way. Yet a basic division of space into sacred and profane hardly does justice to the religious and social realities of the Jerusalem temple. Perhaps, as Mary Douglas has argued, it was as a result of their precarious existence as a minority in a sea of non-Israelites practicing a florid idolatry that the sternly monotheistic Israelites developed to a high degree the boundaries between them and the outside world.[11] Their interest in purity, which involves keeping everything in its proper place, is a reflection of this boundary issue. Even among their internal arrangements the same concern to divide the acceptable from the nonacceptable led to drawing a large number of boundaries between persons, things, times, and places. As far as the latter is concerned, this tendency is clearly seen in the ten zones of holiness that are expressly distinguished in the Mishnaic tractate *Kelim*, moving from the periphery to the center:

1. The land of Israel is holier than all the other lands.
2. The walled cities of the land of Israel are more holy than the land itself.
3. Within the walls of Jerusalem, the locality is still more holy than other cities are.
4. The temple mount is more holy than the wall.
5. The rampart (of the temple) is holier than the mount.
6. The Court of the Women is holier than the rampart.

7. The Court of the Israelites is holier than the Court of the Women.
8. The Court of the Priests is holier than the Court of the Israelites.
9. The space between the porch and the altar is holier than the Court of the Priests.
10. "The Holy of Holies is still more holy than them, since none may enter therein save only the High Priest on the Day of Atonement at the time of the Temple sacrifice" (m. Kelim 1.6–9).[12]

Although the arrangements in Ethiopian churches are not as elaborate as these, they do reflect the same broad impulse to symbolize gradations of holiness in the differentiation of architectural space in the context of the widely held belief in Ethiopia that their country has been sacralized by the presence of the actual ark of the covenant in Aksum. Thus we could adapt the tenfold pattern to an Ethiopian church as follows:

1. The land of Ethiopia is holier than all other lands since it functions as a new Israel.
2. The churches and monasteries of Ethiopia are holier than the land itself. An important source for this belief is the Ethiopian text the *Dersana Ura'el*, which describes how the archangel Urael (also known as Uriel) gathered blood from the chest of Christ on the cross in a vessel and went to Ethiopia, where he scattered it on places that were to be monasteries, thus creating a sacred cosmography.[13]
3. The churchyard is holier than the land outside it.
4. The vestibule (*qene mahlet*) is holier than the churchyard.
5. The nave (*qeddest*) is holier than the vestibule.
6. The inner sanctuary (*maqdash*), holy of holies (*qeddesta qeddusan*), is holier than all the rest since it contains the tabot.

The strong similarity between the Israelite and Ethiopian representations of zones of holiness delineated by boundaries suggests that, just as the Israelite picture may reflect, at least in part, a concern to maintain boundaries between Israelites and the threatening outside world (as Mary Douglas suggested), so too may the Ethiopian. For much of their history from the seventh century CE onward, Christian Ethiopians found themselves surrounded by either Muslim (especially to the north, south, and east) or African (especially to the west and southwest) peoples.

Sacred Time and Memory

Feast Days

The distinctive character of Ethiopian Orthodoxy also depends upon something as fundamental as how time is organized year by year: the Ethiopian calendar. In broad terms, the liturgical calendar (which is also used by the Ethiopian state) is based on the Coptic Church in Egypt. Yet while the Orthodox calendar came from Alexandria, a good deal of it was developed by Emperor Zara Yaqob (who reigned 1434–1468; see chapter 4). It is a solar calendar, accommodated to the annual 365-day cycle of the sun (not a lunar calendar that is adjusted to the phases of the moon). The Ethiopian Orthodox calendar is roughly eight years behind the Gregorian (or Western) calendar, meaning that 1994 EC (Ethiopian Calendar) ran from September 11, 2001, to September 10, 2002. There are twelve months of thirty days each and one intercalated month of five days (or six days every leap year), thus producing the necessary 365 days (or 366 in a leap year). In terms of the Gregorian calendar, the New Year begins on September 11 (or September 12 in a leap year). The months are as follows:

> Maskaram (September 11–October 10)
> Teqemt (from October 11)
> Hedar (from November 10)
> Tahsas (from December 10)
> Terr (from January 9)
> Yakkatit (from February 8)
> Maggabit (from March 10)
> Miyazya (from April 9)
> Genbot (from May 9)
> Sane (from June 8)

Hamle (from July 8)
Nahase (from August 7)
Pagumen (from September 6)

These are the same months as in the Coptic calendar, renamed in Ge'ez. In Ethiopia the beginning of the New Year marks the end of the rainy season, a time associated with harvest and renewal. Pagumen, the short intercalary month, falls at the end of rainy season in early September, just before the renewal of the New Year and the harvest festivities. Those five epagomenal days are neither really in the old year not yet in the new; they are a liminal time.[14]

Superimposed on this calendar is a remarkably rich set of religious feast days and fast days.[15] Ullendorff observed that "there is a prodigious number of feasts in the Abyssinian Church."[16] This means that for the Orthodox Christian diurnal existence unfolds within a religious context. Most time becomes sacred time. For this reason it has been suggested that the calendar is "a system in which bodies, space, and time are mapped, divided, demarcated and otherwise experienced in terms of the temporal geography of ritual."[17]

Like all Christian churches, Ethiopian Orthodoxy has a liturgical year that comprises a major pattern that follows the central activities of Christ (especially Advent, Christmas, Epiphany, Lent, and Easter), together with a variety of other events that celebrate Christ and the saints and, very important in Ethiopia, the archangels. There are nine major feasts of Christ,[18] with those associated with Easter being mobile in the calendar to match the changing date of Easter:

The Annunciation/Incarnation (Maggabit 29 / April 7)
The Nativity (Lidet) (Tahsas 29 / January 7)
The Baptism/Epiphany (Timkat) (Terr 11 / January 19)
The Transfiguration (Dabra Tabor) (Nahasse 13 / August 19)
Palm Sunday (Hosanna)
Great and Holy Friday (Siklet)
Easter (Tensaye)
Ascension (Erget)
Pentecost (Paraklitos)

Timkat celebrates the epiphany of Christ that occurred at his baptism by John in the Jordan when the divine voice from heaven announced that "this is my beloved son" or "you are my beloved son" (Matt 3:17; Mark 1:11; and Luke 3:22). This is one of the most popular feasts in the calendar. It is one of the two occasions when the tabot of a church is taken outside (the other being the feast day of the saint to whom the tabot is consecrated). On the eve of the feast (which lasts for three days), several tabots are carried in imposing processions from each church to some place where there is water, like a lake or a riverbank, in memory of Jesus traveling from Galilee to the Jordan (Matt 3:13). The tabots are placed in a special tent, and songs are sung during the night and a liturgy conducted. In the morning the priests bless the water, scripture passages are read, and three candles (in honor of the Trinity) are set afloat on the water. After prayers, people sprinkle (or sometimes drench) themselves with water, and the tabots are carried back to the churches. One of the most spectacular sites for Timkat is in the impressive stone baths of Emperor Fasilidas in Gondar (figure 7.1). The usually dry pool is filled from a local river for the purpose, and, after certain prayers have been said, male worshippers enter the water in their hundreds to reenact the baptism of Christ.

Figure 7.1. *The festival of Timkat in the baths of Fasilidas, Gondar*

There are also minor feasts of Christ, such as the exaltation of the cross, the circumcision of the Lord, the multiplication of the loaves, the presentation of the Lord, and the entry of the Lord into Egypt.[19] The first of these, the exaltation of the cross, or Mesqel (Ge'ez for "cross"), is observed in other Christian churches but is especially prominent in Ethiopia. It celebrates the discovery of the true cross by Constantine's mother, Helena, in Jerusalem in 326 CE (during her travels in the Holy Land in 326–328 CE). This occurs on Maskaram 17 (or September 27). This is just after the end of the rainy season and the beginning of the New Year, so there is a marked alignment of environmental time and sacred time. It is a feast day that is linked to fertility rituals and, as such, has parallels in non-Christian parts of Ethiopia.[20] On the eve of the feast, people bring the materials for making a bonfire (*demera*). The priest sings, "The Cross has enlightened. It has adorned the heavens with stars, but above all it shows the Sun [i.e., Christ]," and the people answer, "Above all the Cross shows the sun."[21] In due course the bonfire, containing a cross, is lit. Each year large crowds gather for this feast in Mesqel Square in Addis Ababa (figure 7.2). This celebration includes the dramatic reenactment of Helena's discovery of the cross and hundreds of white-garbed priests and deacons

Figure 7.2. *The festival of Mesqel in Mesqel Square, Addis Ababa*

forming the shape of huge cross, while across the country the feast is celebrated in thousands of villages where bonfires are lit.

Mesqel is also the annual focus for the intense attachment that Ethiopian Orthodox Christians have for the cross. We saw in chapter 2 that Ezana put crosses on his coins after his conversion in around 335 CE. That was only shortly after the Christian world had been mesmerized by Helena's discovery of the true cross in Jerusalem. One sees crosses everywhere in Ethiopia. Priests carry staffs with a bronze cross on the top in liturgical contexts. The laity often wear crosses around their necks. So popular is the cross that a number of particular styles of cross have developed, in particular three styles associated with, respectively, Aksum, Lalibela and Gondar (see figure 6.2).

Mary is extremely popular among Ethiopian Orthodox Christians, and there are thirty-three major annual feasts in her honor, relating to her life, her name, her miracles, and her sanctuaries. It was Emperor Zara Yaqob who instituted this number of feasts to honor her. Those commemorating her earlier years (her conception by Anna, her birth, and her presentation in the temple) derive from the early noncanonical Christian work, the *Protoevangelium of James*.

Two important feasts specifically for Mary are those commemorating the Qwesqwam, the flight into Egypt (see the icon in the photograph on the front cover), which is named after the town of that name where the Holy Family stopped on their journey, and her assumption. The Holy Family's flight is commemorated over the period from Maskaram 26 / October 6 until Hedar 6 / November 15, the latter being the actual feast day. This time is called Zamena Tsege, meaning "the season of the flower," since it is after the rainy season when the flowers and the fruits appear. The Assumption (Filseta) occurs on Nahasse 16 / August 22 and is preceded by a fast that runs from August 7 to 21.

There are also numerous feast days for saints, and each is celebrated on a particular day every year. Here "saints" includes the archangels (such as Michael, Gabriel, and Raphael) and angels, Old Testament saints, New Testament saints (apostles, disciples, and holy women), martyrs of the ancient church (especially Egypt), and Ethiopian saints (especially kings [such as Kaleb and Fasilidas] and monks [such as Ewostatewos, Abba Pantalewon, Abba Aragawi, Abba Salama / Frumentius, Abba Libanos, Yared, and Abba Garima]).

Fast Days

Yet sacred time in Ethiopian Orthodoxy is marked not merely by the cycle of feasts. Just as, if not more, central to Orthodox identity is the practice of fasting. In most cases the fasts are followed by festivals, for which they form a necessary preparation. For most believers the fasts are the core of Ethiopian Orthodox practice, and they are regarded as the main point of distinction between Orthodox Christians and the members of other Christian churches, the Protestant ones especially. "In the eyes of most Orthodox Christians I know, certainly in the villages, if you follow the fasts you are a Christian and if you don't you are not, and that's really all there is to it."[22] In fact, the fasts are regular and extensive enough that they become part of the everyday experience of having a body. "In this way temporary, rhythmic prohibitions become a way of maintaining and managing one's bodily state of being." But prohibitions also come to define boundaries of Orthodoxy in relation to other denominations and religions.[23]

The core of a fast is a prohibition on eating meat or animal products (so, a vegan diet, in effect) or engaging in sexual activity. In addition, fasts "generally imply one meal a day to be taken either in the evening or just after midday."[24] If you are attending a liturgy, you cannot take food or water between the beginning of the day and the end of the service, which is 3 p.m. on regular fasting days and 9 a.m. on weekends. There are seven major fasts.[25] Some are compulsory for all, and some only for priests and monks. Here is a sample of these fasts. The Fast of Salvation, compulsory for all Orthodox Christians, is kept on every Wednesday and Friday throughout most to the year unless displaced by a major feast. The Great Fast (Abiy Si'om), also compulsory for all, lasts for the fifty-five days of the Ethiopian Orthodox Lent. Many Orthodox Christians feel exhausted toward the end of this fast and look forward to Easter and the feast that accompanies it. The Fast of Nineveh is kept by everybody and applies to the Monday, Tuesday, and Wednesday of the second week before Lent. The Fast of the Assumption is compulsory for all from Nahase 1 to 16. In contrast, the Fast of Qwesqwam is compulsory only for priests and monks. It lasts for forty days, from Maskaram 26 to the Feast of Qwesqwam on Hedar 6 (as noted above), and commemorates the hardships endured by the Holy Family, Mary especially, during the time of their flight into Egypt. There are 250 fasting days in the year, and it is expected that the clergy will keep all of them, while laity will do as many as they can.

Anthropologist Tom Boylston has observed that Ethiopian Orthodox Christians describe the feeling of fasting in terms of a mixture of tiredness and happiness. This indicates that there is an inward, more individual dimension to the practice, so that "fasting is not simply an activity of rote obedience." He adds, "Fasting is not really a world-denying or world-hating practice, but rather a way for people to do religious work on and through their bodies. Moreover, most fasts have as their culminating act a feast, and should not be considered without this context."[26]

Sacred Action

Eucharistic Liturgy

As with other Orthodox Churches and the Roman Catholic Church, the central liturgical rite in Ethiopian Orthodoxy is the eucharistic liturgy.[27] In both Ge'ez and Amharic it is called the *qeddase* (thanksgiving). The Ethiopian church still uses the ancient service of the early church, and the qeddase is, in fact, equivalent to the ancient Mass of the Catechumens, in which adults receiving instruction in the faith attended Mass until the reading of the Gospel and sermon and were then dismissed (see below), even though these days there are usually no catechumens under preparation for baptism during the Mass. Yet even among baptized Orthodox Christians there are not many who actually receive the Eucharist. Most "Orthodox Christians do not take the Eucharist throughout most of their adult lives. This is because of concerns about purity, and especially the assumption that sexually mature adults are generally not in a fit state for communion." You must fast for eighteen hours, abstain from sexual activity, have no flowing wounds or mucus, and menstruating and postpartum women are not allowed to enter the church at all.[28]

The eucharistic liturgy is celebrated at dawn (but 6 a.m. on Sunday and 7 a.m. on Saturday) and after midday (around 12:30 p.m.) on days of fasting. At Christmas, Epiphany, and Easter it is celebrated at midnight. The ceremony is normally conducted by two priests (the principal celebrant and an assistant celebrant) and three deacons. If clergy are in short supply, one priest and two deacons conduct the service. The eucharistic liturgy is always sung and lasts about two hours. Before each such liturgy the bread and wine are prepared in the *beta lahm* (house of bread). The bread is unleavened. Nuns spend many hours separating by hand the best grains of wheat for use in the Eucharist. The wine is unfermented, made by squeezing dried grapes. This practice of using unfermented wine troubled the early Jesuit missionaries to the country. Once the bread and wine are prepared, they are taken, under the cover of an open liturgical umbrella (*tela*), to the sanctuary of the church in a procession led by the assistant priest and accompanied by two deacons, while a third deacon rings a little bell that announces the start of the Eucharistic celebration.

The qeddase is structured as follows. The rite of preparation commences with the personal preparation of the celebrant. On entering the church the celebrant recites a penitential prayer (known as The Prayer of Absolution of the Son; Fethat Za-Wald), during which the faithful prostrate themselves. He recites other prayers and, having done so, enters the holy of holies through the veiled entrance. He then undertakes the preparation of the sacred vessels and the altar, uttering appropriate prayers. He next says The

Prayer of the Faithful. The priest puts on his vestments and, having washed his hands, begins the Introit, while the congregation sings a hymn. The priest blesses the bread and the wine in the chalice, and the ceremony of incensing occurs.

After all this comes the liturgy of the Word, with the officiants doing the reading from within the holy of holies. There are readings from three "epistles": the first from Paul, the second from the seven Catholic Epistles (James; 1 and 2 Peter; 1, 2, and 3 John; and James) or from the Apocalypse of John, and the third from the Acts of the Apostles. Each reading is introduced by a dialogue among the deacon, priest, and the people and a priestly prayer, and concludes with a hymn sung by the assembly.

After these three readings, the celebrants proceed around the altar while the priest chants the Theotokia (praises to Mary as Theotokos, mother of God). The priest then prays the christological prayer, the Trisagion (the prayer of the "thrice holy": "Holy God, Holy Strong, Holy Immortal, have mercy on us"). This is a prelude to the highly revered Prayer of the Covenant (the Kidan), which Ethiopian tradition regards Jesus as having taught to the apostles and disciples in the period between his resurrection and ascension.[29] The priest utters aloud The Prayer of the Gospel, and the deacons sing the Mesbak (a psalm versicle) that announces the Gospel. Then a procession preparatory to reading the Gospel takes place. The ministers go around the altar, preceding the priest, who carries the open Gospel book, proclaiming "the holy Gospel, the Word of the Son of God, proclaimed by N. [either Matthew, Mark, Luke, or John]." They all step out of the holy of holies, and the people bow toward the Gospel. The priest, standing under an umbrella, then reads the Gospel. Often the homily will be delivered at this stage, although there is an alternative practice of delivering the homily at the end of the qeddase before the final blessing. Any catechumens (that is, those who are being prepared for baptism) present are dismissed at this stage, prior to the liturgy of the faithful (which is called the liturgy of the Eucharist in Roman Catholic churches).

This section of the qeddase begins with prayers of intercession, after which the people sing the creed. The celebrant uncovers the bread and the wine and washes his hands. The prayer The Kiss of Peace (attributed to St. Basil) is recited, and people bow to one another. Then comes the Anaphora, known in the West as the Eucharistic Prayer or the Canon of the Mass. This includes the words commemorating the institution of the Eucharist by Jesus at the Last Supper, the consecration of the bread and wine by the invocation of the Holy Spirit (the *epiclesis*), prayers of intercession, the Our Father, Holy Communion, and the final praises. Before communion the *Book of the Fathers* is read, and if an expert composer of the poetic form known as *qene* (see chapter 6) is present, he will sing a qene about the crucifixion. Psalm 150 is sung during the communion. Immediately after the communion, those who have received the Eucharist drink water to ensure that no part of the Holy Gifts will fall to the ground or remain in the mouth. After the communion the qene is repeated but this time to the accompaniment of sticks (*maqwomia*). Next come hymns after communion, together with another qene, this time in the form of aqwaqwam, or movement with sticks and drums. Last, closing prayers are said. At various times during the liturgy, there are prostrations to the ground.

Practices with a Judaic Dimension

Just as the organization of space and the centrality of the tabot coheres with Jewish ideas, so too do certain practices of the Ethiopian Orthodox Church. The first of these is the practice of circumcision. This is carried out on the eighth day after a male child's birth, as decreed in Genesis 17:12 and Leviticus 12:3. Sometimes female excision is also carried out, but this reflects African and not Jewish practice.[30] Secondly, Ethiopian Orthodoxy adopts many of the Jewish food laws, including those in Leviticus 11 (which bans eating, inter alia, pigs, camels, hares, fish without scales, and birds that are raptors) and Genesis 32:32 (concerning the forbidden sinew). The important source of Ethiopian Orthodox law, the *Fetha Nagast* (The laws of the kings), dating to the thirteenth century CE, actually provides, "Remember what God has commanded you by the mouth of Moses."[31] However, Ethiopians do not employ separate vessels for preparing milk and meat dishes (a rule Jewish people have deduced from Exod 23:19 and 34:26; and Deut 14:21) and used often to offer visiting guests a piece of flesh that had been cut from a living animal, which no Jew could eat.[32] Third, while Ethiopian Orthodox Christians observe Sunday as the principal religious day of the week, some (who maintain the position of Abba Ewostatewos discussed in chapter 3) also hold Saturday in special regard. But this advocacy of a "forty-nine-hour Sabbath" is not binding on all Ethiopian Orthodox Christians.[33] Fourth, the Jewish purity laws in Leviticus 15 are applied to Orthodox believers to the extent that, when they are suffering from one of the forms of impurity mentioned there, they may approach the church building but they may not enter it: they can be seen during services standing outside the church door praying. It must be noted that other Oriental Orthodox churches also adhere to these rules; indeed, they require the faithful to stay at home when they are affected by them.[34]

How are we to explain the various Judaic features that appear in Ethiopian Orthodoxy? One explanation lies in direct historical links. It is possible, for example, that the Syrian Christians who were very influential in the beginnings of Christianity in Ethiopia (see chapter 2) were themselves descendants of Jewish Christ followers of the first and second centuries, that is, like those with whom Paul clashed in Antioch and Galatia, probably because of his negative views toward the continuing role of the Mosaic law in the Christ movement.[35] One sign of Syrian influence is the presence of Syriac loan words in Ge'ez: *orit* (torah or law), *haymanot* (faith), *qurban* (oblation, sacrifice), *salot* (prayer), *maqdas* (sanctuary), and Fasika (Easter).[36] A second form of explanation links the Jewish influences to the major effort to legitimate the Solomonic dynasty that supplanted the Zagwe dynasty by asserting its links to Solomon. To repeat briefly the discussion in chapter 3, the Solomonic kings claimed that Menelik (the son of the queen of Sheba by

Solomon), aided by Israelite young men, including the son of the High Priest, stole the ark of the covenant and the stone tablets given by God to Moses on Sinai and brought them to Ethiopia with one thousand Israelites. With such a tradition to legitimate the dynasty, it is not hard to see that it would be in the interests of the emperors to ensure that Jewish features figured in Orthodox belief, especially features that aligned the structure of the churches and the presence of tabots within to that of the temple of Solomon and the ark of the covenant within its holy of holies.

Some Recent Developments

It has not escaped the attention of many clergy and laity that the Ethiopian Orthodox Church needs to become far more active if it is to maintain itself as the major Christian church in the country, especially faced with the challenge of the rise of Protestantism, including Pentecostal Protestantism. Many initiatives have been launched to do just this.

In the 1950s a number of groups began establishing Sunday school. In 1951–1952 two Coptic Christians set up the first Orthodox Sunday school in Ethiopia in Arat Kilo, Addis Ababa. In addition, a group of students of the Tafari Makonnen School in Addis Ababa began organizing Bible study in 1947. In 1957 they continued this activity in the nearby Meskaye Hizunan Medhane Alem Monastery, and in 1958 they named their organization Teach and Learn (Temro Mastnemar). It has become an extremely active operation, with a wide array of activities. In 1958 students at Addis Ababa University founded Haymanota Abaw [Faith of the fathers] Ethiopian Students Association, which continued with the support of Abunas Basilios and Theophilos. By 1970 it had twenty-one branches with about forty-two thousand members. Its main focus was on adaption to contemporary needs, for example, in liturgical reforms and development activities, while preserving the Orthodox tradition in a manner consonant with the needs of modern youth.[37] It was nationalist in urging Ethiopian youth to guard against foreign influences, but above all it was meant "to address the religious needs of the youth and to cushion its transition successfully in the face of rapid social and economic changes."[38]

Many other associations aimed at renewing the church or simply ensuring its continuing relevance in the face of the pressures of modernity sprang up in the 1960s, 1970s, and 1980s.[39] Many of these called their organization a *mahebar*, and this phenomenon requires a closer look. *Mahebar* means "association" or "society" in Ge'ez. It appears that religious fraternal associations bearing this name have existed for hundreds of years in the Ethiopian Orthodox Church. The original purpose of a mahebar was to honor a particular saint, typically by collecting money to host feasts on the saint's day. Members of the mahebar would meet once a month (on the saint's day) in the house of each member in turn. As mahebars could embrace members from neighboring parishes, they were a powerful device for promoting fellowship between Christians living at a remove from one another. They also provided help to other parish projects in their area. In the early twentieth century, with the arrival of capitalism leading to a more monetarized local economy, these associations began to require membership fees.[40] The mahebar model allowed the development of "a popular and influential lay movement within the life of the church."[41] They are outside the control of the hierarchy and give the laity space and freedom to develop useful initiatives. Their importance increased when the Derg took power, and since that time they have grown in number and in the size and range of activities they undertake.[42]

A particularly significant association is the Mahebara Qeddusan (Association of the Righteous). This was formed in 1991, at the end of the Derg regime. A large number of students had been sent to the Belate military training camp to be trained to fight the EPRDF. One night a number of Orthodox students met in a hall and decided to form the Mahebara Qeddusan. A few days later Addis Ababa fell to the EPRDF, but the students pushed on with this organization. Abuna Paulos permitted them to build a large headquarters in Addis Ababa near the patriarchate compound. They are a renewal movement within Ethiopian Orthodoxy with official sanction. Their stated mission statements include helping Orthodox students in higher education to understand their faith; aiding the transmission of the heritage of Orthodoxy from generation to generation (for example, in monasteries and church schools); engaging in an active publishing campaign across a range of media;[43] supporting the Orthodox Church financially and in other ways; and encouraging the study of the Orthodox Church, especially by young scholars.[44] It now has thousands of members who retain their membership throughout their lives and pay 2 percent of their income to the association. It has become an effective agency for renewing the church. Nevertheless, it tends to be doctrinally and spiritually conservative and has a research section that is said, inter alia, to have published accounts of attempts by evangelicals and Muslims to subvert the church and the state.[45] While, from one Protestant perspective, it appears to be a "highly aggressive and more militant movement,"[46] it was always likely that the rapid growth of the Protestant churches in Ethiopia would stimulate countervailing pressures and structures on the part of Orthodoxy. In particular, the fact that conversion to Pentecostal churches still seems mainly to occur among Orthodox believers partly explains the appearance of "more confrontational and fundamentalist reactions in the Orthodox camp, such as the strict return to tradition preached by the influential *Mahebara Qeddusan* movement."[47]

Also notable is the launch, since 2000, of the church's own missionary activity in Ethiopia to occupy a space hitherto largely the preserve of the Protestant churches and organizations, indigenous and foreign. Gospel-spreading councils have been established in many places, and missionary work is also undertaken by Sunday school people, theological students, and others. New monasteries have been established, especially in the South, both to promote Orthodox spirituality but also to engage in missionary activity. This work includes efforts to evangelize in different Ethiopian languages. Hitherto the overwhelmingly dominant languages were Ge'ez and Amharic, and this was a real and unnecessary obstacle to Orthodox evangelism.[48]

A final measure is the recent expansion of preaching in the Ethiopian Orthodox Church. The church has two services, in the morning and the afternoon, in which preaching is delivered in Amharic. The afternoon service is particularly popular and occurs daily in thousands of churches across the country. This service tends to be characterized by extensive biblical preaching related to contemporary contexts. Sometimes the preaching is recorded on tapes or CDs, and these are popular among the faithful.[49] This preaching, to judge from the rich array of samples provided by Keon-Sang An, indicates both the power of the distinctive Ethiopian Orthodox approach to biblical interpretation and the great skill of the preachers in bringing this to bear on contemporary issues, not least the challenges posed to Orthodox beliefs (concerning tabots, for example).[50] The role of the Bible and biblical knowledge in Christian faith were long regarded, with some justification, by Protestant missionaries and churches in Ethiopia as problematically underemphasized by the Orthodox Church. The emphasis now being placed by Orthodoxy on widespread biblical preaching to the laity, coupled with the existence of its unique *andemta* commentary tradition and well-trained clerics who know much scripture by heart, suggests that it has now fully realized the extent to which the Bible is an asset and not a liability in its mission.

One contested area in which Ethiopian Orthodoxy has adapted itself to the changing social and religious context in the country is Pentecostalism, whose history in Ethiopia is addressed in chapter 8. Under the influence of Protestant Pentecostalism, a number of charismatic movements have developed within Ethiopian Orthodoxy, especially in the last quarter of the twentieth century. Yet they are routinely a point of contention within Orthodoxy. Some of them, for example, proclaim a different biblical canon, closer to the Protestant biblical canon, and question some Orthodox literature, such as the lives of the saints.[51] More seriously, these charismatic groups are seen by some Orthodox believers as instruments for their youth to join Protestant churches. Some, indeed, have left the church and become independent Pentecostal churches.

Arguably the most prominent example of this phenomenon is the Emmanuel Fellowship, which began as a charismatic prayer fellowship in Nazareth in 1991 and left the Orthodox Church in 1995. Thereafter, it became increasingly Protestant, constituting itself as the Emmanuel Fellowship Church, and finally joined the (Protestant) Evangelical Churches' Fellowship in 2004.[52] It now has three hundred churches and about seventy-nine thousand members.[53]

New religious movements in Africa have frequently begun life by splitting away from their parent church, with most examples coming from missionary churches.[54] When a new movement arises in a church, it is common for its new attitudes, new idioms, and new ventures of faith to be highly disturbing to other members of the church.[55] The clergy are likely to be particularly troubled because their position and status are tied to the existing status quo.[56] Nevertheless, and this is an issue that will be further considered in chapter 10, it is not inevitably the case that a new movement will break away, quickly or at all. For example, the Jamaa (Family) charismatic movement was begun among the Luba of Katanga in Zaire in 1945, but despite certain unorthodox features its twenty thousand adherents remained almost entirely within the Roman Catholic Church because of its missionaries' sympathetic treatment for nearly three decades. It began to arouse opposition from the bishops in the 1970s, but even into the 1980s some members of the movement insisted on attending Roman Catholic Masses.[57] In line with the desire by the members of some new movements to remain within the parent religion, there are still some charismatic groups within Ethiopian Orthodoxy who wish to maintain that affiliation but keep a low profile on account of their precarious position.[58] Perhaps the church will be able to reach a form of accommodation with those pursuing a charismatic path while retaining their lifelong allegiance to Orthodoxy, an outcome that is likely to bring new energy to this ancient faith.

PART FOUR

OTHER ETHIOPIAN CHRISTIANITIES

8

Protestantism

History

By far the greatest change in Ethiopian Christianity in the past few centuries has been the arrival of evangelical and, in many cases, Pentecostal Christianity. This growth in Protestant churches has partly been at the expense of the Orthodox Church. The statistics are striking. In 1994, when the population of Ethiopia was fifty-five million, Christians constituted 61.6 percent of the population, with the Orthodox constituting 50.6 percent and Protestants 10.1 percent. Yet, by the time of the 2007 census, of Ethiopia's seventy-four million people, 43.5 percent were Orthodox, 18.6 percent were Protestant, 33.9 percent were Muslim, 2.6 percent were members of traditional African religions, 0.7 percent were Catholic, and others made up 0.6 percent. In absolute numbers, between 1994 and 2007 the Orthodox Church had increased from twenty-nine million to thirty-two million members, and the Protestant churches from six million to fourteen million. So both branches of Christianity expanded as the population grew, but Protestantism expanded at a much faster rate. It is worth noting, however, that the percentages of Orthodox and Protestant Christians in the population had not changed much by the time of the 2013 census, at which point the Orthodox believers comprised

43.2 percent of the population (41,691,000), and Protestants 19.1 percent (18,433,000).[1] This suggests that by 2013 the period of dramatic Protestant expansion vis-à-vis Orthodoxy had ended.

For much of its history Orthodoxy was the official religion of the state and worked closely with the emperor and state officials in supporting Ethiopian culture and national identity. The emperors generally viewed themselves as protectors of Ethiopian Orthodoxy. We saw in chapter 4, for example, how in the nineteenth century Ethiopian emperors, keen to enlarge the area under their political control, also aided the expansion of the church by the forced integration of Muslims and members of African religions. This process represented the common phenomenon of the coincidence of interests between the state and a monopolistic or dominant church.[2]

As a national church, Ethiopian Orthodoxy largely accepted the political order in which it was located, and it functioned as a conservative force in society. It drew its members, most of whom entered the church through baptism shortly after birth, from all social strata, including the aristocracy. It offered a means to grace and salvation that focused on its priesthood and on sacraments and liturgies that were long and embodied stately ritual forms. It was a hierarchical church, especially to the extent that the abuna had paramount authority, expressed in particular in his unique power to ordain priests. When the Protestant churches reached Ethiopia, however, they introduced powerful alternative modes of Christianity that were not aligned to the imperial regime. They recruited (at least initially) through the conscious conversion of adults. They were often anti-sacramental, anti-clerical and anti-hierarchical, and they stressed the importance of personal experience and a direct encounter with Jesus. They tended to be composed of small, at times autonomous groups. The contrast they provided with Ethiopian Orthodoxy was quite pronounced.

The Arrival and Growth of Evangelical Christianity to the 1960s

The earliest Protestant missionary in Ethiopia was from Germany. Peter Heyling arrived in Gondar (via Egypt) in 1634. This was during the reign of Emperor Fasilidas, who expelled the Jesuits from the country. Heyling's aim was to "reawaken the derelict churches of the Orient to genuine evangelical life."[3] Whereas the Jesuit Mendes had wanted to compel the Ethiopians to become Roman Catholics, with death the penalty for those who refused, Heyling aimed to revitalize Orthodoxy. He hoped to have it "focus on its scriptural origins, reform, and be endowed with a heightened sense of evangelization in accord with the doctrine of salvation." In line with the broad approach taken by the Protestant reformers, Heyling translated the Gospel of John into Amharic.[4] He remained in Ethiopia until 1652 (an impressive period considering the fate of the Jesuits) and was killed in Egypt by the Pasha. But on his departure from Ethiopia, his followers formed a brotherhood of devout people that later became known as the Evangelical Association. They did not intend to separate from the Orthodox Church and persisted for some two hundred years, even though they were persecuted by Tewodros II, Yohannes IV, and Menelik II.[5]

In 1829 two missionaries from the (Anglican) Church Missionary Society, Samuel Gobat (figure 8.1) and Christian Kugler, arrived in Tigray. Like Heyling, their aim was to work collaboratively with the national church, helping it with renewal and internal transformation. Kugler made little attempt to adapt to life in Ethiopia, but Gobat did—wearing Ethiopian dress, sharing food and lodging, and seeking to meet and talk to people wherever he went.[6] They distributed thousands of copies of scripture in Amharic but generally had little impact. Kugler died a year after his arrival, and Gobat went back to England. Later Gobat returned to Ethiopia, traveling with Johann Krapf to Shoa, an area settled by the Oromo. The local king, however, wanted artisans and technical experts, not preachers. But Krapf became very interested in the Oromo. He translated part of the New Testament for them into vernacular Oromo and conceived and popularized the thought that forming a Christian community among the Oromo was central to the evangelization of Central Africa. Aided by a Falasha, an Ethiopian Jew, from Gondar, Mikael Aragawi, who had converted, Krapf

Figure 8.1.
Samuel Gobat

also published a much-improved Amharic Bible, and this would prove crucial in the work of the Protestant missions in Ethiopia.[7]

During his reign (1855–1868), Emperor Tewodros welcomed Protestant missionaries from Europe on the condition that they trained his people in handicrafts and technical skills and did not interfere with the role of the Orthodox Church as a key component in maintaining national identity. In 1855 a group known as Pilgrim Missions arrived at Tewodros' court. It offered technical help but was not permitted to engage in evangelical activity. The one exception among its number was Martin Flad. He decided to concentrate on converting the Falasha, and both the emperor and the abuna agreed to this. A community of Christians was established among the Falasha, and they were probably the first evangelical Protestants in Ethiopia. By 1912 there were two thousand of them.[8]

Under Yohannes IV (reigned 1871–1889) the situation became far less welcoming to missionary activity. The practice of pious craftsmen being sent from Europe to serve the emperors came to a halt, and Flad was ejected from the country. But there were now several indigenous missionaries who were able to carry on the work in his absence. Yohannes did not see the need for missionaries in a country that to his mind was already Christian enough, and he believed that national unity might be threatened by competing Christian communities. This latter factor induced him to declare that the Orthodox Tewahedo faith was the only permitted theological position. He required the missionaries in Ethiopia to leave. But some of them retired only so far as Eritrea.[9]

In 1866 the Swedish Evangelical Mission had opened a mission in Massawa, on the Eritrean coast, as part of a wider push into the Red Sea area. These missionaries established good relations with the Orthodox priests in the Hamassien region and also converted ex-slaves, mostly Oromo, to work as local missionaries in various parts of Ethiopia. In 1872 they established a Bible training school at Imkullu. As a result, Christian evangelical communities were established, first in Eritrea and later in Ethiopia, especially in the region of Wellega.[10] In the late 1870s they experienced significant persecution because of their views.

The next emperor, Menelik II (reigned 1889–1913), was initially sympathetic to Protestant missionaries, especially if they came with technical skills, but later began to oppose them under Orthodox pressure. But by then the Swedish missionaries, from their establishments on the Red Sea coast, had begun to make progress in Addis Ababa, Menelik's new capital, and in the Wellega area. For this purpose they relied on indigenous missionaries in the form of Orthodox priests from Eritrea who had not surrendered their Orthodox tradition nor sundered their ties with their local churches. They had adopted Protestant views on salvation through personal faith in Jesus Christ. One of the converts and graduates of Imkullu was Onesimus Nesib, an ex-slave. Aided by another ex-slave who had trained at Imkullu, the woman Aster Gano, he completed the first translation of the Bible into Oromo.[11]

The year 1904 saw the arrival in Ethiopia of the highly effective Swedish Lutheran missionary Karl Cederqvist. He worked with Onesimus Nesib in the Wellega region and in Addis Ababa. Cederqvist received permission from Menelik to establish a mission station in Addis Ababa, and thereafter missionaries were allowed to enter Ethiopia. Cederqvist established a congregation and built a school and a medical center. He worked at building up the evangelical movement across the nation. In 1919 he died while tending patients suffering from Spanish flu. His devotion to service won him the respect of the then-young emperor Haile Selassie, who (as noted in chapter 4) was regent from 1916 to 1930 and emperor from 1930 to 1974.[12]

Haile Selassie wanted to provide education and health care to as many people as possible, and, since the government had insufficient resources, he regarded European and US missions as an alternative means to achieve this aim. Under his progressive policies, he therefore granted considerable freedom to foreign missionaries in the 1920s and 1930s. At times the Orthodox Church opposed their initiatives.[13] Nevertheless, many foreign missions established operations in Ethiopia's South, Southeast, and Southwest. One significant entrant was the Sudan Interior Mission (SIM) from the United States in 1928, which later employed Thomas Lambie, a Presbyterian missionary from the United States, who had arrived in 1918. A feature of Lambie's work was the effective integration of the provision of health, educational, and social services and evangelism. He played a big role in improving medical facilities in the country.[14] From the start the SIM urged its converts to form their own congregations separate from the Orthodox Church, whereas at the time Anglican and Lutheran missionaries tended to encourage converts to join the Orthodox Church. So the SIM converts met in a house, with no tabot and without an ordained priest. This represented a radical departure from Orthodoxy. To an extent, the SIM connected with indigenous developments, such as preaching by local prophets in marketplaces and so on, that preceded its arrival.[15]

The last Protestant group to enter Ethiopia in the period before the Italian occupation was the Bible Churchmen's Missionary

Society, which started at Addis Ababa in 1934. Its aim was help the Ethiopian Orthodox Church return to biblical foundations and spiritual renewal. It produced Christian literature and opened Bible schools.[16] While aiding the missionary endeavors of the Orthodox Church, it generated opposition from within it, and interest in studying at its schools eventually waned.[17]

As noted in chapter 4, the Italian occupation from 1936 to 1941 led to the suppression of Protestant Christianity and the expulsion of foreign missionaries. Yet Italian repression had the opposite effect of the one intended, since the indigenous evangelical communities flourished rather than collapsing. The evangelical Christians felt bound to preserve, indeed, to spread the faith, and their leaders began actively interpreting the Bible to cope with the new exigencies of their situation. They developed an indigenous style of preaching that paid great attention to a traditional concern of Ethiopian people: the need to be freed of evil forces that cause illness and misfortune. New styles of hymnody, including antiphonal singing, were developed. They even began organizing themselves at a national level with a view to an alliance of evangelical Christians. When the SIM missionaries left during the Italian period, they had made about one hundred converts. When they returned in 1941, that number had risen to the tens of thousands![18]

As noted in chapter 4, in 1944 Haile Selassie had divided the country into "closed" and "open" areas as far as missionary activity was concerned, while the capital, Addis Ababa, was declared open to all. The development of an umbrella organization for all evangelical Christians continued after the expulsion of the Italians, and an association of evangelicals was formed. But this intra-Protestant ecumenical movement soon petered out when confronted with two obstacles. The first was a major program of evangelization by the Ethiopian Orthodox Church, and the second was the desire of returning missionaries from the United States and Europe to put the interests of their denominations over the establishment of a united evangelical church in Ethiopia.[19]

During the period 1938–1941, one aspect of Karl Cederqvist's work bore rich fruit. Prior to his death in 1919, he had collaborated with Onesimus Nesib and the priests Gebre Ewostatewos and Gebre Selassie to unite scattered evangelical believers in southern Ethiopia into an embryonic evangelical community from which the first Ethiopian evangelical church would emerge.[20] In 1938 the leaders of evangelical churches of Lutheran background announced their intention to form an independent church under Ethiopian leadership. In 1941 this aim was achieved. In 1959 the church was officially recognized as the Ethiopian Evangelical Church of Mekane Yesus, better known as the Mekane Yesus Church.[21] Mekane Yesus means "place of Jesus." It is now one of the largest parts of the World Lutheran Federation, with several million members. As already noted, SIM arrived in Ethiopia in 1928. In 1963 the SIM churches set up the Yewengel Amagnoch Andenet Hebert (Evangelical Believers' Association). From this emerged the Kale Heywet Church, which eventually developed a Pentecostal emphasis.[22] It now has some seven million members.[23] Kale Heywet means "Word of Life."

One group of missionaries who arrived after World War II and who proved hugely successful were the Mennonites. Arriving in Addis Ababa in 1945 and choosing Nazareth (also called Adama) in central Ethiopia as their primary site, they focused on establishing missions in urban settings and in places with large populations in the rural areas, for example, large cotton plantations. They ran excellent Christian bookstores, established schools (including one for the blind in Addis Ababa), and built a hospital and medical training centers (where the Bible was taught alongside medical courses). Sunday schools that covered other activities like art, crafts, music, and English proved a big attraction to local young people, who thus came under the influence of evangelical faith. Many of these young converts were from Orthodox families. They believed that in their Orthodox context the Bible had not been explained to them adequately, and they were concerned about the behavior and infighting of the priests (and the poverty they experienced) and moral laxity and insufficient fervency of faith among the laity. They were attracted to important features of evangelical Christianity: strict morality; abstaining from alcohol, drugs, and sexual misconduct; and the mutual love and solidarity the evangelical Christians expressed for one another. In Ethiopia, just as elsewhere in the world, the 1950s and 1960s witnessed a surge of modernity and a sense of rebellion by youth against what were seen to be the restraining structures and values of the past. In such a context, it was not difficult for young Ethiopians exposed to modernity (mainly in urban areas) to see Orthodoxy as invested in the past, while evangelical Christianity looked to the future.[24] As the number of converts in the Mennonite areas increased, an impetus began toward the establishment of a national Mennonite Church in Ethiopia. In 1962 the first formal meeting of the Meserete Kristos Church took place, Meserete Kristos meaning "Christ's Foundation." In due course, Milion Belete became chairman of the church and was ordained as its first pastor. Previously, the pastors had been foreign missionaries.[25] It now has about 250,000 baptized members and a worshipping community of some 500,000.

The 1960s witnessed a number of phenomena that greatly aided the expansion of Protestantism in Ethiopia. One was the dramatic increase in the availability of translations of the Bible into Amharic and other Ethiopian languages, with the entire Bible in Amharic (printed in London) becoming available in Addis Ababa in 1962. A second was the explosion in the writing and performance of new hymns that brought biblical text together with lived experience. A third was the establishment of the Radio Voice of the Gospel by the Lutheran World Federation in Addis Ababa in 1963 and its widely influential broadcasting until taken over the by Derg in 1977. A fourth was the arrival of university-oriented missionary activities in Addis Ababa that managed to bring the evangelical message to large numbers of some of the brightest young people in the country. A fifth was Billy Graham's successful crusade in 1960.[26] But the sixth, perhaps the most significant, was the establishment of Pentecostalism in Ethiopian Protestantism.

Pentecostal Christianity

The New Testament Picture: Experience of the Spirit

Pentecostal Christianity means those forms of the faith in which the faithful believe that at worship gatherings the Holy Spirit comes upon the congregation, with the Spirit's presence manifested in exciting spiritual gifts such as glossolalia (Greek for "speaking in tongues," a form of non-articulate utterance), interpretation of glossolalia, prophecy (articulate discourse), kinetic movements of various parts of the body (or, on the contrary, trance-like states), visions, auditions, miraculous cures, and exorcism of evil spirits. These phenomena are usefully referred to as "charismatic," since they are regarded as "charisms" (Greek: *charismata*), or "gifts" of the Holy Spirit. People who experience such phenomena often believe that God has been within them and have a sense of euphoria afterward. The name Pentecostalism derives from the experience of the very early Christ movement on the feast of Pentecost (called Shavuot, "Weeks," in Hebrew), which fell fifty days (*pentecostē* being the Greek word for "fiftieth") after the feast of Passover, which in that year had been the occasion of the death and resurrection of Jesus. The story of Pentecost is told in Acts 2:1-13, in a way that focuses on the phenomenon of speaking in tongues. Here we are told that on the feast of Pentecost, when all the Christ followers were gathered in one place:

> Suddenly a sound came from heaven like the rush of a mighty wind, and it filled all the house where they were sitting. And there appeared to them tongues as of fire, distributed and resting on each one of them. And they were all filled with the Holy Spirit and began to speak in other tongues, as the Spirit gave them utterance. (Acts 2:3-4 RSV).

Other Jews from other places in the Mediterranean world then living in Jerusalem were attracted to the sound, and they were amazed since they heard Galileans speaking to each of them in their own language: Parthians and Medes, Elamites, people from

Mesopotamia and Cappadocia, Pontus and Asia, Egypt, and so on (Acts 2:5-11). It is often said that in Pentecostal congregations today the same phenomenon occurs, that is, people speaking another language they have never learned under the inspiration of the Holy Spirit. The technical term for this is xenoglossy. Close study of contemporary Pentecostal congregations, however, has shown that xenoglossy never occurs. What occurs is glossolalia, an inarticulate but dramatic and often tuneful utterance.[27]

A far better source for charismatic phenomena in the New Testament than Acts 2:1-13 is what Paul tells us about them in 1 Corinthians 12–14. Paul was an actual witness to, indeed exponent of, charismatic phenomena that were occurring in his own congregations, while Luke was writing decades after the Pentecost event, possibly in the 80s or 90s of the first century CE. It is not clear that Luke himself had even witnessed charismatic phenomena, which may explain why he falls into the common mistake of confusing glossolalia for xenoglossy. Paul, however, made no such mistake. Although he gave thanks to God that he spoke in tongues more than anyone (1 Cor 14:18), he fully appreciated that glossolalia was non-articulate discourse (in other words, not a foreign language that the person concerned had never previously acquired). This is why he said it needed interpretation: "So with yourselves; if you utter speech in a tongue that is not intelligible, how will any one know what is said? For you will be speaking into the air" (1 Cor 14:9 RSV) and also that "if I pray in a tongue, my spirit prays but my mind is unfruitful" (1 Cor 14:14 RSV). It seems that another way to describe glossolalia is as "the tongues of angels," since at one point Paul mentions his ability to speak in the tongues of human beings and the tongues of angels in the one statement (1 Cor 13:1).[28]

When Paul mentions the Holy Spirit, he is not thinking just of a theological category or entity but of a powerful force present in creation that can become personally present to those attending a meeting of a Christ-movement group with a dramatic demonstration of charismatic phenomena, signs, and miracles. Thus, he asks his Galatian addressees:

> Let me ask you only this: Did you receive the Spirit by works of the law, or by hearing with faith? Are you so foolish? Having begun with the Spirit, are you now ending with the flesh? Did you experience so many things in vain?—if it really is in vain. Does he who supplies the Spirit to you and works miracles (*dunameis*) among you do so by works of the law, or by hearing with faith? (Gal 3:2-5 RSV).

Similarly, he can remind the Corinthians that "the signs of the true apostle were worked among you in all patience, with signs (*sēmeia*) and wonders (*terata*) and mighty works (*dunameis*)" (2 Cor 12:12 RSV). He also tells the Romans that his work among the Gentiles has proceeded "by the power of signs (*sēmeia*) and wonders (*terata*), by the power of the Holy Spirit" (Rom 15:19 RSV). It is probably the case that biblical scholars, with some notable exceptions,[29] pay too little attention to the charismatic and miraculous nature of Paul's ministry. This almost certainly reflects the long-standing animosity of most mainstream Christian denominations, which have tended to oppose the at times unruly and status-leveling dimension to contemporary manifestations of the Spirit. Ethiopian Pentecostalism represents one particular example of the situation, as James Dunn has accurately described it:

> Against the mechanical sacramentalism of extreme Catholicism and the dead biblicist orthodoxy of extreme Protestantism they [sc. Pentecostals] have shifted the focus of attention to the *experience* of the Spirit. Our examination of the NT evidence has shown that they were wholly justified in this. That the Spirit, and particularly the gift of the Spirit, was a *fact of experience* in the lives of the earliest Christians has been too obvious to require elaboration.[30]

History of Pentecostalism in Ethiopia

The beginnings of Pentecostalism in Ethiopia are explicable on the basis of some external influence coupled with a very powerful indigenous adoption of Pentecostal Christianity. In March 1934 three women from the Elim Bible Institute and the Assembly of

God Church in New York—Bertha Dommermuth, Ruth Shippey, and Ellen French—arrived in Ethiopia. They appear to have been the first Pentecostal missionaries to reach the country. They began to preach on the Holy Spirit and its gifts, while also themselves practicing Pentecostal faith, including by speaking in tongues. By 1937 they were reporting revivals in which some young people were experiencing baptism in the Spirit. One of these was Fikre, the daughter of Qes Bademe Yalew, the famous Orthodox priest who was prominent in the establishment of the Mekane Yesus Church. Then came the Italian occupation (1935–1941), with the Italians as strongly opposed to the Pentecostal missionaries as they were to the other Protestant missionaries in Ethiopia. In 1938 the Assembly of God group was compelled to return to the United States. It seems that most of the Ethiopians who had become Pentecostal under its influence either died during the Italian occupation or lost their zeal for this form of Christianity, so it is hard to connect the activities of the three women with the outbreak of Pentecostalism that was to occur in Ethiopia in the 1960s. More direct external influences can be traced in the early 1950s.[31]

The first Pentecostal missionaries to establish a long-term presence in Ethiopia were the Finnish couple Anna-Lüsa and Sanfrid Mattson, who arrived in Addis Ababa in 1951. They received a permit to establish a vocational school in Wolmera, 35 kilometers west of Addis Ababa. A year later they set up a second station in Mercato, the commercial hub of Addis Ababa. Other Finnish Pentecostal missionaries followed.

In 1959 Swedish Pentecostal missionary activity began. Especially important was the Swedish Philadelphia Church Mission, established in the southern town of Awasa in 1960. At Awasa a vocational school was set up, but the missionaries also conducted annual Bible summer conferences lasting several weeks that were attended by students from all over the country on their summer vacation. A further influence came from the American evangelist Kenneth Oglesby and his family. Oglesby was a long-term friend of Emperor Haile Selassie, and the emperor allowed him to come to

Ethiopia in 1956. By the mid-1960s a number of Ethiopians were receiving baptism in the Holy Spirit and were starting local revival groups. Of particular note was the visit by the Kenyan Pentecostal evangelist Chacha Omahe to both the Awasa Bible Conference and the Finnish mission in Addis Ababa in the summer of 1965. But there were also several other events during the 1960s at which charismatic phenomena occurred, so there is some competition for their claim to have inaugurated Pentecostalism in Ethiopia.[32]

A number of the expanding Pentecostal movements converged around the university student movement in Addis Ababa that had become a major focus of evangelical missionary activities. The Haile Selassie I University in Addis Ababa proved to be particularly significant as a context for the growth of Pentecostalism. The formation by four students of a group devoted to prayer and fellowship in a rented house in Arat Kilo, near Menelik II School, in 1966 proved to be a decisive event. They attracted others and soon had to move to a larger house closer to the Sedest Kilo campus, which was the hub of the university students' activities. The next step came in setting up a chapel, which led to a further increase in numbers.[33] A four-day conference held in Addis Ababa in 1966 attracted Pentecostal students from all over Ethiopia; its theme was "The Gospel for Ethiopia by Ethiopians." The conference at Awasa the previous year formed an important impetus for this conference.[34]

Activities such as these led to the establishment of the first national Pentecostal church in 1967, the Full Gospel Believers' Church, to which I will return further below. The fact that the first seven elders of this church were inducted with the help of Swedish Pentecostal missionaries led to conflict with the Finnish mission in Addis Ababa, which had lost some of its following to the university student movement, including some of those now ordained as elders by the Swedes.[35]

While the birth and development of the Pentecostal movement in Addis Ababa was the direct result of contact with other missionaries, another focus of expansion, in the eastern city of Harar, appears to have been a locally grown phenomenon. The city of Harar hosted a number of national training institutions, and the large number of students there provided fertile soil for the growth of Pentecostalism. Students at the Harar Teacher Training Institute had their first Pentecostal experience, manifested in glossolalia, in 1964. They were mainly Orthodox Christians, although some came from evangelical Protestant backgrounds. The initiating event seems to have been the alleged miraculous cure of two of the students and their subsequent efforts to make sense of this in relation to the activity of the Holy Spirit. The Harar movement was indigenous, with no direct external influence or foreign missionary being involved.[36]

There was also a flowering of Pentecostalism in the city of Nazareth, where the Mennonites had established their center of operations. It began among high school students in the Atse Gelawedros High School. But the extent to which it was or not influenced by foreign missionaries is contested. The students, most of whom were Orthodox Christians, founded a group called Semay Berhan (Heavenly Light). They devoted themselves to Bible study and to intense readings and discussions. They were particularly interested in scriptural texts concerning the power of the Spirit. Some even practiced fasting for days on end. At some point they began to receive the Holy Spirit, and among them this was manifested partly in screaming that they believed indicated the exorcism of evil spirits. They began to attract opposition from mainstream Orthodox quarters, and the numbers joining the group also led to concerns among their fellow students, teachers, and people in the community. In 1964 these tensions culminated in a riot that led to the temporary suspension of some of the leaders. But in due course they were readmitted, and many of them went on to Haile Selassie I University in Addis Ababa. At some point they made contact with local Mennonite missionaries. The debate as to how indigenous this movement was turns on how influential the Mennonites were during the early stages.[37] It does appear, however, that the students encountered baptism in the Spirit in their own meetings and did not receive it from the Mennonites.[38]

The arrival of Pentecostalism as a major force in Ethiopian Protestantism can be dated roughly to the creation of the Mulu Wengel [Full Gospel] Church in 1966/1967. Ethiopian Pentecostals, most of them young and many university students, held meetings in Awasa in 1965 and Addis Ababa in 1966. Although some favored continuing with Pentecostalism as a renewal movement, another group wanted to found a new and separate Pentecostal church and forged on with that project. It was decided to ask Swedish ministers to ordain ministers in the new church, in spite of a concern in some quarters that this would tar the new church and Pentecostalism generally with association with foreign influences. The issue of a name also caused some controversy, but eventually the group settled on Ye Mulu Wengel Amagnoch Andenet Mahaber (The Full Gospel Believers' Association), or Mulu Wengel Church for short. This was the name submitted to the government for official registration of the church, but the application was refused. This, in effect, pushed the new church into operating illegally. In spite of this, it was very active. It attracted members of the emerging elite but also developed a strong musical tradition that attracted well-known Ethiopian musicians to its ranks. Pentecostal singing eschewed the antiphon chanting of Orthodoxy and moved into solo and choir forms of gospel songs that proved extremely popular, even beyond the Pentecostal networks. They were even given a regular slot on the Radio Voice of the Gospel.[39]

As early as 1967 the new church began to experience serious persecution. There was a particularly serious incident in Dabra Zeit in 1967, when a large crowd of local people attacked a gathering of hundreds of youths belonging to the Pentecostal movement. It is likely that the name Pente, employed as a term of abuse by outsiders, was first directed to Pentecostal Christians in the aftermath of the Dabra Zeit incident.[40] Tibebe Meshete has suggested that many other Ethiopians, especially Orthodox Christians, believed that the new church with its screaming and shouting during prayer times and its healing services offended against the value of *chewanet*, "the reserve and gentility supposed to reside at the root of the Ethiopian persona, and were thus viewed as countercultural and antisocial."[41] The Ethiopian Orthodox Church also regarded Pentecostalism as deeply opposed to its values and position in the national life and identity, and when Abuna Theophilos was invested into his position in 1972 he delivered an address in which he undertook "to oppose and endeavour to eradicate any movement or teaching that is contrary or against the Orthodox Church."[42] Protestants, Pentecostals especially, reasonably took this as a threat. By 1972 the Pentecostals had, moreover, already suffered considerably, with their meetings attacked and broken up by armed mobs, while members were arrested and imprisoned.[43] It was in the context of these attacks that the name Pente, initially used as a term of derogation by outsiders, became a term of self-designation by Pentecostals. Similarly, in the late first or early second century CE, the word Christianos, originally a derogatory, outsider term meaning something like "Christ-lackey," was taken up by Christ followers as a convenient way to refer to themselves.[44] Ironically, not only was the persecution not successful in extinguishing the Mulu Wengel Church (which exists to this day in great numbers),[45] but it actually spread the teaching of Pentecostalism throughout other Protestant churches in Ethiopia. Many of the Pentecostals were given refuge during this time in the other churches and brought their charismatic preaching and activities with them. The Meserete Kristos Church, for example, took in the Pentecostal choir called Zion and was deeply influenced by it. In due course the church itself became charismatic.[46]

Pentecostalism seems to be particularly effective in elaborating religious and cultural responses to transformations generated in society by modernity and globalization. It certainly seems to be the case that the forces of modernization experienced by students at the university in Addis Ababa during Haile Selassie's reign were a causal factor in their moving toward Pentecostal forms of Christianity. For Ethiopians in the cities, this was a faith that seemed to provide answers to the material, political, ideological, and ontological insecurity produced by Ethiopia's insertion into the processes of neoliberal globalization.[47]

Yet Pentecostalism also spread to the rural regions and became very popular there, and for somewhat different reasons. During the

1970s, to cite one example, weavers from the highlands of Gamo, who were already Protestant, traveled to cities such as Goba Town in Bale and there encountered Pentecostalism in the Mulu Wengel Church. They were attracted by the vibrant singing and energy but were most impressed by the exorcisms and healings they witnessed. When they returned to their homes in the Gamo mountains, they took these practices back with them, especially the practice of sending away spirits that were causing illness "in the name of Jesus" (*be Yesus sim*). Exorcisms became so important to them that they eventually broke from the Kale Heywet Church and got help to join the Mulu Wengel Church. So although they encountered the Pentecostal faith in the city, they put it into practice in the countryside.[48] In due course (after the revolution of 1974 described below), the church pressured its members to dissociate themselves from all the traditional ways of dealing with spirits (see the discussion of prayer scrolls in chapter 6) and only rely upon the use of Jesus' name. They also broke away from other traditional forms of behavior (including the distribution of food in feasts provided by wealthier members of the community) and began to stress the role of activities by individuals before God, such as becoming independent of others by trading. Thus spiritual transformation through the direct experience of the Spirit became the pathway to other forms of transformation where those involved built new relations, new economies, and new communities. Membership in the Pentecostal Church, which entailed gaining power over traditional spirits, helped people escape from traditional redistributive practices and also legitimized the accumulation of wealth. With this came a major transformation of lifestyle and behavior.[49]

Protestant Christianity and the Revolution of 1974

The revolution of 1974 began with an uprising in February 1974, and the military, who stepped in to take charge, proceeded fairly cautiously in the next few months. The draft constitution of August 1974 announced the separation of church and state, a measure deplored by the Orthodox Church. On September 11, 1974, however, Abuna Theophilos used his traditional (Ethiopian) New Year's Day broadcast to bless the revolutionaries and to define the emerging political forces as a "holy movement," while eschewing the usual and constitutionally demanded eulogy for the emperor and his family, presumably sealing the emperor's fate. Haile Selassie was deposed the next day.[50] But such cooperation from the abuna did little to help his church. The separation of church and state was duly implemented, ending a unity that had lasted more than sixteen centuries from the time of the Christian kingdom of Aksum. By November 1974 the Derg was fully in operation. In 1975 the land holdings of the Orthodox Church were nationalized.

In the early days of the revolution, the disestablishment of the Orthodox Church and statements made by the revolutionary leaders concerning religious freedom gave hope to the evangelical churches, especially the seriously oppressed Mulu Wengel Church, that their situation was about to improve. Some streams of Christian thought were open to the idea that socialism might be beneficial for Ethiopia, especially as a way of alleviating the extreme poverty suffered by so many, and that perhaps it was also capable of reconciliation with Christianity. But this was not something that was easy to achieve. The focus on personal conversion and piety among the Protestant churches and the lack of deep theological training for many of its leaders meant that there had been little focus on bringing the Gospel to bear on social and economic issues.[51] Nevertheless, interesting initiatives emerged, such as the Council for the Cooperation of Churches in Ethiopia that was formed in October 1976. It was conceived as a forum for bringing together (for the first time ever) the three main Christian groups in Ethiopia (Orthodox, Protestant, Catholic) to create a corporate voice for faith groups to address the new political, social, and economic realities of Ethiopia. The council came out of an earlier initiative of Qes Gudina Tumsa, a US-trained theologian and a leader of the Evangelical Church of Mekane Yesus, and the World Lutheran Federation in organizing an ecumenical colloquium at the Mekane Yesus Seminary the previous year on the theme of Christianity and socialism. As things turned out, however, the council did not survive long, with both the Orthodox and Catholic Churches pulling out. While Gudina Tumsa had a sense of heightened social concern, he did not himself consider Christianity and socialism compatible. He paid the ultimate price for his faith, for on July 28, 1979, he was abducted by the secret police and murdered the same night.[52]

With the passage of time, however, the attitude of the Derg hardened toward the Protestant churches. Church leaders were imprisoned and, at times, executed or, indeed, murdered without any legal process. The Derg even went after Pentecostal musicians, with the well-known singer and evangelist Tesfaye Gabiso spending seven years in prison without trial, where he was subject to mistreatment and torture.[53] Property of all sorts—churches, schools, and administrative buildings—was confiscated, congregations were harassed, and meetings in private homes forbidden. Mass propaganda that attacked Christianity but sang the praises of Marxism was widely used, and organizations were set up for certain groups, such as youth and women, as an alternative to Christian organizations, to indoctrinate them in the ideology of the regime.[54] Two Pentecostal churches, the Meserete Kristos Church and the Mulu Wengel Church, were subject to particularly savage persecution. They were both led by educated members of the rising urban elite, who were passionate in their convictions and represented a particular challenge to the regime. When the true nature of the Derg revealed itself, both churches went underground, employing a home-based mode of organization. In these clandestine cells they provided extensive programs of teaching and created songs to express their faith and their experience.[55]

As we saw in chapter 4, the Derg collapsed in 1991. Its efforts to suppress or extinguish evangelical, including Pentecostal, Christianity had precisely the opposite effect. What appears to have happened is that the increasing severity of the Derg's policies led to growing disillusionment among large numbers of the population, some of whom joined the Protestant denominations for spiritual nourishment at this time. It is possible that the very traditional nature of Orthodoxy and the more personal nature of Protestantism made the latter a more attractive option.[56] The number of evangelical Christians grew significantly in the seventeen years of the regime. In the early 1960s Protestants accounted for less than 1 percent of the population. By 1984 this figure had risen to 5.4 percent and in 1994 to 10.2 percent.[57] During the period of the Derg, Protestantism went from being mainly rural to a largely urban phenomenon, and it moved out of its traditional southern bases to spread across all of Ethiopia. Its leadership went through a process of indigenization as the missionary leaders of the past were replaced by Ethiopians.[58] Additionally, the Derg period witnessed the proliferation of Pentecostalism into the mainstream Protestant churches.[59] One visible sign of this was that the word Pente, which had previously referred only to Pentecostals, was now applied to all Protestants and became a term of self-designation.[60]

The coming to power of the Ethiopian People's Revolutionary Democratic Front in 1991 was discussed in chapter 4. Many of the church buildings that had been confiscated under the Derg were returned to their original owners.[61] As a result of the EPRDF's policy of religious freedom, Pentecostal churches have emerged as a highly visible element in Ethiopian Protestantism, not least of all because their theology and practices have permeated mainstream Protestantism. Across the Protestant churches, speaking in tongues (glossolalia), ecstatic praise, prophesy, exorcisms, and healing prayers are now commonplace. In addition, the mainstream Protestant churches have included references to Pentecostal beliefs and practices in their official documents, while this process has found an institutional reflection in the establishment of the Evangelical Churches Fellowship of Ethiopia, which embraces Pentecostals and mainline Protestants.

Other developments since 1991 are worth noting here. Perhaps most prominent among them is that in the climate of freedom created by the 1995 Federal Constitution there has been a new wave of Pentecostal Christianity leading to the establishment of several neo-Pentecostal or neo-charismatic churches. These churches have been associated with the broad phenomenon of African "spirit" movements, emphasizing the working of the Spirit in their midst. Examples include the Beza International Church, the You-Go City Church, the Exodus Apostolic Reformation Church, and the Unic 7000 Church. They tend to keep themselves separate from the main network representing evangelical and Pentecostal churches, the Evangelical Churches Fellowship of Ethiopia.[62] Many of these independent Pentecostal churches have been founded and continue to be led by individual "prophets," "apostles," or television evangelists.

The Current Situation

One writer on Ethiopian Christianity has made the following observation about the presence of Protestantism in the country:

> The result of Evangelical evangelism is a second style of Christianity in Ethiopia. Alongside the Orthodox Church which has been identified with Ethiopia throughout its history as a state, is now a growing number of independent Evangelical churches.[63]

Protestant denominations vary greatly, from very small to very large, and from those that are independent to those that have links to worldwide Christian churches. The Protestant landscape can, however, be divided conveniently into three main parts. First, there are the traditional Evangelical denominations, like the Lutheran Mekane Yesus Church and the Baptist-aligned Kale Heywet Church (both with more than four million members) and the smaller Mennonite Meserete Kristos (with around 250,000 members). Second, there are the well-established Pentecostal churches, such as the Mulu Wengel Church. Third come the new independent churches and ministries that have sprung into existence since religious freedom was enunciated in the 1995 Federal Constitution.[64]

As noted at the start of this chapter, the Protestant churches offer a very different way of being a Christian to Orthodoxy, a critical issue being the mode of recruitment to the church, by birth in Orthodoxy but often by conscious choice and "conversion" as an adult for Protestantism. Whereas Orthodoxy holds its adherents in strong ritual and cultural patterns, such as fasts, festivals, funeral practices, and the maintenance of an ancient language for the liturgy (Ge'ez), Protestantism uses local languages and forms of worship and prayer that fit into, and vary with, the local setting. The Orthodox Church offers a communal solidarity based on ancient tradition, whereas the Protestant churches tend to exhibit a more individualistic type of faith.[65]

Two other significant issues emerge when we dig beneath the surface of Protestantism in Ethiopia. In the first place, Protestantism has a different understanding of the human person in society than does Orthodoxy. Whereas the latter expects its adherents to remain in the faith from birth to death, Protestantism, by its very nature, valorizes the notion that persons are unique individuals and should be able to change their religious outlook and worldview without the risk of repercussions. A person is accountable only to him- or herself and God for a decision on religious affiliation. This also means that people are to be judged more by their character than by their ethnic background or political affiliation. This creates a clear line of demarcation from the central instincts of Ethiopian Orthodoxy. It also means that marginalized people may find a home in Protestantism that is not readily available elsewhere. In the development of Protestantism in the country, this also has meant that traditional patterns of leadership have been opened up to progressive young people, men and women.

Second, the sundering of church and state by the Derg after their sixteen centuries' union, which has been maintained by the EPRDF, has created a space for Protestantism, expressed especially in the language of freedom. Whereas some Protestant leaders, for example, Gudina Tumsa, argued that such freedom went beyond being free to worship as one liked and to avoid eternal damnation to include liberation from economic and political oppression, that has hardly become a majority view. More typical has been the development of *semayawi zeginet* (heavenly citizenship) as a response to the scientific materialism and oppression of the Derg period. This is based on what Paul says in Philippians 3:20: "But our citizenship is in heaven and from it we await a Savior, the Lord Jesus Christ" (ESV). This idea originated in the idea of Protestants as an oppressed minority, even stigmatized as *mette* (foreigners), so they replied by viewing themselves as homegrown aliens in line with Pauline thought. The notion of a heavenly citizenship provides them with an alternative and compensating social structure, one that focuses solely on faith and disregards ethnicity, social class, gender, or economic status. Thus, on the one hand, *semayawi zeginet* has provided Protestants with a sense of community and room to maneuver vis-à-vis the state. On the other hand, their situation under the Derg and this emerging notion of *semayawi zeginet* meant many Protestant churches insulated themselves from engaging in public issues. They had created a comfort zone that was largely interested in spiritual salvation.[66] Some Protestants were even critical of the traditional work of the Lutheran Mekane Yesus and the Kale Heywet Churches in areas of health and education as being too focused on material aspects of the human condition.[67] So pronounced has been the Protestant disinterest in the public sphere that, when the Parliament recently discussed liberalizing the law on abortion, there was not a single Protestant MP who opposed it, whereas strong opposition came from Muslims.[68] The emphasis on spiritual salvation has not only been evident in a lack of concern with social and political issues but also in the very limited development of a theology focused on such issues, which is "a handicap that continues to hamper the church's contribution to Ethiopian society at large."[69]

The appointment in April 2018 of the new prime minister, Abiy Ahmed, a former Muslim who turned to Pentecostal Protestantism, brings a new dynamic to this picture. For he provides an example to the Protestant churches of the need to seriously engage with political, social, and economic issues and of the potential benefits of such engagement. There is reason to believe that he has begun to have this effect, since Protestant pastors have taken to the media to discuss this question, and young Ethiopians have also begun to grapple with it. Rather than persisting with their previous insulation from politics,[70] there is now a possibility that the Protestant churches will move in the direction pioneered by the new prime minister. Engagement of this kind will consist both of Protestantism's active involvement ("praxis," in the language of liberation theology) and also the project of "making deep theological reflections of itself and its wider role in the socioeconomic and political environment of Ethiopian society."[71]

Pentecostal Protestants are located in two main areas of Ethiopia. One concentration, with some 1.5 percent of the total, is found in the two cities of Addis Ababa and Bahir Dar, often taking the form of the new churches and having connections with global Pentecostalism.[72] This concentration may reflect the attractions of a more modern form of religion and the community reconfiguration in urban space that is conducive to a break with the tradition represented in Orthodoxy. The other, and main, concentration is in rural areas in the Southwest. This is the mainly Muslim area that was conquered by the Ethiopian emperors Yohannes IV and Menelik II in the late nineteenth century, with a feudal style of landholding imposed on the people by the state, and with Orthodox churches, seen by the locals as representing the religion of the conqueror, established. In these areas evangelical Christianity, inaugurated by missionaries speaking, conducting services, and distributing Bibles in local languages (as opposed to the Ge'ez of Orthodox services), represented one way in which the conquered could assert their identity. Some 96 percent of Pentecostals now live in this area.[73] Some of the reasons for the appeal of Pentecostalism in the countryside were considered above. The largest Pentecostal churches with a Trinitarian theology are the Full Gospel [Mulu Wengel] Believers Church and the Hiwot Berhan Church of Ethiopia, with about 500,000 members each.[74]

In the past two decades Pentecostal theology and practices have penetrated deeply into mainstream Protestantism, so that most Protestant churches have adopted central Pentecostal ideas in their theologies and regulations. They now employ concepts such as the "the baptism in the Holy Spirit" and often provide detailed regulations for charismatic practices, such as speaking in tongues, prophecy, and the laying on of hands.[75] Music is one area where the influence of Pentecostalism has been particularly noticeable. Pentecostal music was an indigenous phenomenon from the start, not relying on translations of foreign works but using popular music of contemporary Ethiopia, complemented by original lyrics. This approach has transformed the music of the mainline Protestant churches and has become a part of the wider Ethiopian culture. Finally, Pentecostal exorcisms connect with Ethiopian cosmology, by acknowledging the traditional link between evil spirits and illness and misfortune and by providing a new way of dealing with them in Jesus' name that seems more powerful than the holy water of the Orthodox priest or the prayer scroll of the Orthodox dabtara in contexts where Western medicine is all too often unobtainable.[76]

The theological alliance between the mainstream Protestants and the Pentecostals now has an organizational correlate in the form of the Evangelical Churches Fellowship of Ethiopia, originally founded in 1976,[77] during the dangerous communist regime. This is the only significant ecumenical body among Protestants, and almost all of the major (that is, Trinitarian) churches participate in it. The fellowship is an umbrella organization that facilitates theological discussion and also fosters cooperation in areas, such as evangelism and development projects, and on very practical matters, such as burial grounds. To some extent it seeks a common representation of Protestants in the political arena.[78]

Finally, earlier issues with a lack of theological training for the members of the Protestant churches, even for ministerial staff, have been squarely addressed. One major step was the foundation of institutions such as the Evangelical Training College, which was set up (under another guise) in 1983 at the instigation of the

Kale Heywet Church. In 1991 this college obtained its current name and began a bachelor's degree in theology aimed at training servant leaders for the Protestant churches. It also provides other types of theological programs and is now educating three hundred students per semester.[79] There are also a number of other, smaller Bible colleges. At the postgraduate level is the Ethiopian Graduate School of Theology, located in a large, new, seven-story building in Addis Ababa that opened in 2014. It was founded in 1997 as a joint venture between the Kale Heywet Church, the Evangelical Mekane Yesus Church, and the Evangelical Churches Fellowship of Ethiopia.[80] The first class graduated in 2001, and its annual enrollment now exceeds two hundred students. Many of its graduates go on to theological and biblical doctorates at leading universities abroad. Last, the recognition by the Ethiopian Graduate School of Theology of its place in the long history of Christianity in Ethiopia includes hosting an annual series of public lectures, called the St. Frumentius Lectures, which are delivered by eminent Ethiopian and international church leaders and scholars.

9

Catholicism

The Number of Catholics in Ethiopia

In 2014 there were, according to the Catholic Church itself, some 764,000 Catholics in Ethiopia, representing 0.8 percent of a population of 96,506,000.[1] According to another source (which has a slightly lower number of Catholics but the same total for the whole population), at 0.7 percent of the population, they represented the smallest category by number of the main religions in Ethiopia, with the largest group being the Orthodox at 43.2 percent (41,691,000), then Muslims at 34.4 percent (33,198,000), then Protestants at 19.1 percent (18,433,000), and then folk religions at 2.6 percent (2,509,000).[2] On this latter view, Catholics accounted for 1.25 percent of the Christian population of the country, making this too small a religion, apparently, for two academic authors to even mention in their discussion of post-Derg Christianity in Ethiopia; indeed, at one point, they refer to "the two Christian blocks," when really there are three.[3] The Catholic population was spread out among the various regions in the country as follows:

Ecclesiastical Jurisdiction	Number of Catholic Faithful
1. Addis Ababa (Archdiocese)	27,713
2. Adrigat (Eparchy)	22,172
3. Harar (Apostolic Vicariate)	21,855
4. Emdeber (Eparchy)	17,196
5. Hosanna (Apostolic Vicariate)	141,699
6. Soddo (Apostolic Vicariate)	187,662
7. Meki (Apostolic Vicariate)	27,570
8. Gambella (Apostolic Vicariate)	12,000
9. Hawassa (Apostolic Vicariate)	218,119
10. Jimma–Bonga (Apostolic Vicariate)	42,268
11. Nekemte (Apostolic Vicariate)	45,000
12. Robe (Apostolic Prefecture)	890
Total	764,144

Another eparchate was established at Bahir-Dessie in 2015.[4] In relation to these figures and the historical information to follow, a brief explanation of the Catholic Church's system of territorial jurisdiction is needed. A diocese is an established, administrative area presided over by a bishop and divided into parishes. An archdiocese is a diocese with greater size or historical significance that is presided over by an archbishop. In Catholic churches that employ an Eastern rite, an eparchy is a territorial diocese presided over by a bishop called an eparch. An apostolic vicariate is an area in a missionary region where a diocese has not yet been established but where it is hoped that there will in due course be enough Catholics to do so. An apostolic vicariate is normally led by a vicar apostolic, who is usually a bishop. An apostolic prefecture, lastly, is a missionary area at a pre-diocesan stage that is led by a prefect apostolic, who does not usually have episcopal status. In Ethiopia an ecclesiastic who is head of a diocese/archdiocese, eparchy, or apostolic vicariate and has episcopal status is (roughly in line with Ethiopian Orthodox practice) addressed as *abuna* (Ge'ez for "our father").

At the same time, there was a rather different distribution among Eritrea's 6,536,000 inhabitants, with a larger proportion, 4.6 percent (301,000) being Catholic, 57.6 percent (3,765,000) Orthodox, 36.6 percent (2,392,000) Muslim, and only 0.7 percent (45,750) Protestant.[5] The Catholic population in Ethiopia is both miniscule as a fraction of the total population and is regarded by many as a very recent arrival in Ethiopia. This situation recently prompted one Catholic leader to make the wry observation that many people in Ethiopia view it more as an NGO than as a church.[6] The prevalence of this perception depends both on the recent history of Catholicism in Ethiopia and the way it operates there, both of which features now require some explanation.

The head of the Catholic Church in Ethiopia is Cardinal Archbishop Berhaneyesus Demerew Souraphiel (1948–). Born in Harar, he became a member of the Vincentian Order, and, after completing a bachelor of theology at Kings College London, he was ordained a priest in 1976 in Ethiopia. He suffered imprisonment under the Derg from 1979 to 1980. He was consecrated a bishop in 1998, appointed an archbishop in 1999, and created a cardinal by Pope Francis in 2015.[7]

History of the Catholic Church in Ethiopia since 1837

The expulsion of the Jesuits from Ethiopia in the 1630s was discussed in chapter 3. Desultory efforts by Rome to win Ethiopian converts continued thereafter.[8] Two Capuchins who arrived in 1638 were immediately exposed and publicly executed in Gondar. Two French Franciscans who entered the country during the reign of Emperor Yostos (1711–1716) were discovered and executed in Gondar. In 1752 three other Catholic missionaries were imprisoned for nine months. In 1787 another abortive attempt, this time to found a mission in northern Ethiopia, was unsuccessful. It was not until around the 1840s that a permanent Catholic presence in Ethiopia was established.

In 1839 Pope Gregory XVI appointed Giustino de Jacobis (1800–1860), a priest of the (Vincentian) Order of the Mission, as prefect apostolic of Abyssinia with the responsibility of founding missions in the country. He worked mainly in the central and northern highlands and had considerable success, in recognition of which he was appointed titular bishop of Nilopilis in 1847 and vicar apostolic shortly afterward. He aroused considerable antipathy among the Orthodox clergy, not surprisingly nursing bitter memories of the periods of Jesuit proselytization, and was subject to persecution and imprisonment. Nevertheless, in addition to founding his missions, he made many converts to Catholicism, built schools for training Ethiopian clergy, and ordained many of them priests.[9]

Perhaps the most notable feature of de Jacobis' approach was his belief in the need to adapt closely to the prevailing practices and culture of Ethiopia and Ethiopian Orthodoxy. In this he acted in the manner that St. Ignatius Loyola had originally and prophetically advised for the Jesuits who went to Ethiopia, advice that had been taken seriously and successfully by Pedro Páez but utterly disregarded, with catastrophic consequences, by Alfonso Mendes. It appears that Rome itself fully appreciated the lesson to be learned from Mendes' disastrous approach, since the decree of June 1847 appointing de Jacobis as vicar apostolic of Abyssinia explicitly mentioned that he would carry out "all the sacred functions according to the Abyssinian rite."[10] Not surprisingly, then, de Jacobis took the task of inculturation seriously, especially by establishing a Catholic rite of Mass closely based on the Orthodox form, even to the extent of most of it being said in Ge'ez.[11] He "lived with the Ethiopians as a brother among brothers, even adopting the external lifestyle of an Ethiopian monk."[12]

Guglielmo Massaia (1809–1889) was a Capuchin Franciscan who was appointed the vicar apostolic of the Apostolic Vicariate of Galla for the Oromo, meaning that he would work mainly in the interior of the country. He was raised to episcopal status in 1846 and reached the country in that year. He was immensely active in that role, was frequently banished from the country, and frequently returned. He left behind a long and detailed account of his missionary work in Ethiopia.[13]

Massaia adopted a radically different approach to enculturation than did de Jacobis. He worked in the Oromo regions (which were less subject to the influence of Ethiopian Orthodoxy) and was somewhat paternalist in comparison with de Jacobis.[14] He developed a Western, Latin rite for his converts.[15] It has been suggested that he estimated Oromo culture and religion to be sufficiently different from the classical Christian culture of Ethiopian Orthodoxy to justify this step. He regarded his vicariate as being conducted *in partibus infidelium* (in the regions of unbelievers), in an area of traditional African religions, rather than in an Orthodox region. But added to this was the factor that Massaia was rather lacking in sympathy for the Ethiopian rite in particular and the Oriental rites in general. Unlike the "brotherly" approach of de Jacobis, his was "fatherly," or even paternalistic. Indeed, he spent the second decade of his time in Ethiopia in the court of Menelik II, functioning almost as his political advisor. However, he always opposed intervention in Ethiopia by European powers that might curb or curtail Ethiopian independence, and he had learned to appreciate and respect Ethiopian identity.[16]

As a result, both the Eastern rite and the Roman rite were adopted by the original leaders of the one Roman Catholic Church in

Ethiopia. The existence of both an Eastern and a Western liturgy in Ethiopian Catholicism, remarkably within the one ecclesiastical structure, remains a distinctive aspect and, as we will see below, challenge to the church in the country to this day. The merits of these two founders of Ethiopian Catholicism have not passed unnoticed by the Catholic Church. Pope Paul VI canonized de Jacobis in 1975, while Pope Francis conferred the title venerable on Massaia in 2016.

One surprising feature of the ministries of both de Jacobis and Massaia and their immediate successors was their failure to appreciate the apostolate for women in the Ethiopian mission. It is somewhat ironic, therefore, that the first female congregation to come to Ethiopian was the female arm of de Jacobis' own Vincentian Order, the Daughters of Charity, who arrived in Keren in 1878.[17] During the late nineteenth and early twentieth centuries, many other European Catholic religious orders were established in Ethiopia. In the 1920s there was considerable discussion about establishing a Catholic monastery in the country modeled on those of Ethiopian Orthodoxy, but the result was a rather disappointing establishment of a "Catholic monastery in Ethiopia" rather than a "Catholic Abyssinian monastery."[18] By 2004 there would be fifty-three Catholic religious orders present in Ethiopia, and all of them were Western in origin.[19]

During the period of the Italian occupation (1936–1941), the number of churches using the Latin rite increased. After the Second World War, however, the Ethiopian government divided the country into areas that were "closed" or "open" in relation to religious activities. The Catholic Church was not allowed to conduct pastoral activity in the closed regions, which included the area of the Vicariate of Abyssinia, covering much of the old Orthodox heartland in the North. Pending stabilization of the situation, the priests were moved from Adrigat to Addis Ababa. One of them was Abba Hailemariam Kahsay. When the vicariate was replaced by the Apostolic Exarchate of Adrigat in 1951, he was made the first eparch, which meant he had episcopal status; indeed, he was the only bishop in the whole country. He invited many religious congregations to Ethiopia, and this gave new life to Catholicism in the South. He later returned to Adrigat and died there in 1970.[20] This should be seen in the context of the large increase in the number of Catholic orders and religious congregations becoming active in Ethiopia in the second half of the nineteenth century.[21] This appears to have led to some conversions to Catholicism. In 1942, when the population of Ethiopia was some 18,000,000, there were 44,816 Catholics, or 0.2 percent of the total. Twenty-two years later, in 1964, there were 128,105 Catholics in a population of 20,000,000, meaning the Catholic proportion had grown to 0.6 percent.

During the Derg regime (1974–1987), an effort was made to get the Catholic Church banned from Ethiopia on the grounds of its being an imported religion. Although the case was dropped, its very existence revealed a concern with Catholicism as a foreign importation in style, culture, tradition, and overall operation.[22]

As noted previously, Eritrea achieved independence in 1993. At that time about half the Catholics in Ethiopia and Eritrea found themselves in that new country. In 1995 Pope John Paul II created two new eparchies in Eritrea at Keren and Barentu, in addition to the preexisting Metropolitan Eparchy of Asmara, and in January 2015 Pope Francis created a separate metropolitan church for Eritrea.[23]

The Current Position of the Catholic Church in Ethiopia: Challenges

As noted above, the Roman Catholic Church in Ethiopia maintains both an Eastern and a Western rite. As far as the Eastern rite is concerned, most worshippers do not understand Ge'ez, which means its status is like that of Latin in the Western rite of Roman Catholicism before the Second Vatican Council. This position is ameliorated somewhat by conducting part of the services, the scriptural readings, for example, in the local language. The Eastern rite lasts for two to three hours, while the Western rite can be concluded in forty-five minutes. The action of the Eastern rite focuses in particular on the clergy, deacons, and assistants on the altar. As in Ethiopian Orthodox services, the primary attitude is reverence and worship, not community building, as in the post–Vatican II Western rite. Although Ethiopian culture tends to frown upon ostentation, the clergy are dressed splendidly during the liturgy, and vestments are more Orthodox in style than Roman. The Catholic liturgical year, like that of the Orthodox Church, is structured around the traditional Ethiopian church calendar that derives from the ancient Coptic calendar and the Julian (pre-Gregorian) Roman calendar.[24]

But there are differences between the Catholic Eastern rite in the country and Ethiopian Orthodoxy. Whereas Orthodox Mass-goers tend to receive communion primarily as children or in old age (while generally refraining during years of sexual activity, including for married people), Ethiopian Catholics are not so restrained and are happy that the Eucharist is more accessible to them. At Catholic liturgies the women usually sit separately from men, although this is a pattern is more strictly observed in Orthodox churches, which have different entrances for men and women.[25]

Catholics in Ethiopia describe their church as less restrictive and more "modern" and see it as bridging the modern and the traditional. They tend to describe their faith in relation to Orthodoxy rather than in contrast with it; sometimes they agree with it, while at other times they diverge. They often describe themselves as more "liberal" in terms of fasting or the fact that they do not remove their shoes when going into church. They speak of their faith as one that utilizes catechesis to inculcate the meaning of beliefs, in contrast with Orthodoxy. They often suggest that the primary difference is theological, in that they accept God as fully human and fully divine, unlike their understanding of Ethiopian Orthodox miaphysite theology. However, they distinguish themselves from Protestants, especially Pentecostals or Jehovah's

Witnesses, whose faith is seen as too foreign, with such groups having become very prominent in Ethiopia in recent decades.[26]

Nevertheless, the coexistence of the Eastern and Roman rites in the Catholic Church in Ethiopia, which might represent a richness of the system, continues to be a source of tension and ambiguity. In the late twentieth century, there was an aspiration that the Ethiopian Catholic Church would eventually follow one rite, the Ethiopian. Indeed, when in September 1997 the bishops of Ethiopia and Eritrea made their regular, *ad limina* visit to Rome, Pope John Paul II in his address to them observed, "Efforts to gain a deeper understanding of the history and development of the Alexandrian rite should continue, so that the common Christian tradition of the region can contribute to the journey to unity, both within the Catholic community and with the other Churches."[27] Yet, during the development of the Catholic Church in Ethiopia, there had been a tendency for the missionaries from abroad to implant their own culture rather than respecting the centuries-old Ethiopian Christian cultural heritage and tradition. Sometimes Ethiopians were actually required to adopt European names if they became Catholics, even though this led to ridicule among and alienation from their family and friends. These problems were inevitably more acute in areas where the Roman rite was practiced. In some places this type of evangelization led to the creation of Catholic communities that were living largely outside the Ethiopian context. One legacy of this tendency is that, whereas Orthodox Christians support their church financially, Catholics often expect support from their church.[28] A more serious example of the separation of Catholicism from Ethiopian Orthodoxy lies in the area of monasticism. Today there are more than eight hundred monasteries and thousands of monks in Ethiopia.[29] They live lives of remarkable asceticism, dwelling in simple huts and eating very simple food in small amounts. The modes of religious life in the Catholic Church that were introduced in the mid-nineteenth century and thereafter and persist today are very different and, moreover, not easily identified as Ethiopian.

Abuna Mussie, the Franciscan Capuchin eparch of Emdebir, put the matter like this in 2007:

> Catholic religious communities are recognized as foreigners on sight. Their standard of education is higher; their knowledge of the Ethiopian culture and tradition rather limited; their religious garments different; their spirituality less demanding; their lifestyle on a par with the middle class to the point that some young people may perceive it as a human promotion and opt for it on this understanding. In many instances Catholic religious are seen more as social workers than as religious in the monastic sense of the word. Thus there is the challenge to find their identity within the context of the centuries-old monastic tradition of Ethiopia.[30]

Even more problematic are members of religious orders who have abandoned their habit and taken to wearing civilian clothing since, in a country that still appreciates the value of symbols, this step appears to involve belittling the value of their religious vocation.[31] A further dimension of the bi-ritual nature of Ethiopian Catholicism is that there are very few communities practicing the Eastern rite in areas such as Soddo-Hosanna, Hawassa, Meki, Nekemt, Jimma-Bonga, and Gambela. Most of the Catholics here came from the Orthodox Church yet are unable to maintain their rite, Christian culture, and tradition.[32]

Not only has this tension in Catholicism continued, but it has, if anything, become more evident. At the political level the federalist position of the EPRDF, with its negativity to the notion of a dominant Amhara and Orthodox culture, has given new life to old ethnic and historical divisions.[33] Since the cultural unity of Ethiopia is no longer seen as a goal, it is difficult to press the case for the unification of the two rites under the Eastern banner. In addition, unification has been further hampered by the agitation of certain elements in the Eastern rite to "purge" it of Roman features.[34]

In principal, the existence of two rites should be an advantage to the Catholic Church. In the context of a pluralistic society, where people explore different modes of faith, having two such imposing liturgical rites available seems valuable, since this facilitates options in line with the advice of the late Pope John Paul II that the church should breathe from "the two lungs" of the East and the West.[35] Yet the abiding problem of the Western and un-Ethiopian connections of the Roman rite seems likely to persist and to frustrate any early solution to this issue that goes back to the beginnings of Catholicism in Ethiopia.

Pentecostalism, which is both a feature of Protestantism in the country and has taken hold among some Orthodox Christians (see chapters 7 and 8), has also made its appearance in the form of a Catholic charismatic renewal movement in the Ethiopian Catholic church. This has caused tension. Those who do not appreciate these movements tend to marginalize them. They fear that they are overemphasizing feelings and sensational experiences. They also criticize them for not paying enough attention to quiet prayers, the sacraments, and the eucharistic liturgy. Most seriously, some Catholics regard the charismatic movement as a means whereby Catholic youth join Protestant denominations. It is likely that the answer to such concerns lies in the development of a stronger pastoral approach to the charismatic movements and a stronger youth ministry. Moreover, there are Catholic faithful who have returned to the church or become more fervent in how they practice the faith thanks to their experience in Catholic charismatic movements.[36]

The Current Position of the Catholic Church in Ethiopia: Strengths

A notable strength of the Catholic Church is the large number of clergy and religious and lay catechists for a comparatively small Catholic population. The following is a detailed statement of "pastoral agents" of the Catholic Church according to its directory for 2014:

Ecclesiastical Jurisdiction	Diocesan Clergy	Religious Priests	Catechists
1. Addis Ababa	32	108	60
2. Adrigat	72	18	34
3. Harar	14	11	45
4. Emdeber	22	5	62
5. Hosanna	43	11	958
6. Soddo	26	29	747
7. Meki	20	18	140
8. Gambella	12	1	96
9. Hawassa	19	30	579
10. Jimma-Bonga	13	10	150
11. Nekemte	35	5	190
12. Robe	2	3	10
Totals	310	249	3,071[37]

It is worth noting that this means that in 2014 there were 559 priests for a population of 764,144, or one priest for every 1,367 Catholics. It is unclear why nuns and religious brothers do not appear in these figures, unless they are included under the heading "Catechists." In 2014 Ethiopia had 766 female religious (of whom 476 were Ethiopian and the rest from abroad) and 352 male religious (of whom 234 were Ethiopian and the others from abroad).[38]

Pope John Paul II observed to the Ethiopian and Eritrean bishops visiting Rome in 1997 that the Catholic Church is particularly valued for its health care and social services.[39] This observation can be related to the facts on the ground in Ethiopia. The church runs health clinics, centers for the promotion of women, HIV/AIDS centers, and other institutions, often staffed by nuns and tending to operate at full capacity.[40] In 2014 there were roughly one hundred

Catholic health-care institutions in Ethiopia. Four were hospitals (one of which also had a nursing school), while there were sixteen health centers, two speciality centers, sixty-three clinics, eighteen hospices, and six HIV/AIDS counseling and service centers. This network of staff and facilities allows the Catholic Church to provide health-care services (in line with the government's health-care policy) to more than seven million people per year all over the country, or about 7.3 percent of the total population (that is, ten times the Catholic share of the population).[41]

A large part of the social service provided by the Catholic Church consists of educational institutions. In 2012 the number of students served by Catholic schools was 170,000. Interestingly, only 13.8 percent of them were Catholics, with 36.9 percent Orthodox, 18.2 percent Protestant, 10 percent Muslim, and 21.1 percent not identified by religion. They were taught by 3,624 teachers, aided by 1,614 administrative staff.[42] A significant new initiative is the creation of the Ethiopian Catholic University of St Thomas Aquinas in Addis Ababa on land given to it by the government. It will have an initial focus on engineering and medicine, and some buildings have already been erected.

The liveliest intellectual center for Catholicism in Ethiopia is the Capuchin Franciscan Institute of Philosophy and Theology in Gulale, Addis Ababa. It was inaugurated in 1970. In due course it became, in effect, the seminary for all diocesan and religious priests in Ethiopia, with the exception of those from the Eparchy of Adigrat, which has its own seminary. The institute is also a center for publication of books on Ethiopian Christianity (often in English),[43] and it has an active program publishing translations of classics of the Western and Eastern traditions (such as Augustine's *Confessions*) into Amharic. Significant conferences are held at the institute on a regular basis.

Moving beyond the impressive services rendered to Ethiopia in health care and education, the Ethiopian Catholic Church is particularly open to ecumenical discussions, especially compared with the more "proselytizing" attitudes of some other Christian churches in the country. Although small in numbers, it is in a good position to promote dialogue between the various Christian denominations (see chapter 10). In part this is because it is too small to pose much of a threat and because it is very close to the Orthodox Church in doctrine and close to the Protestant churches in terms of its Western formation and outlook.[44]

Ultimately, the role of the Catholic Church might be to serve as an outward-looking, creative minority, confident in its own identity and fostering the faith of its members, yet supporting and developing initiatives for the benefit of all Ethiopians, not just in relation to health, education, and interreligious dialogue but in newer areas of social concern, like climate change.[45]

PART FIVE

CONCLUSION

10

The Future of Christianity in Ethiopia

The Context

To explore what the future might hold for the Christian churches of Ethiopia—Orthodox, Protestant, and Catholic—it is necessary to situate the discussion in relation to the main challenges and opportunities thrown up by the unique context in which they find themselves. It is a context shaped by the country's national politics; by its topography; by the long hands of memory and history; by the social and economic issues and pressures that Ethiopia, like all developing nations, faces; and, as well, by the distinctive theologies and identities of the churches and by their relationship with Islam. Some of these issues are generated in the world beyond the churches, while others arise from the relationships between the churches themselves.

The major challenges and opportunities for the Christian churches, and indeed for Islam, have come at the political level—from actions of the national government in Ethiopia. In 1991 the Ethiopian People's Revolutionary Democratic Front introduced policies that recognized religious freedom while maintaining a sharp division between religion and the (secular) state. This inevitably eroded the position of the Ethiopian Orthodox Church, while strengthening the Protestant, Muslim, and, indeed, Catholic communities. In short, by its actions the government created a fluid and competitive arena for the various religions. One consequence has been the rapid growth of the Protestant churches in comparison with the Orthodox Church in the 1990s and early 2000s. Yet that growth was sourced not only from Orthodox believers becoming Protestant but from the Protestant churches attracting a higher proportion of the rapidly growing population through their doors and from conversions among Muslims. In any event, the extremely rapid growth of Protestantism has slowed considerably in the last decade (see chapter 8).

But it would be a mistake to assume that since 1991 the various religions in Ethiopia have entirely escaped from government interference. In the interests of maintaining its political power, the EPRDF government took various steps to monitor and even control the various religious communities.[1] During 2011–2014 the government's determination to maintain its power vis-à-vis the religions became very evident in its controversies with Ethiopian Muslims.[2] There was something of a crisis in 2012, in particular, with Muslim protests in Addis Ababa that the EPRDF government was interfering in Muslim affairs. The Muslims complained that the government was trying to pack the Supreme Council of Islamic Affairs with persons loyal to government policy and to promote (with little previous consultation) the views of the small, moderate al-Ahbash Islamic movement that was based in Lebanon but had links to Harar, Ethiopia. The government rejected this criticism and claimed that a small Islamic faction was trying to turn Ethiopia into an Islamic state. It also arrested seventy-five Muslims, including the leaders of the group critical of it, and this worsened the situation.[3] Nevertheless, the past two decades have witnessed an increase in the political power of the lowland periphery, with large Muslim populations, vis-à-vis the Christian highlands with its Orthodox majority, and this has arguably begun to shift the balance of power toward Islamic political interests.[4]

Since 1991 Muslims have become much more prominent, economically and politically, and are represented in all the levels of ruling party and government.[5]

After the grimly oppressive years of the Derg, the establishment of ethnic federalism and religious freedom by the EPRDF has coincided with the rise of globalization, and this has led to the arrival of many religious organizations from abroad. In addition, increasing urbanization has resulted in larger populations in towns and cities detached from their traditional geographic and cultural settings. These people are more likely to be open to joining one of the new movements offering their wares in an increasingly crowded religious marketplace.

A major new factor in considering the future of Christianity in Ethiopia arrived on April 2, 2018, with the appointment of a new and charismatic prime minister, Abiy Ahmed—a Protestant whose father is Muslim and mother Orthodox. For nearly sixteen centuries the Ethiopian state and the Ethiopian Orthodox Church were closely aligned in ruling Ethiopia and in protecting its unique culture and traditions. That period came to a dramatic end with the revolution of 1974. Now, forty-five years later, the country has an openly Christian leader. His public expression of thanks to God in a speech on his appointment in 2018 constituted a dramatic difference from the discourse of any political leader in Ethiopia since the overthrow of Haile Selassie in 1974 and was warmly welcomed by a majority of the citizens in what remains, in spite of everything, a deeply religious Ethiopia.[6] The years since 1991, when the EPRDF assumed power, have seen increased ethnic compartmentalization and some interreligious violence. Not surprisingly for someone whose doctorate was on the resolution of religious conflict, Ahmed takes the view that "the fierce urgency of now" that confronts Ethiopia is national reconciliation.[7] In his inaugural speech he made many appeals to the notion of Ethiopiawinet (Ethiopianness). This is a concept with a longstanding history in Ethiopia, although some intellectuals doubt it exists. Girma

Mohammed notes, however, that for many ordinary Ethiopian citizens Ethiopiawinet is an idea that transcends historical debates:

> It not only exists, but it is a matter of survival, common belonging and celebration. Religiously, it emphasises the unity of humanity by weaving together Islamic and Christian teachings. Ethically, it offers moral guidance by critiquing the imperfections of earthly life. Politically, it urges negotiation and the striking of a balance between what is good to me and what is good to my ethnic and religious neighbour.[8]

It is a reality that finds expression, for example, when an Ethiopian athlete wins an international track and field event.

In addition, Ahmed uses another forward-looking concept to encapsulate the social harmony he seeks to encourage, namely, *medemer*, which literally means "being added to" and which stresses the beauty of blending.[9] He has explained medemer as follows:

> Tender love instead of abject cruelty, peace instead of conflict, love over hate, forgiveness over holding grudges, pulling instead of pushing. Peace to be the mother of prosperity, one will stay a pipe dream without the other. . . . Handled wisely our differences are our assets. What "Medemer" does not like is conflict instead of cooperation, banning instead of accommodation, polemics instead of discussion and acquiring fame through war by killing each other instead of resolution through a healthy debate.[10]

Medemer is a concept that appeals to the moral outlooks of Christianity, Islam, and indigenous African religions while not being so freighted with the distinctive beliefs or identity of any one of them as to alienate the others or, indeed, people of goodwill with no faith at all. Like Ethiopiawinet, medemer is a highly astute superordinate moral outlook with room for all Ethiopians in its embrace. One must not, however, forget that Ahmed faces immense challenges to his reforming agenda that may yet derail it, graphic evidence of which was the discharge of a grenade at a rally in Addis Ababa where he was speaking on June 23, 2018.

The approach being taken by Ahmed to reconciling various groups in Ethiopia coheres closely (although perhaps unintentionally) with a major source of thinking in social psychological research today on the resolution of conflict. This is provided by social identity theory, as originally developed by Henri Tajfel and John Turner at the University of Bristol, England, in the 1970s and 1980s.[11] Social identity theory focuses on the ways in which individuals acquire identity from belonging to groups in the context of a very wide array of intergroup and intragroup phenomena, including the issue of conflict between or within groups. One promising answer offered by social identity theory to the question of how to reconcile groups in conflict has been to advocate that the two or more groups concerned activate an existing identity that is common to all of them or, if necessary, invent such a common identity. This is called recategorization or the "common ingroup identity" approach, and experience suggests that it only works if the subgroup identities concerned are not threatened in the process, since that arouses animosities to the whole project.[12]

Great leaders often instinctively grasp the core of this approach even when they have not been exposed to social identity theory. Such was the case with Nelson Mandela when he managed to persuade "black" and "colored" South Africans to unite with "white" South Africans around the South African rugby team during the 1995 Rugby World Cup in South Africa, even though the team had formerly been almost exclusively "white." As a sign of his understanding the need to protect ingroup identities in this process, Mandela persuaded the South African rugby officials to allow the team to continue wearing designs (associated with Afrikaner identity) they had worn previously. South Africa won the tournament.[13] Similarly, Ahmed's advocacy of the concepts of Ethiopiawinet and medemer as a means reconciling Ethiopia's ethnic and religious groups represents another example of the activation of aspects of an existing common ingroup identity under which they can all rally but without threat to their current subgroup identities. This may provide an approach to ecumenism to which I will return below.

The Position of Orthodoxy

Orthodoxy has been negatively affected by these new trends and has reacted to them with revivalist and para-church movements, daily evening preaching, and other activities (see chapter 7). Some dimensions of this reaction have been anti-ecumenical compared with the situation in the past, as is evident, for example, in the fact that, whereas Anglican clergy were once invited to preach at the Orthodox Holy Trinity Cathedral in Addis Ababa, by 2014 that had become unthinkable.[14] Aid organizations, many of them faith based, came to Ethiopia to assist with various natural disasters and gained considerable influence. Among the Orthodox perceptions grew that these organizations were the vanguard of Protestant influence in their areas, and at daily evening prayers in Orthodox churches preachers condemned "wolves in sheep's clothing who came to steal the faithful."[15] There is evidence that some members of the Orthodox Church engage in active opposition to Protestant churches in their areas. It has been reported, for example, that in June 2017 a congregation of the Full Gospel Church that was meeting in a house in Tikil Dingaye, 20 kilometers outside Gondar—a house it had purchased when refused permission to build a church—was attacked by a mob of Orthodox believers, allegedly from the Mahebara Qeddusan movement (see chapter 7), with property destroyed and members of the congregation assaulted.[16] At the same time, it appears that the Orthodox Church continues to be the subject of unfounded charges by Protestant preachers, for example, that the presence of tabots in its churches represents a form of idolatry[17] or that the Orthodox worship Mary.

Nevertheless, the Ethiopian Orthodox Church retains a strategic position in the life of the country because of its access to the hearts and minds of nearly half of the population. It has a strong bureaucracy and strong institutions and has a tradition as an eco-friendly organization. Visionary programs could assist in the process of transformation that it has already begun. Ideally, it should aim at a rapprochement with global culture while maintaining its distinct identity. Part of this would entail reinterpreting its theology and ethics in the light of the contemporary situation, no doubt accompanied by training programs for clergy, officials, and laypeople.[18]

The Position of Protestantism

Protestantism is now firmly established in Ethiopia as the spiritual home of nearly one-fifth of population, even if the rate of growth it achieved in the years up to 2007 (especially in relation to Orthodoxy) is unlikely to be repeated. At the same time, the Protestant churches are maturing in other ways that will solidify their position in the religious landscape of Ethiopia. Chief among these is the development of robust institutions providing theological education at preuniversity, undergraduate and postgraduate levels (see chapter 8).

As noted above, Pentecostal ideas have successfully migrated into the mainline Protestant churches. It is significant, therefore, that, as one looks forward, it is Pentecostalism and the Pentecostal churches, among the diverse aspects of Ethiopian Protestantism, that are likely to face some of the biggest challenges. One commentator has noted that the Pente trajectories have come to exemplify the contemporary struggle by Ethiopians to define their identity against the unresolved issues of ethnic federalism, to renovate traditional practices of equilibrium between adhesion and dissidence vis-à-vis a feared political authority, and to cope with the contradictions of the country's engagement with the neoliberal economy.[19] While the efforts of Prime Minister Ahmed to bridge ethnic and religious boundaries in Ethiopia under a narrative embracing powerful concepts like Ethiopiawinet and medemer may offer assistance with all of these questions, they will not simply disappear overnight from the experience and concerns of Pentecostal Christians.

In addition, it may prove difficult for the Pente movement to continue its exceptional rate of expansion (at least until 2007).[20] For the Pentecostal churches share a problem common to all new religious organizations: how to recruit a second generation (and subsequent generations) to the movement in succession to their parents.[21] More specifically, as far as the numerous Pentecostal churches are concerned, their internal divisions and proliferation of churches together with their individualistic approach to religion and "the spiritual nomadism of the faithful" represent obstacles to their transmitting their faith to their offspring.[22] Yet there is a particular problem with Pentecostalism. As the great sociologist Max Weber recognized, charisma tends to become "routinized," in that the direct personal and charismatic relationship between the initial leader of the movement and his or her followers is, over time, replaced by institutional forms of leadership, bureaucracy, for example. Moreover, in relation to charismatic religious movements, there is a tendency for the initial excitement and energy of the earliest stages of the movement, when the members enjoyed a direct experience of the Spirit, with the various phenomena associated with it, to fade over time.[23]

Relations among the Christian Churches: The Current Picture

Many of the contextual factors mentioned above have had a negative impact on relations among the Christian churches in Ethiopia. At least until the appointment of Abiy Ahmed as prime minister in April 2018, the evidence suggests that Ethiopia was not a favorable environment for ecumenical sentiments and, indeed, that most of the numerous churches and ecclesial communities were "engulfed in mutual institutional antagonism and rancor which undermine the very essence or mission of Christianity in Ethiopia."[24] While most (but not all) of the Protestant churches had a common forum in the Evangelical Churches Fellowship of Ethiopia, very little indeed has occurred to bring together the Orthodox, Protestant, and Roman Catholic Churches. We must acknowledge, therefore, that Ethiopian Christianity has been seriously riven. To put the matter in theological terms, the answer in Ethiopia to Paul's question, "Is Christ divided?" (1 Cor 1:13 RSV) has, indubitably, been yes. While all Ethiopian Christians have been baptized into Christ (Rom 6:3), the consequences of that reality have not been much seen in the field of relations among the three Christian groupings. The worst aspect of this situation is that the urgent problems facing Ethiopia have thus been denied the benefit of a combined Christian response.

Until very recently the situation seemed to be getting worse rather than improving, as suggested by the drying up of invitations for Anglican clerics to preach in the Orthodox Holy Trinity Cathedral in Addis Ababa, mentioned above. One observer had suggested, "The evolution of ecumenical relationships among different Christian denominations towards more tensions is a matter of growing concern."[25] At present, ecumenical activities are not visible at official levels. The only ecumenical institution that seems to have flourished is the Bible Society.[26] It has a board with twenty-four members, eight of whom are Orthodox, eight Protestant, and eight Catholic. The Bible Society has also launched an initiative to create a platform for the Orthodox, Protestant, and Catholic Churches to come together to consult and deliberate on current issues. This is called the Trinitarian Forum and has one gathering per annum. If needed, the participants make recommendations to the government on useful matters, such as the need to include ethics in the public schools' curriculum.[27] There are also some ecumenical charitable activities, and the research group at the Capuchin Franciscan Institute of Philosophy and Theology in Gulale, Addis Ababa (mentioned in chapter 9), is ecumenical. Abiy Ahmed's strong interest in ending intra- and interreligious tension and conflict and in mobilizing Christianity to work on issues of poverty and justice provides grounds for optimism that a new dawn of ecumenism may be about to break in Ethiopia.

A Way Forward I: Christian Ecumenism

The best answer to the Ethiopian problem of Christian churches at war with one another is a renewed effort at ecumenism. But, prior to the commencement of such an ecumenical endeavor beyond the current activities sponsored by the Bible Society, it would help if the churches took stock of their current positions and drew the lessons to be learned from them. This will take courageous, even charismatic, leadership, but perhaps the example of Ethiopia's new prime minister will be an object lesson in what is possible.

There are already voices across the Christian spectrum in Ethiopia who suggest that there are many paths to God and that it would be desirable for members of the various Christian groupings to show humility and respect toward one another. For those who find this view theologically problematic (in spite of all Christians being baptized into Christ), another way to make a similar point is to affirm that the three Christian groupings in Ethiopia are well established and are not under major threat from the others. They can all afford to relax a little. It would be desirable for due acknowledgment to be made of the condition of modernity, or even postmodernity, in which all the Christian churches find themselves, with people able to elect which religious affiliation they choose and willing to accept the social consequences of moving from one Christian affiliation to another. Rancorous criticism on theological or other grounds may achieve very little except in damaging trust and in souring the atmosphere for dialogue, which makes significant collaboration on important issues very difficult. Except for the work of the Bible Society, that is precisely where Ethiopian Christianity finds itself today. But we know from the remarkable scenes of joy across Ethiopia and Eritrea in July 2018 when the two countries ended their long decades of conflict with inspired leadership from the two leaders, Prime Minister Abiy Ahmed and President Isaias Afwerki, what happens when bitterness and rancor are dropped in favor of peace and reconciliation. Afwerki commented during lunch with Ahmed when the peace had been declared, "Words cannot express the joy we are feeling now. We are one people. Whoever forgets that does not understand our situation."[28] This is a sentiment with equal applicability to Ethiopia's Christians should they wish to rise to the challenge.

There are specific issues that might usefully be addressed. For Orthodox Christians, it is highly likely that the old days, when they ruled the country with the national government and largely had a religious monopoly, are gone forever, even if the new prime minister wants them to have more autonomy. Seeking to exercise ecclesial power as in the past is unlikely to be a good long-term strategy, in spite of occasionally producing short-term tactical outcomes (like persuading the civic authorities to veto a Protestant church being built in a town). Such power as remains of this kind will eventually erode, and the legacy of bitterness left by its previous exercise may tarnish the image and effectiveness of the church for years to come. There is now a group of Protestant churches in the country with half as many adherents as Orthodoxy, and there is nothing much the latter can do about it. Indeed, the Orthodox Church can afford to be much more relaxed about the growth of Protestantism. In the past decade that growth has slowed dramatically, and the measures taken by Orthodoxy in response to Protestantism, such as we have seen so far, are clearly having an effect in stabilizing Orthodoxy and in slowing defections to Protestantism. It will also be harder for Orthodox Christians to have a negative view of Protestants when so many of them are being regularly asked to pray for the Protestant prime minister who reunited their church after nearly three decades of separation.

The severe Protestant criticism of Orthodoxy that has occurred in the past can perhaps now be tempered with tolerance and a realization of the realities of the situation. Orthodox Christians do not worship Mary, and the tabots in their churches are not idols. Suggestions that the Orthodox Church discourages familiarity with the Bible among the laity would appear to have passed their use-by date, at least to the extent that every afternoon crowds gather to hear heavily biblical sermons in thousands of churches across the country and that the Orthodox Church is an equal partner in the work of the Bible Society. Protestant criticism of Orthodox fasting practices fails to recognize the extent to which they entail living the faith bodily and spiritually in a profound recognition of the transcendent God. The pronounced asceticism of Ethiopian monks who usually make do on one (modest) meal a day in the service of getting ever closer to God—in a world so obsessed with material goods—might usefully prompt respect and admiration, not disparagement. It will do no harm to the Protestant churches, indeed, it will raise them in wider estimation if their members can take to heart the sentiment recently expressed by Ethiopia's Protestant prime minister: "It is impossible to think of Ethiopia without taking note of the Ethiopian Orthodox Tewahedo Church, which is both great and sacred."[29]

What would the mechanics of an ecumenical initiative look like? The Trinitarian Forum, sponsored by the Bible Society, although fairly inchoate, certainly reveals the possibilities. As noted above, one potent means to reconcile different groups, which applies to religions as much as any other form of group, is to recategorize the participants into a new group, to create a new ingroup identity, or to activate an existing one. This approach offers a vantage point for considering a proposal on ecumenism in Ethiopia made recently by a group of Catholic theologians:

> The faithful and clergy from various confessions are waiting anxiously and with hope for the emergence of a better ecumenical encounter among the Churches and their Church leaders. It would be a blessing for Ethiopia if the Church leaders were to be more open to the urgent call from diverse groups in the country and were to launch a theological dialogue dealing with various ecclesiological issues.[30]

The major qualification one might offer to this hunger for ecumenical engagement is that, to begin with, the matters to be discussed should probably not be ecclesiological. Ecclesiology is an area of maximum difference among the three types of Christianity, and beginning a discussion there will produce only immediate disagreement. In a diplomatic negotiation, the parties usually begin with topics on which they agree. This allows the participants to get to know one another and, hopefully, to learn to respect and even trust one another. The social identity approach suggests that this could then lead into some common expression of identity, perhaps involving the establishment of an umbrella organization addressing a particular issue. In Ethiopia one starting point might be social and economic questions, especially in relation to assisting the poor, the sick, and the uneducated. If a theological topic were to be assayed in due course, it should probably be baptism. Addressing Christology or the theology of the Holy Spirit might provoke discord rather than bringing the parties together.

As noted above, at present the Bible Society in Ethiopia is the main sponsor of the very limited ecumenical engagements across the Christian churches. While recognizing the distrust many Ethiopian Orthodox Christians still have toward Catholics by reason of the Jesuit episode in the seventeenth century, the Catholic Church may have a useful role to play in helping to promote such dialogue among the Christian traditions in Ethiopia. This is because its small size minimizes the threat it poses to Orthodoxy and Protestantism and because, as noted in chapter 9, it shares virtually all its doctrines with the former and a Western outlook on many matters with the latter. The Second Vatican Council has made such a brokerage role possible by its replacement, in the 1964 document *Unitatis Redintegratio* (The Restoration of Unity), of the old principle *extra ecclesiam nulla salus* (no salvation outside the church) with a new affection for the Orthodox Churches and a new openness to the Protestant churches.

A Way Forward II: Relations with Islam

One increasingly pressing matter is the changing nature of Islam in Ethiopia. Leaving aside the times when Ethiopia has been engaged in war with neighboring Muslim states, especially in the sixteenth century, and the efforts of nineteenth-century emperors to convert Muslims in conquered southern regions to Christianity, the country has largely experienced the "continuation of the tradition of peaceful coexistence between the Christian and Muslim communities."[31] There have, in fact, been good relations between Muslims and Ethiopians since the very beginnings of Islam. One of Muhammad's first converts was a freed slave of Ethiopian parents. Moreover, a tradition, generally accepted as historical, records that the prophet advised a group of his followers to seek safety from persecution by the Quraysh tribe of Mecca in al-Habasa (Abyssinia), as the Ethiopian regions were then known to the Arabs. There they were received with kindness by the Ethiopian king. This episode is known as the first *hejra* (a journey to escape persecution). Less likely to be historical is the extra feature that the Ethiopian king became a Muslim.[32] Islam subsequently entered Ethiopia from a number of directions and flourished there, in many diverse ways and with numerous local variations. Among the various streams of Islam in Ethiopia, however, the Sufi tradition has played a prominent role.[33] Sufi Islam in Ethiopia has traditionally been a tolerant religion, and this has been conducive to good relations with the other faiths, Orthodoxy especially.[34]

Girma Mohammed has recently explained the generally good Christian-Muslim relations that have characterized Ethiopia in some detail. It is necessary, however, to begin by distinguishing between attitudes at the political level and attitudes among ordinary Christians and Muslims living together in local communities. Until 1974 the Ethiopian state was characterized by a very hierarchical organization with the emperor, as head of state, and the abuna, as head of the national religion, at the top of the pyramid. They were followed by the nobility, the military, the ordinary citizens, and finally slaves. The emperors governed the provinces through local strongmen who considered themselves as minor kings; that is why a major title of the emperor was *negusa nagast*, "king of kings." The attitudes of the political elite toward Muslims were neither smooth nor overtly violent. They patronized and demeaned Muslims as "honorary guests," even though many Muslim communities went back centuries, and sometimes Muslims fought back, in an effort to occupy the center ground.

But among ordinary citizens there has been a long-standing tradition of solidarity. The key to this solidarity has been a rejection of the notion of toleration in favor of acceptance. Toleration is seen in a negative light since it assumes strong uneasiness with the presence of an individual or group coupled with a recognition that he, she, or they are legitimate adversaries. Toleration means having the power to interfere in someone's behavior yet choosing not to. This feature of toleration lessens its role in the Ethiopian moral framework that tends to select either outright rejection where social norms are breached or principled acceptance (when the positive outweighs the negative). Acceptance dwells on the positive dimensions of the other rather than on his or her negative dimensions. In the event that Christians and Muslims are engaged in negotiating an issue, the emphasis is placed on societal norms relating to moderation, solidarity, respect, and fairness, while the respective (and different) theological underpinnings of those norms are not brought to the surface. One aspect of this is that mission as between Orthodoxy and Islam has not been very significant in Ethiopia and, indeed, is often regarded as dangerous. There has been a tendency to treat the universalist claims of the two religions as a matter for the divine realm and not for day-to-day interaction, where people have invested rather in sociocultural hybridity, principled acceptance, and accommodation of diversity, rather than in mission. Theological consistency is sacrificed on the altar of social pragmatism. Even though Christians and Muslims in Ethiopia forbid intermarriage, this does happen and is, in fact, common (an example being Prime Minister Ahmed), since interfaith marriage without conversion is largely tolerated. In addition, the adherents of both religions have embodied belief in the Ethiopian national identity—Ethiopiawinet. This concept was described above, but it embraces tradition, pride, faith, patriotism, religion, community, festivities, strong moral values, reservation, endurance, and so on. Subscribing to this national identity tends to suppress social or political activism in the name of any particular religion.[35]

However, the common assertions of the good relations that have existed between Orthodoxy and Islam in Ethiopia have neglected the fact that the former has long provided the ideological underpinning of the meaning of Ethiopia and has historically defined Islam and other Christian confessions as the "others." Thus, the celebrated image of Ethiopia as an example of harmonious Christian-Muslim relations must be related to the dominant position of Orthodox Christianity.[36] In any event, the situation has now become very different. Developments in the latter part of the twentieth century have reduced the church's hegemonic position and, together with a more active and visible Muslim community, have produced a highly complex religious landscape in which religious boundaries are increasingly contested.

In spite of the traditional good relations between Muslims and Christians and the appointment in 2018 of a popular prime minister whose father is Muslim, many Ethiopians consider that the traditional nature of Islam in the country is at risk of being pushed in a more radical direction by the exposure of Ethiopian Muslims to influences from abroad. Hundreds of thousands of Ethiopians travel annually to work in Middle Eastern countries and return influenced by the Islamic ideas that they encounter there. In addition, Muslim organizations from abroad are becoming increasingly active in Ethiopia. The country has witnessed the construction of numerous new mosques, madrassas, and orphanages, especially from funds originating in Saudi Arabia.[37] Also apparent is the introduction of more radical Islamic ideas alongside those inspired by Sufi tolerance.[38] While the extent to which the country's Muslims are actually becoming radical is a matter of debate and governmental overreaction could aggravate the problem, there seems little doubt that processes of radicalization are occurring.[39] There is a growing number of Ethiopian Islamic scholars, who are fluent in both Arabic and Amharic, who have studied in Saudi Arabia and then returned to Ethiopia as part of the Wahhabi movement. Others have studied at Al-Azhar University in Cairo. Some strongly oppose the traditional practices in Ethiopia connected with Sufi Islam and in a few cases may have encouraged the desecration of traditional Oromo Sufi Muslim tombs. There are conflicting reports as to just how much influence the Wahhabi movement has in Ethiopia, and some Muslims and Christians downplay their influence. But they do seem to carry sway among the young, poor, and unemployed, and these represent a large proportion of the population.[40] A recent survey showed that 65 percent of Ethiopian Muslims were in favor of making sharia the official law of the land.[41] The EPRDF government has attempted to keep a fairly strong grip on Islam, especially via its control of the Islamic Affairs Supreme Council (the Majlis). Muslim protests in 2012, demanding especially that the members of the Majlis be elected by the Muslim community, drew tough countermeasures by the government. The risk is that the government will overreact to the perceived danger of Islamic radicalism and make the whole situation worse.[42]

Of most relevance to this volume is that on occasion there have been instances of violence by Muslims against Christians. In January 2011, in the largely Muslim town of Besheno (near Alaba), evangelical Christians were subject to harassment after Muslims posted notices on the doors of Christian homes saying they "should convert, leave the city or face death." In November 2011 a group of Muslim students burned down St. Arsema Orthodox Church in Qoto Baloso. Also in 2011 Muslims attacked Protestant churches in the Asendabo area, when a rumor was spread that a Qur'an had been defiled. While it was not possible to confirm or deny the truth of this, the rumor alone led to clashes (with one dead, six injured), displacement (of four thousand people), and the destruction of fifty-one churches. This kind of overreaction seems to indicate an emerging everyday distrust between religious groups, in a context where religion is becoming polemicized in Ethiopia, with incidents instigated by a few militants achieving a rapid mass following. In the past, however, religious mob violence was uncommon.[43] Phenomena such as these raise an apprehension of "the threat posed by radicalized Islam" that "previously had no foothold in our country."[44]

In this difficult situation it would seem that there is scope for a mutually beneficial dialogue between Christianity and Islam.

If the Christian churches of Ethiopia can come together in some ecumenical enterprise that entails the reactivation or creation of a new common identity, it is also possible that the participants could then reach out to Muslims to create a new superordinate social and religious category, a broader ingroup identity, embracing Christianity and Islam. While one could imagine this taking many forms (for example, the place of religion in the public square), it is likely that in the early stages at least, while a joint exploration of the concepts of Ethiopiawinet and medemer might initiate the discussion, the emphasis might then progress to some practical activities that all parties could jointly undertake. It is not impossible that at a later point there might be a theological discussion on the nature of God, although here the Christian participants will need to be alive to the concern on the part of many Muslims that the Christian triune God is really an instance of tritheism. Given that there are so many happy Christian-Muslim marriages in Ethiopia, it is reasonable to assume that the negotiation of a larger joint identity between the Christian churches and Islam might be successful.

Notes

Chapter 1: Locating Ethiopian Christianity

1. Salome is mentioned as traveling with the Holy Family to Egypt in the sixth- or seventh-century work *The History of Joseph the Carpenter* (for the text, see http://www.newadvent.org/fathers/0805.htm).
2. Munro-Hay 2002: 156.
3. Kaplan 2007.
4. Binns 2005: 104.
5. Voigt 2003: 59.
6. Munro-Hay 2002: 15.
7. Ullendorff 1990: 22–23.
8. Ullendorff 1990: 25.
9. See https://www.britannica.com/place/Ethiopia/Soils, accessed January 17, 2018.
10. Ullendorff 1990: 26.
11. See https://www.britannica.com/place/Ethiopia/Soils, accessed January 17, 2018.
12. See Romm 1992.

13 See Phillipson 2012: 9–22.
14 Phillipson 2012: 24.
15 Phillipson 2012: 24.
16 Information provided to the author and Angus Pryor by one of the excavation team onsite on March 13, 2017.
17 See Wolf et al. 2010.
18 For the text and a German translation, see Nebes 2010: 216.
19 For the text and a German translation, see Nebes 2010: 226.
20 Nebes 2010: 226–27.
21 On the political history, see Nebes 2010: 230.
22 Nebes 2010: 223.
23 In relation to the naming the maternal line, see Nebes 2010: 219.
24 Wolf, in a PowerPoint presentation supplied to the author.
25 Wolf et al. 2010: 190.
26 Wolf et al. 2015: 43.
27 Wolf et al. 2015: 33.
28 Phillipson 2012: 40–41.
29 Phillipson 2012: 41.
30 Ziethen 2007: 19.
31 On Kush, see Breyer 2007.
32 For one example, see http://www.gizapyramids.org/static/pdf%20library/bmfa_pdfs/bmfa21_1923_11to27.pdf (accessed July 18, 2018).
33 Munro-Hay 1991: 79 and 224 (which has the text of the inscriptions).
34 Phillipson 2012: 41–44.
35 Phillipson 2012: 44.
36 Thelamon 1981: 44.
37 Fattovich (2010) suggests 50 BCE, while Phillipson (2012: 69) prefers the first half of the first century CE.
38 See the edition by Casson 1989, with introduction, Greek text and translation and notes. For the mid-first-century date of the work, see Casson 1989: 7.
39 Casson 1989: 8.
40 *Periplus Maris Erythrae* 4–6; see Casson 1989: 51–55.
41 Pliny the Elder, *Natural History*, 6.34.
42 So Phillipson 2012: 73. But he errs in thinking that Adulis could have been part of a different kingdom ruled by Zoscales, since Aksum was the mother city (*metropolis*: see above) of whatever political entity of which Adulis was part. The various possibilities are discussed by Casson 1989: 109–10.
43 The inscription is RIE 180; see Phillipson 2012: 79.
44 See Phillipson 2012: 82 for a list.
45 See Fattovich 2003: 174; and Phillipson 2012: 74–78.
46 Mani, *Kephalaion* 77. On Mani, see BeDuhn 2017.
47 Thelamon 1981: 67.

48 For the text of the inscription, see Munro-Hay 1991: 222–23.
49 For the inscriptional remains, see RIE.
50 Hahn 1999: 432–33.
51 See Hahn 1999: 433; Munro-Hay 1991: 221–32; and RIE.
52 Hahn 1999: 433–34.
53 This is type 35 in Munro-Hay and Juel-Jensen 1995. See the discussion of this coin in Munro-Hay and Juel-Jensen 1995: 119–21.

Chapter 2: The Advent of Christianity in Ethiopia

1 For a discussion of how Rufinus understood "Further India" (*India ulterior*) as covering a large Red Sea region that included Ethiopia, see Thelamon 1981: 49–54.
2 Rufinus, *Ecclesiastical History*, I.9–10. Translation by the author. For the Latin text, see Mommsen 1903–1909: 971–73; cited by Thelamon 1981: 39–40. For a French translation, see Thelamon 1981: 39–41. There is a detailed discussion of this text in Thelamon 1981: 37–83.
3 Thelamon 1981: 44.
4 Thelamon 1981: 39.
5 Thelamon 1981: 45. Similarly, Rufinus cites one Bacurius for his account of the conversion of the peoples of the Iberian Peninsula, and there is independent evidence for the existence of Bacurius (ibid.).
6 Munro-Hay 1991: 204.
7 See Thelamon 1981: 61 (citing Jerome, *Chron. Ad an.* 328 [PL 27. 497]); and Hahn 1999: 435 (citing a work by the eleventh-century Byzantine historian Cedrenus, *Chron. Anno xxi Constantini*, which Hahn regards as probably based on a lost part of the *Res Gestae* of Ammianus Marcellinus).
8 Robin 2017: xliii.
9 Colin 2017: 1.
10 Fiaccadori 2014: 484–85.
11 Thelamon 1981: 45–47, 61.
12 See Thelamon 1981: 61; and the works cited in note 7.
13 At the start of their sojourn in Aksum, Frumentius and Edesius were "young boys" (*pueruli*) yet old enough to read and write quite well and to be given responsibilities by the king, suggesting about twelve years of age. By the time the king died, they had become "young men" (*adulescentes*). This means, typically, between fifteen and thirty years old (although they could be older). They then had to wait while the prince, the queen's "young son" (*parvus filius*), a "boy" (*puer*) came of age. We should allow about five to ten years. The minimum period Frumentius and would have been in Aksum altogether was therefore ten years, at the maximum perhaps twenty. Thelamon (1981: 61) suggests ten to twelve years.

14 Thelamon (1981: 61) notes the importance of keeping these events within Constantine's reign, while also pointing out that Rufinus had a theological reason to do so: to keep this activity out of the reign of Constantine's (heretical) son, Constantius II (62).
15 See Thelamon 1981: 62 (citing the *Chronicon* of the Festal Letters and the *Historia acephala*). Thelamon also notes that Athanasius was in Alexandria from November 27, 337, to April 16, 339, but Constantine died on May 22, 337.
16 Robin 2017: xxxi–xxxii.
17 For the summary of the letter, see 32C (Szymusiak 1958: 121). For the text of the letter see 636B–637A (Szymusiak 1958: 125–26). Szymusiak provides the Greek text and a French translation.
18 Robin 2017: xxxii.
19 Thelamon 1981.
20 Thelamon 1981: 64.
21 Defense to Constantius 636B.
22 Munro-Hay 2003.
23 Robin 2017: xlvi–xlvii.
24 Phillipson 2012: 83.
25 See Munro-Hay 1991: 225–26 for the text of the inscription.
26 Munro-Hay 1991: 206, and see the Ezana inscriptions on pp. 224–32.
27 Munro-Hay 1991: 77 and 205. For the coinage of Ousanas, see Munro-Hay and Juel-Jensen 1995: 103–18.
28 Munro-Hay 1991: 205–6.
29 Thelamon 1981: 70.
30 Thelamon 1981: 66.
31 Thelamon 1981: 72.
32 Thelamon 1981: 75.
33 Hahn 2003. For this type of coin, also see type 49 in Munro-Hay and Juel-Jensen 1995, discussed at pp. 136–39.
34 This is type 50 in Munro-Hay and Juel-Jensen 1995: 139–41.
35 RIE 187 records the Agwezat campaign (Ezana is not specifically mentioned in the inscription, the beginning and end of which are lost, but he is likely to have been the king at the time [Munro-Hay 1991: 226]), and RIE 188, that against the Tsarane. English translations for these can be found in Munro-Hay 1991: 226–27.
36 Munro-Hay 1991: 196–98.
37 Munro-Hay 1991: 198.
38 Munro-Hay 1991: 225.
39 The Ge'ez version is RIE 189 and the Greek is RIE 271.
40 ET from Munro-Hay 1991: 227, but adding "I" before "Ezana" in accordance with the Ge'ez.
41 ET by Munro-Hay 1991: 228–29, occasionally modified by the author against the Ge'ez text.

42 This is RIE 271. For a discussion of this inscription, see Anfray et al. 1970; and RIE 15–21.
43 Although the Greek adds the Atiadotai to the list, making four oppressed peoples.
44 See Caquot and Nautin in Anfray et al. 1970: 270.
45 Caquot and Nautin in Anfray et al. 1970: 270–271.
46 Phillipson 2012: 93–94.
47 Levine 1972 [1965]: 16.

Chapter 3: Fifth to Seventeenth Centuries

1 For photos of these coins and discussion thereon, see Munro-Hay and Juel-Jensen 1995: Ouazebas (types 54–58 and pp. 147–52), Eon (type 59 and pp. 152–56), Mehadeyis (types 67–70 and pp. 160–65), Ebana (types 71–72ii and pp. 166–79), Nezana (types 77–79 and pp. 178–84), Nezool (types 82–83 and pp. 185–88), Ousas (types 84–86 and pp. 188–92), and Ousanas (types 87–90 and pp. 192–98). As far as Mehadeyis is concerned, on these coins the legends are in unvocalized Ge'ez, and his name appears as MHDYS, so that "Mehadeyis" is Munro-Hay's reasonable suggestion for how the name was vocalized (1991: 81).
2 See Munro-Hay and Juel-Jensen 1995: 160–61.
3 Munro-Hay and Juel-Jensen 1995: 181–84.
4 Munro-Hay and Juel-Jensen 1995: 185–93.
5 Munro-Hay and Juel-Jensen 1995: 195.
6 For an English translation, see Munro-Hay 1991: 230.
7 Fiaccadori 2007: 329.
8 Munro-Hay 1991: 230.
9 See Ullendorff 1990: 52; Fiaccadori 2007: 329–30; and Colin 2017: LII.
10 See McCrindle 1897: iii–x.
11 McCrindle 1897: 50–68.
12 *Patrologia Graeca* 88, column 98; McCrindle 1897: 120.
13 McCrindle 1897: 55–56. There were actually two inscriptions (which Cosmas mistakenly thought was a continuous text). One (= RIE 276) was by Ptolemy III Euergetes (reigned 246–222 BCE) to record his victories in Asia. The other (= RIE 277) was by a non-Christian king of Adulis (or, more probably, Aksum), which is clear from the thanks he offers to the god Ares (Mahrem in Ge'ez, as we have seen in chapter 2).
14 Henze 2000: 38.
15 Tamrat 1972: 23.
16 Fiaccadori 2007: 330.
17 Colin 2017: L.
18 Tamrat 1972: 24.

19 Isaac 2012: 21. On Pachomius, see Goehring 2017.
20 Tamrat 1972: 23–24.
21 Colin 2017: LII.
22 Brita 2010.
23 Ullendorff 1990: 54–55.
24 Tamrat 1972: 34–41; and Ullendorff 1990: 55–59.
25 Tamrat 1972: 41–45; and Ullendorff 1990: 59–61.
26 Tamrat 1972: 58.
27 Derat 2007: 478.
28 Derat 2007: 477.
29 Finneran 2007: 482.
30 Wondmagegnehu and Motovu 1970: 6.
31 Ullendorff 1990: 62.
32 Marrassini 2007: 366.
33 See Isaac 2012: 131.
34 Marrassini 2007: 367.
35 Pankhurst 2005: 208; Kaplan 2010: 688.
36 Kaplan 2010: 688.
37 Tamrat 1972: 68.
38 For a sample of texts in the *Royal Chronicles*, see Pankhurst 1967.
39 Ullendorff 1990: 62–63.
40 Colin 2015: IX.
41 Ancel and Ficquet 2015: 65.
42 Ancel and Ficquet 2015: 66.
43 Ancel and Ficquet 2015: 66.
44 Ancel and Ficquet 2015: 65.
45 See Tamrat 1972: 107–112.
46 Tamrat 1972: 116.
47 For a detailed account of the reign of Amda Seyon, see Tamrat 1972: 73–106.
48 Kaplan 2003: 553. For a detailed treatment of the Falasha, see Kaplan 1992 and Quirin 1992.
49 Kaplan 2003: 552.
50 Kaplan 2003: 553.
51 Ullendorff 1990: 65–66.
52 Tamrat 1972: 222.
53 Isaac 2012: 258–59.
54 Tamrat 1972: 230–31.
55 Isaac 2012: 256.
56 For the material in this paragraph (except where otherwise indicated), see Tamrat 1972: 231–47.
57 Kaplan 2003: 554.
58 The story of the progressive Portuguese maritime expansion is told extremely well (using large-scale ship models) in the Navy Museum in Lisbon (http://ccm.marinha.pt/pt/museu/).

59 Caraman 1985: 5.
60 Caraman 1985: 5.
61 Marcus 2002: 14, 26–27, 33.
62 Caraman 1985: 4.
63 See Tamrat 1972: 31–33; and Ullendorff 1990: 68.
64 See Caraman 1985: 6; and Ullendorff 1990: 68.
65 The story is told by Francisco Alvares (Beckingham et anor. 1961:2: 413–415).
66 Ullendorff 1990: 68–69.
67 See Beckingham et anor. 1961.
68 Caraman 1985: 6.
69 *True Relation*, chapter 22 (Beckingham et anor. 1961: 1:109–10). Alvares was mistaken about the timeline for baptism. In Ethiopian Orthodoxy girls are baptized eighty days after birth, not sixty. The basis for this tradition is a combination of Leviticus 12:1-7 and Jubilees 3:9-11, the latter describing Adam as being brought into Eden forty days after his birth and Eve being brought in eighty days after her birth. (I am indebted to Daniel Assefa for this information.)
70 *True Relation*, chapter 26 (Beckingham et anor. 1961: 1:119–20).
71 *True Relation*, chapter 9, of the account of the return journey to Portugal (Beckingham et anor. 1961:2: 510–11).
72 *True Relation*, chapter 110 (Beckingham et anor. 1961: 2:389–30).
73 *True Relation*, chapter 110 (Beckingham et anor. 1961: 2:394–95).
74 *True Relation*, chapter 9, of the account of the return journey to Portugal (Beckingham et anor. 1961: 2:508–9).
75 *True Relation*, chapter 99 (Beckingham et anor. 1961: 2:357).
76 *True Relation*, chapter 5 (Beckingham et anor. 1961: 1:63–64).
77 *True Relation*, chapter 9, of the account of the return journey to Portugal (Beckingham et anor. 1961: 2:510).
78 See the French translation by René Basset published in 1897.
79 Caraman 1985: 8.
80 See the edition of Boavida et al. 2011.
81 See Boavida et al. 2011: 1:270–85.
82 See Boavida et al. 2011: 1: 288–91.
83 Ullendorff 1990: 70.
84 Caraman 1985: 9.
85 Ullendorff 1990: 72–73. For a detailed treatment, see Pankhurst 1997.
86 Caraman 1985: 10.
87 Caraman 1985: 123–24.
88 Caraman 1985: 11.
89 Caraman 1985: 12.
90 Caraman 1985: 13.
91 Caraman 1985: 12–13.
92 Caraman 1985: 13–14.

93   Caraman 1985: 14.
94   Caraman 1985: 15.
95   Caraman 1985: 17.
96   Caraman 1985: 44.
97   Ullendorff 1990: 5.
98   Ullendorff 1990: 6. For an edited translation of this work, see Boavida et al. 2011.
99   Caraman 1985: 52–54.
100 Caraman 1985: 67–68.
101 Caraman 1985: 81.
102 Caraman 1985: 85.
103 Caraman 1985: 119–20.
104 Caraman 1985: 131–32.
105 Caraman 1985: 137–39.
106 Caraman 1985: 141–42.
107 Caraman 1985: 142–43.
108 Caramam 1985: 148.
109 Caraman 1985: 149–50.
110 Caramn 1985: 150–51.
111 Caraman 1985: 152–58.

Chapter 4: Mid-seventeenth Century to the Present

1   Beckingham et anor. 1961: 1:267–68 and 1961: 2:437–38.
2   For these details, see Tamrat 1972: 268–75, with a plan of the encampment on 270.
3   See Caraman 1985: 126–27.
4   Munro-Hay 2002: 121.
5   Kaplan 2003: 554.
6   Kaplan 2003: 554.
7   Ullendorff 1990: 76.
8   Ullendorff 1990: 76–79.
9   Ullendorff 1990: 79.
10 Kaplan 2003: 554.
11 Kaplan 2003: 555. For somewhat different views on the effect of the missionaries on the Falasha, see Kaplan 1992; and Quirin 1992.
12 Kaplan 2003: 555.
13 Ancel and Ficquet 2015: 67.
14 Ancel and Ficquet 2015: 68.
15 See https://www.vam.ac.uk/event/14gkkD4W/maqdala-1868-updated.
16 Ancel and Ficquet 2015: 68.
17 Ullendorff 1990: 85–87.

18 Ullendorff 1990: 87.
19 For a description of this church, see Munro-Hay 2002: 142–46.
20 Ullendorff 1990: 88–89.
21 Ullendorff 1990: 89–90.
22 Ullendorff 1990: 90–91.
23 Munro-Hay 2002: 35.
24 *Fetha Nagast*, chapter 31, p. 175 of the translation, available online (http://www.ethiopianorthodox.org/biography/02thelawofkings.pdf; accessed July 13, 2018). The scripture quoted is from Lev 25:44-45.
25 Pankhurst 2010: 673.
26 Miran 2010: 675.
27 Busorf 2010: 678.
28 Marcus 2002: 120.
29 *Fetha Nagast*, chapter 10, p. 66, of the translation of the text, available online (http://www.ethiopianorthodox.org/biography/01thelawofkings.pdf; accessed July 13, 2018).
30 Eshete 2009: 85–93.
31 Smidt 2010: 681.
32 On the rise of the Derg, see Markakis 2011: 161–69; and Marcus 2002: 181–96.
33 Eshete 2009: 94–95.
34 Smidt 2010: 681.
35 Ullendorff 1990: 103.
36 Marcus 2002: 169–72.
37 Eshete 2009: 201. For a discussion of feudalism in Ethiopian agriculture, see Cohen 1974. Keller (1988: 55–59) considers the appropriateness of referring to parts of Ethiopian rural society as "feudal" even though it diverged in certain respects from European feudalism.
38 Keller 1988: 54–55.
39 Eshette 2009: 197–99.
40 Markakis 2011: 169.
41 Abbink 2014: 348.
42 Markakis 2011: 169–70.
43 Chaillot 2005: 429.
44 Haustein 2011: 190.
45 Loubser (2002: 383) suggests one-third; for the other suggestions, see Keller (1988: 55), following Cohen 1974.
46 Keller 1988: 55.
47 Aalen 2011: 135.
48 Markakis 2011: 172–73.
49 Markakis 2011: 186.
50 Markakis 2011: 186.
51 Haustein and Østebø 2011: 756.

52 Abbink 2014: 348.
53 Haustein and Østebø 2011: 756; Markakis 2011: 187.
54 Haustein and Østebø 2011: 769n23.
55 Engedayehu 2014: 120.
56 Markakis 2011: 187.
57 Haustein and Østebø 2011: 756.
58 Markakis 2011: 230; Marcus 2002: 231–32.
59 Abbink 2014: 348.
60 Haustein and Østebø 2011: 756.
61 Abbink 2014: 349.
62 Haustein and Østebø 2011: 756.
63 Chaillot 2005: 429; Loubser 2002: 385.
64 Abbink 2014: 348.
65 For the initial outline of this thesis, see https://www.siitube.com/dr-abiy-ahmed-phd-proposal_d05cd47bf.html.
66 Haustein and Østebø 2011: 760.
67 Engedayehu 2014: 121–22.
68 Not Princeton University, as Haustein and Østebø (2011: 760) suggest.
69 Haustein and Østebø 2011: 760.
70 Haustein and Østebø 2011: 769n23.
71 Engedayehu 2014: 120.
72 Engedayehu 2014: 119.
73 Engedayehu 2014: 124–25.
74 Haustein and Østebø 2011: 760–61.
75 See http://www.tadias.com/08/01/2018/abune-merkorios-ethiopias-4th-patriarch-returns-after-27-years-in-exile/ (accessed August 5, 2018).
76 Personal communication from Daniel Assefa in Addis Ababa, August 5, 2018.

Chapter 5: Intellectual and Literary Traditions

1 Isaac 2012: 234.
2 Isaac 2012: 231.
3 See Stuckenbruck 2013: 16–20.
4 Judith McKenzie in McKenzie and Watson 2016: 1.
5 Watson in McKenzie and Watson, 2016: 145.
6 Watson in McKenzie and Watson, 2016: 147.
7 Watson in McKenzie and Watson, 2016: 149.
8 Watson in McKenzie and Watson, 2016: 169.
9 Colin 2017: IX.
10 See Bausi and Camplani 2016. They have named the Ge'ez text of the history of the Patriarchate, and a Latin version covering similar material, *Historia Episcopatus Alexandriae*.

11 This is document 34 in the thirty-six documents contained in the manuscript, as rearranged into its probable original order (Bausi and Camplani 2016: 251).
12 For the text, see http://www.seanmultimedia.com/Pie_Pachomius_Rule_1.html.
13 Isaac 2012: 241.
14 See Negash n.d. (post-1991).
15 Isaac 2012: 242–43. For a discussion of the *Gadla Lalibela*, see Pankhurst and Pankhust 2006.
16 Pankhurst and Pankhurst 2006: 46.
17 Huntingford 1965.
18 Isaac 2012: 243–44.
19 Isaac 2012: 244.
20 Ullendorff 1990: 61 (first quotation) and 1968: 1975 (second quotation).
21 Budge 2013: 58.
22 Budge 2013: 59.
23 Marrassini 2007.
24 Isaac 2012: 245–56. See the translation by E. A. Wallis Budge (2004 [1935]).
25 Isaac 2012: 246–47.
26 Isaac 2012: 247.
27 For the narrative of Alexander, see the description in Mercier 1997: 49–50; and the text itself in Budge 1968 [1896].
28 Isaac 2012: 248–49.
29 Isaac 2012: 250–51.
30 Ullendorff 1990: 143.
31 Isaac 2012: 252–53.
32 For a discussion of this *Gadl*, see Colin 2017: LXII–LXVII, and, for the text, see 38–74.
33 Colin 2017: 62.
34 Isaac 2012: 253.
35 See Colin 2017: XLIX–LVI (discussion) and 6–37 (text of the homily).
36 Ullendorff 1990: 143.
37 Isaac 2012: 257–59.
38 Ullendorff 1990: 141.
39 Isaac 2012: 259.
40 See Ullendorff 1990: 144; and Isaac 2012: 261.
41 Isaac 2012: 262–63.
42 For the text (in Ge'ez) and a French translation, see Donzel 1969.
43 There is an English translation of the text in Levine 1993.
44 Ullendorff 1990: 145.
45 Isaac 2012: 265.
46 Ullendorff 1990: 74; Pankhurst 2001: 95.
47 Ullendorff 1990: 145–46.

48 Isaac 2012: 266–67.
49 There is an English translation by Charles (1913). He was reliant on the manuscript as published with a French translation by Zoternberg in 1883.
50 For an online translation of this work, see http://www.ethiopianorthodox.org/biography/01thelawofkings.pdf.
51 Domnic 2010: 1–2.
52 Isaac 2012: 273–74.
53 Edemariam 2018: 115.
54 Levine 1972 [1965]: 42; Isaac 2012: 261.
55 Levine 1972 [1965]: 8.
56 Chaillot 2002: 87.
57 Binns 2013: 40.
58 Levine 1972 [1965]: 5; Binns 2013: 41.
59 See this explanation in a short 2003 essay on *qene* by G. E. Gorfu (http://www.meskot.com/qene.htm; accessed April 18, 2018).
60 The expression appears as the title of a book by Donald Levine on tradition and innovation in Ethiopian culture (1972 [1965]).
61 Binns 2013: 42.
62 For this example and the explanations, see Levine 1972 [1965]: 6.
63 Levine 1972 [1965]: 7.
64 Binns 2005: 104.
65 The situation may be changing, however. In March 2017 the rural roads of Tigray Province in northern Ethiopia were filled each morning and afternoon with long lines of uniformed children walking, often for several miles, to school in nearby towns for either the morning or the afternoon teaching shift.
66 Binns 2005: 112.
67 Comment made at a lecture given by Christine Chaillot to the Anglo-Ethiopian Society, on Tuesday, March 15, 2005 (https://anglo-ethiopian.org/publications/articles.php?type=L&reference=publications/articles/2005summer/tradeducationlecture.php; accessed April 17, 2018).
68 Isaac 2012: 92–93.
69 Binns 2005: 110.
70 Binns 2005: 111.
71 Binns 2005: 107.
72 See Chaillot 2002: 83; and Isaac 2012: 93–94.
73 Binns 2005: 105–6.
74 Edemariam 2018: 23.
75 So Isaac 2012: 94. Chaillot (2002: 84) states that to become a deacon or a priest, young boys can go to the school of music (*zema*) or the school of liturgy (*bet qeddase*), although the former is more common. Isaac regards *qeddase* as a subcategory of *zema*.
76 On this material, see Chaillot 2002: 85–87.

77 Binns 2005: 110.
78 Chaillot 2002: 90.
79 Binns 2005: 109.
80 Chaillot 2002: 88.
81 Chaillot 2002: 89.
82 Isaac 2012: 95.
83 Leslau 2010: 195.
84 Isaac 2012: 95.
85 Edemariam 2018: 22.
86 Binns 2005: 110.
87 Roger Cowley published pioneering research into the andemta in the 1970s and 1980s (1972; 1983; 1988), and scholars such as Daniel Assefa (2017) and Ralph Lee (2014; 2017) have now taken up the baton. Also see the comprehensive monograph by Keon-Sang An (2015).
88 Chaillot 2002: 91–92.
89 Isaac 2012: 97.

Chapter 6: Art, Architecture, and Music

1 On the pigments, see Marx 2010: 91–92.
2 For the organization of this material into eight periods and for many of the details of the discussion, see the website of Jacopo Gnisci, a member of the Hiob Ludolf Centre for Ethiopian Studies at the University of Hamburg, who specializes in art history (https://www.khanacademy.org/humanities/art-africa/east-africa2/ethiopia/a/christian-ethiopian-art; accessed on March 23, 2018).
3 Watson in McKenzie and Watson 2016: 197.
4 McKenzie in McKenzie and Watson 2016: 61–62.
5 See the image on McKenzie and Watson 2016: 182. The image is discussed by Watson (in McKenzie and Watson 2016: 182–85).
6 For the church of Dabra Selam, see Mercier 2001: 46–47.
7 See Munro-Hay 2002: 203–6; and https://upload.wikimedia.org/wikipedia/commons/8/85/Lalibella_Cross.jpg.
8 Mercier 2001: 50–51.
9 For an investigation of his Marian icons, see Heldman 1994.
10 Mercier 2001: 51–56.
11 Mercier 2001: 56–57.
12 Mercier 2001: 57–59.
13 Mercier 2001: 57–59.
14 Mercier 2001: 60–62.
15 Mercier 2001: 64–65.
16 Mercier 2001: 62–63.

17 Johnson 2011: 53.
18 Mercier 2001: 64.
19 Mercier 2001: 66.
20 Mercier 2001: 66.
21 Mercier 2001: 66.
22 On this subject, see Balicka-Witakowska 2010.
23 This paragraph is based on Chaillot 2002: 130–31.
24 Munro-Hay 2002: 145.
25 Mercier 2001: 45.
26 Mercier 1997: 46.
27 Mann 2001: 118.
28 Mercier 1997: 41.
29 Mercier 1997: 48.
30 Kirsten Windmuller-Luna, https://www.metmuseum.org/toah/hd/heal/hd_heal.htm (accessed March 21, 2018). This prayer begins: "Net of Solomon that he extended over the demons like a net over the fishes of the sea, saying Sadqael, Adnael, Remel" (Mercier 1997: 48).
31 For the narrative of Alexander, see the description in Mercier 1997: 49–50; and the text itself in Budge 1968.
32 Mercier 1997: 79. Phanuel does not, surprisingly, figure among the seven archangels listed with their functions in 1 Enoch 20:1-8, but he is mentioned later in the text, in fourth place (after Michael, Raphael, and Gabriel in 1 Enoch 40:7 and 9), as "driving away satans" and as being "in charge of the repentance to hope of those who inherit everlasting life."
33 Mercier 1997: 94–95.
34 Mercier 1997: 79.
35 The discussion in this section is largely dependent on Johnson 2011.
36 See the discussion of his work in Silverman 1999.
37 Johnson 2011: 102.
38 Johnson 2011: 177.
39 In this section I have relied especially on Chaillot 2002; Appleyard 2007; Munro-Hay 2002; Ullendorf 1990; and my own personal observations.
40 Phillipson 2009: 37–38.
41 Phillipson 2009: 39.
42 Phillipson 2009: 63–64.
43 Phillipson 2009: 123–24.
44 Phillipson 2009: 179–81.
45 Mercier 2001: 48.
46 See Appleyard 2007: 134.
47 See the discussion of this church in Phillipson 2009: 160–65.
48 Munro-Hay 2002: 50.
49 See Antohin 2014.
50 Ullendorf 1990: 105.

51. See the image on the cover of Esler 2017b and the discussion of the religious and social function of such an image on pp. 1–5.
52. The Hebrew for this expression is *beth-lehem*.
53. This story is similar to that of the Scottish hero Robert the Bruce, who learned perseverance from watching a spider repeatedly trying to swing from one roof beam to another.
54. For a good account of Yared within Ethiopian tradition, see http://www.st-gabriel.org/Styared/gab_yared_music.htm (accessed July 15, 2018), based on Belai Giday, *Ethiopian Civilization*.
55. See the Ethiopian Orthodox Church website: http://www.ethiopianorthodox.org/english/church/music.html (accessed July 15, 2018).
56. Ullendorff 1990: 167.
57. Binns 2017: 172–73.
58. Binns 2017: 172.
59. The first piece is at https://www.youtube.com/watch?v=KE-ycqs0gPc; and the second is at https://www.youtube.com/watch?v=BnSUJffsRLA (accessed on July 15, 2018).
60. Kaufman-Shelemay 2003.
61. Binns 2013: 39–40.
62. Kaufman-Shelemay 2003.

Chapter 7: Theology

1. Isaac 2012: 27 and 41.
2. Isaac 2012: 30.
3. Isaac 2012: 29. But the monk is allowed to talk to people through a gate (as the author has personally observed)!
4. Isaac 2012: 29.
5. Chaillot 2002: 102–3; Munro-Hay 2002: 49–50.
6. Isaac 2012: 28–29.
7. Boylston 2018: 25.
8. See Antohin 2014.
9. Eliade 1959: 26.
10. Eliade 1959: 38–40.
11. Douglas 1966: 124.
12. Blackman 1983: 32–34.
13. For the Ge'ez text and a French translation, see Caquot 1955.
14. Boylston 2018: 54.
15. I have depended heavily on Chaillot 2002: 114–25 in relation to the calendar and festivals.
16. Ullendorff 1990: 101.
17. Boylston 2018: 37.
18. See Fritsch 1999: 94; and Chaillot 2002: 116.

19 See Fritsch 1999: 95.
20 Boylston 2018: 40.
21 See the details in Chaillot 2002: 116–17.
22 Boylston 2018: 42.
23 Boylston 2018: 8.
24 Ullendorff 1990: 102.
25 They are listed by Boylston 2018: 55n1, who is reliant on Fritsch 2001. For a shorter treatment, see Fritsch 1999: 107–11.
26 Boylston 2018: 43–44.
27 For this section I have drawn on Fritsch 1999: 78–80; Chaillot 2002: 104–9; and two Orthodox websites: http://www.ethiopianorthodox.org/english/church/divineliturgydoc.html; and http://www.ethiopianorthodox.org/english/ethiopian/worship.html.
28 Boylston 2018: 5.
29 The text forms part of the *Mashafa Kidan*, dating from the fifth century CE (Fritsch 1999: 79n26).
30 Pedersen 1999: 204–5.
31 Isaac 2012: 28.
32 Pedersen 1999: 206.
33 Pedersen 1999: 207–8.
34 Pedersen 1999: 205–6.
35 Isaac 2012: 37.
36 Isaac 2012: 37–38. The other explanation is that these words have a Jewish rather than a Jewish-Christian provenance (ibid.).
37 Chaillot 2002: 64–65.
38 Eshete 2009: 58–59.
39 Chaillot 2002: 66–67.
40 Schaefer 2007.
41 Binns 2017: 241.
42 Binns 2017: 241–242.
43 For details of their publications, see Chaillot 2002: 68.
44 See https://eotcmk.org/e/.
45 Binns 2017: 242–43.
46 Eshete 2009: 313.
47 Fantini 2015: 142 (note that Fantini transliterates the name of the organization as *Mahbere Qiddusan*, but I have modified it as here for the sake of consistency).
48 Chaillot 2002: 53–54.
49 An 2015: 158.
50 An provides detailed analysis of some of the eighty sermons he attended in 2008 and 2009 (2015: 157–217).
51 Personal communication, Daniel Assefa (August 5, 2018).
52 Haustein 2014: 120.

53 See the church's website: http://www.ethiopiaemmanuel.org/About-Us (accessed August 15, 2018).
54 Barrett 1968.
55 Barrett 1968: 183.
56 Barrett 1968: 219.
57 See Fabian 1994.
58 Haustein 2014: 120.

Chapter 8: Protestantism

1 McFarland 2018d.
2 Berger and Luckmann 1967: 140.
3 Werner Raupp, *Dictionary of African Christian Biography*, https://dacb.org/stories/egypt/heyling-peter/.
4 Eshete 2009: 65–66.
5 Launhardt 2010: 223–24.
6 Binns 2017: 211.
7 Eshete 2009: 66–67.
8 Eshete 2009: 67–69.
9 Eshete 2009: 69–70.
10 Eshete 2009: 70–71.
11 Eshete 2009: 71–72.
12 Eshete 2009: 72–73.
13 Launhardt 2010: 224.
14 Launhardt 2010: 224.
15 Eshete 2009: 75–83.
16 Launhardt 2010: 225.
17 Eshete 2009: 104–5.
18 Eshete 2009: 85–93.
19 Eshete 2009: 93–99.
20 Eshete 2009: 73.
21 Eshete 2009: 99.
22 For an explanation of how this occurred, see Eshete 2013.
23 Eshete 2013: 161.
24 Eshete 2009: 106–16.
25 Eshete 2009: 116–21.
26 For a discussion of these issues, see Eshete 2009: 124–42.
27 See Goodman 1972: 148–52.
28 For a fuller discussion of this subject, see Esler 1994: 37–51.
29 See the admirable discussion in Dunn 1970.
30 Dunn 1970: 225.
31 For this discussion, see Eshete 2009: 147–52.

32 For this material, see Eshete 2009: 152–54 and 164; and Haustein 2011: 14. For a discussion of Chacha Omahe, see Haustein 2011: 69–79.
33 Eshete 2009: 161–62. Haustein offers a more critical account of the transition from the first residence to the second (2011: 118–25).
34 Eshete 2009: 163–65.
35 Haustein 2011: 14.
36 Eshete 2009: 154–56. Also see Haustein 2011: 92–99.
37 On the Nazareth movement, see Eshete 2009: 156–57; and Haustein 2011: 108–18.
38 On the baptism of the Spirit being endogenous, see Haustein 2011: 111.
39 For the material in this paragraph, see Eshete 2009: 169–75; and Haustein 2011: 124–42.
40 Fantini 2015: 129.
41 Eshete 2009: 175.
42 Haustein 2011: 152. He notes that there are other versions of what Theophilos said at the time, but their purport is similar to this.
43 Eshete 2009: 175–86.
44 Elliott 2000: 793.
45 The largest church in Addis Ababa is that of the Mulu Wengel Church, at Ketena Hulett, which seats five thousand worshippers (Binns 2017: 223).
46 Eshete 2009: 188.
47 Fantini 2015: 132–33.
48 Freeman 2013: 4–5 (London School of Economics online version).
49 Freeman 2013: 6–10 (London School of Economics online version).
50 Haustein 2011: 189.
51 Eshete 2009: 215–16.
52 For Qes Gudina Tumsa, see Eshete 2009: 225–30; and Haustein 2011: 193–94.
53 Haustein 2011: 199.
54 Eshete 2009: 219.
55 Eshete 2009: 253–72.
56 Personal communication, Girma Mohammed (August 13, 2018).
57 Haustein and Fantini 2013: 150.
58 Eshete 2009: 301–2.
59 Haustein and Fantini 2013: 155.
60 Eshete 2009: 303.
61 See Haustein 2011: 219–26.
62 Fantini 2015: 128.
63 Binns 2017: 223.
64 Fantini 2015: 125–28.
65 Binns 2017: 225.
66 See Girma 2018a: 7–8 (online version).
67 Personal communication, Girma Mohammed (August 13, 2018).

68 Personal communication, Girma Mohammed (August 13, 2018).
69 Eshete 2009: 303.
70 Personal communication, Girma Mohammed (August 13, 2018).
71 Eshete 2009: 304.
72 Dewel 2016: 10–11.
73 Dewel 2016: 10–11.
74 Haustein 2014: 119.
75 Haustein 2014: 120.
76 Haustein 2014: 123.
77 See http://www.ecfethiopia.org/history.htm (accessed August 17, 2018).
78 Haustein 2014: 120–21.
79 See https://etcollege.org/?page_id=22 (accessed August 16, 2018).
80 See https://egst.edu.et/?page_id=1762 (accessed August 16, 2018).

Chapter 9: Catholicism

1 The Ethiopian Catholic Church Directory for 2014, cited in Ethiopian Catholic Secretariat, Pastoral Activities Commission 2015: 78–79.
2 See https://www.catholicsandcultures.org/ethiopia (accessed August 31, 2018).
3 Haustein and Østebø 2011: 765.
4 See http://www.cnewa.org/source-images/Roberson-eastcath-statistics/eastcatholic-stat17.pdf (accessed July 4, 2018).
5 McFarland 2018d. Opinions differ on the number of Christians in Eritrea, and some suggest that Protestants could represent as much as 2 percent of the total. It should be noted here that most Protestant churches in Eritrea have been subject to repression in recent decades.
6 Abuna Mussie, OFM, Cap. Eparch of Emdebir, Conference of Major Religious Superiors (of Ethiopia) (2007: 100).
7 See https://press.vatican.va/content/salastampa/en/documentation/cardinali_biografie/cardinali_bio_souraphiel_bd.html (accessed July 4, 2018).
8 For a detailed history of Catholicism in Ethiopia since the sixteenth century, see Alberto 2013.
9 Ott 1910.
10 Agenzia Fides 2008: 6, citing from *La Missione dei Minori Cappuccini in Eritrea* (1894–1952) (Rome, 1953), 363.
11 For a modern version of the Eastern Rite Catholic Mass in Ethiopia, see the text at https://www.catholicsandcultures.org/sites/default/files/documents/ethiopian_rite.pdf.
12 Núñez 2015: 68.
13 Massaia 1883–1895.

14 Núñez 2015: 68.
15 Teklehaymanot et al. 2003: 700–701.
16 Núñez 2015: 68.
17 Núñez 2015: 69–70.
18 Mussie 2007: 98–99.
19 Mussie 2007: 100.
20 Agenzia Fides 2008.
21 Berga 2015: 49.
22 Mussie 2007: 100.
23 Roberson 2018.
24 See https://www.catholicsandcultures.org/ethiopia/worship (accessed August 19, 2018).
25 See https://www.catholicsandcultures.org/ethiopia/worship (accessed August 19, 2018).
26 See https://www.catholicsandcultures.org/ethiopia-catholicism-shaped-orthodoxy-ancient-legacies (accessed August 19, 2018).
27 John Paul II 1997: paragraph 5.
28 Mussie 2007: 93.
29 Mussie 2007: 95.
30 Mussie 2007: 97.
31 Mussie 2007: 101.
32 Mussie 2007: 102.
33 Núñez 2015: 72; Berga 2015: 6.
34 Núñez 2015: 72.
35 Berga 2015: 49. In his encyclical *Ut unum sint* of May 25, 1995, Pope John Paul II repeated one of his favorite expressions in relation to coexistence of the churches of the East and the West that "the Church must breathe with her two lungs" (paragraph 54).
36 Personal communications from Daniel Assefa, August 2018.
37 Ethiopian Catholic Secretariat, Pastoral Activities Commission 2015: 78–79.
38 Núñez 2015: 70 (citing the Catholic Church Directory of 2014).
39 John Paul II 1997: paragraph 4.
40 Mussie 2007: 101.
41 Ethiopian Catholic Secretariat, Pastoral Activities Commission 2015: 103–4.
42 Ethiopian Catholic Secretariat, Pastoral Activities Commission 2015: 102.
43 For example, Alberto 2013.
44 Núñez 2015: 71.
45 Berga 2015: 50.

Chapter 10: The Future of Christianity in Ethiopia

1 Haustein and Østebø 2011.
2 Shinn 2014.

3   Shinn 2014.
4   Shinn 2014.
5   Abbink 2014: 352.
6   Personal communication, Girma Mohammed (August 13, 2018).
7   Girma 2018b.
8   Girma 2018c.
9   Girma 2018c.
10 Quoted at https://ecadforum.com/2018/07/20/ethiopia-discourse-on-the-concept-of-medemer/ (accessed August 13, 2018).
11 See Tajfel 1978 for the key ideas in social identity theory. For an early overview, see Hogg and Abrams 1988; and, for a recent summary, see Esler 2014.
12 See Gaertner et al. 1993.
13 The whole story is inspiringly told in the film *Invictus* (2009), based on John Carlin's 2008 book *Playing the Enemy: Nelson Mandela and the Game That Made a Nation*.
14 Berga et al. 2015: 123.
15 Berga et al. 2015: 123.
16 See WorldWatchMonitor.org, for August 2017 (https://www.worldwatchmonitor.org/2017/08/ethiopia-church-attacked-told-close-member-arrested-inciting-religious-clashes/; accessed August 4, 2018).
17 See An 2015: 162–66, discussing a recent Orthodox sermon on the ark of the covenant, where the preacher aimed to defend the tabots in Ethiopian churches against the Protestant claim that they are idols.
18 Loubser 2002: 388–89.
19 Fantini 2015: 141.
20 Fantini 2015: 141.
21 This is a central question in Berger and Luckmann 1967.
22 Fantini 2015: 142.
23 Goodman 1972: 95–96.
24 Berga et al. 2015: 121.
25 Fantini 2015: 142.
26 Berga et al. 2015: 122.
27 Personal communication, Girma Mohammed (August 17, 2018).
28 See https://www.theguardian.com/world/2018/jul/15/ethiopia-eritrea-abiy-ahmed-charismatic-young-peacemaker (accessed August 5, 2018).
29 See https://www.news24.com/Africa/News/ethiopias-torn-orthodox-church-reunites-after-27-years-20180727 (accessed August 5, 2018).
30 Berga et al. 2015: 128.
31 Ahmed 2007: 207.
32 Ahmed 2007: 202.
33 Ahmed and Gori 2007: 199.
34 Berga et al. 2015: 130.
35 See Girma 2017.

36 Østebø 2017.
37 Abbink 2014: 358.
38 Berga et al. 2015: 130.
39 See Weldemariam 2012.
40 Shinn 2014.
41 Abbink 2014: 258.
42 Fantaw 2012.
43 For these details, see Abbink 2014: 351 and the evidence he cites.
44 Anonymous 2015: 135, an author associated with the Roman Catholic Archdiocese of Addis Ababa.

Bibliography

Aalen, Lovise. 2011. *The Politics of Ethnicity in Ethiopia: Actors, Power and Mobilisation under Ethnic Federalism*. African Social Studies. Leiden: Brill.

Abbink, Jon. 2011. "Religion in Public Spaces: Emerging Christian-Muslim Polemics in Ethiopia." *African Affairs* 110, no. 439: 253–74. https://research.vu.nl/ws/portalfiles/portal/2979285/274014.pdf.

———. 2014. "Religious Freedom and the Political Order: The Ethiopian 'Secular' State and the Containment of Muslim Identity Politics." *Journal of East African Studies* 3:346–65.

Agenzia Fides (Agenzia della Congregazione per l'Evangelizzazione dei Populi). 2008. "The Catholic Church in Ethiopia: A Brief History of Evangelisation." In *Dossier by Fides News Service*. May 3, 2008. Rome: Vatican.

Ahmed, Hussein. 2007. "History of Islam in Ethiopia." In EA 3:202–8.

Ahmed, Hussein, and Alessandro Gori. 2007. "Islam." In EA 3:198–202.

Alberto, Antonios, OFM Cap. 2013. *A Modern and Contemporary History of the Catholic Church in Ethiopia (16th–20th Centuries)*. Ethiopian Review of Cultures 6. Addis Ababa: Capuchin Franciscan Institute of Philosophy and Theology.

An, Keon-Sang. 2015. *An Ethiopian Reading of the Bible: Biblical Interpretation of the Ethiopian Orthodox Tewahido Church*. African Society of Missiology, Monograph Series. Eugene, Ore.: Wipf and Stock.

Ancel, Stéphane, and Éloi Ficquet. 2015. "The Ethiopian Orthodox Tewahedo Church and the Challenges of Modernity." In Prunier and Ficquet 2015, 63–91.

Anfray, Francis, André Caquot, and Pierre Nautin. 1970. "Une nouvelle inscription grecque d'Ezana, roi d'Axoum." *Journal des Savants* 4:260–74.

Antohin, Alexandra Sellassie. 2014. "Expressions of Sacred Promise: Ritual and Devotion in Ethiopian Orthodox Praxis." PhD diss., University College London, London.

Anonymous. 2015. "Additional Information." In Ethiopian Catholic Secretariat, Pastoral Activities Commission 2015, 132–35.

Appleyard, David. 2007. "Ethiopian Christianity." In Parry 2007, 117–36.

Assefa, Daniel. 2017. "The Animal Apocalypse (1 Enoch 85-90) in the Light of Ethiopian Traditional Commentary: The Case of 'Open' and 'Closed' Eyes." In Esler 2017a, 61–69.

Balicka-Witakowska, Ewa. 2010. "Painting: II. Main Subjects of Ethiopian Painting." In EA 4:92–94.

Barrett, D. B. 1968. *Schism and Renewal in Africa: An Analysis of Six Thousand Contemporary Religious Movements*. Nairobi: Oxford University Press.

Basset, René, ed. and trans. 1897–1901. *Histoire de la conquête de l'Abyssinie (XVI siècle), par Chihab ed-Din Ahmed ben Abd el-Qader surnommé Arab-Faqih*. Paris: Ernest Leroux.

Bausi, Alessandro, and Alberto Camplani. 2016. "The History of the Episcopate of Alexandria (HEpA): Editio Minor of the Fragments Preserved in the Aksumite Collection and in the Codex Veronensis LX (58)." *Adamantius: Journal of the Italian Research Group on "Origen and the Alexandrian Tradition"* 22:249–302.

Bausi, Alessandro, in cooperation with Siegbert Uhlig. 2014. *Encyclopaedia Aethiopica*. Vol. 5, *Y–Z*, addenda, index. Wiesbaden: Harrassowitz Verlag.

BeDuhn, Jason David. 2017. "Manichaeism." In Esler 2017b, 921–39.

Beckingham, C. F., and G. W. B. Huntingford. 1961. *The Prester John of the Indies: A True Relation of the Lands of the Prester John, Being the Narrative of the Portuguese Embassy to Ethiopia in 1520, the Translation of Lord*

Stanley of Alderley (1881); Revised and Edited with Additional Material. 2 vols. Cambridge: Hakluyt Society.

Berga, Petros, Fr. 2015. "Which Mission: Today for the Catholic Church in Ethiopia: A Diocesan Perspective." In Comboni Missionary Sisters et al. 2015, 46–53.

Berga, Petros, Fr., Fr. Worku Demeke, and Fr. Telebirhan Yematay. 2015. "Ecumenical Dialogue in Ethiopia." Ethiopian Catholic Secretariat, Pastoral Activities Commission 2015: 121–31.

Berger, Peter L., and Luckmann, Thomas. 1967. *The Social Construction of Reality: A Treatise in the Sociology of Knowledge*. Garden City, N.Y.: Doubleday.

Bernand, Etienne, et al. 1991–2000. *Recueil des inscriptions de l'Ethiopie des périodes pré-axoumite et axoumite*. 3 vols. Paris: Academie des Inscriptions et Belles-Lettres.

Biasio, Elisabeth. 2013. "Ethiopia and Eritrea." Oxford Art Online. Oxford: Oxford University Press.

Binns, John. 2005. "Theological Education in the Ethiopian Orthodox Church." *International Journal for the Study of the Christian Church* 2:103–13.

———. 2013. "Out of Ethiopia—A New Way of Doing Theology." *International Journal for the Study of the Christian Church* 13:33–47.

———. 2017. *The Orthodox Church of Ethiopia—A History*. London: I. B. Tauris.

Boavida, Isabel, Hervé Pennec, and Manuel João Ramos, eds. 2011. *Pedro Páez's History of Ethiopia, 1622*. 2 vols. Translated by Christopher J. Tribe. London: Ashgate for the Hakluyt Society.

Boylston, Tom. 2018. *The Stranger at the Feast: Prohibition and Mediation in an Orthodox Christian Community*. Oakland: University of California Press.

Breyer, Francis. 2007. "Kush." In Uhlig 2007: 458–60.

Budge, E. A. Wallis. 1928. *The Book of the Saints of the Ethiopian Church: A Translation of the Ethiopic Synaxarium; Made from the Manuscripts Oriental 660 and 661 in the British Museum*. Cambridge: Cambridge University Press.

———. 1968 [1896]. *The Life and Exploits of Alexander the Great*. New York: Benjamin Blom. Original 1896 publication in London by C. J. Clay.

———. 2004 [1935]. *The Book of the Mysteries of the Heaven and Earth: And Other Works of Bakhayla Mikael (Zosimas)*. Lake Worth, Fla.: Ibis Press.

———. 2013. *The Kebra Nagast*. Reprint of the 1922 translation by Sir E. A. Wallis Budge. Rookhope, UK: Aziloth Books.

Busorf, Dirk. 2010. "Slave Raiding in the 19th Century." EA 4:676–78.
Caquot, André. 1955. "L'homélie en l'honneur de l'archange Ouriel (Dersāna Urā'ēl)." *Annales d'Ethiopie* 1:61–88.
Caraman, Philip. 1985. *The Lost Empire: The Story of the Jesuits in Ethiopia 1555–1634.* London: Sidgwick and Jackson.
Casson, Lionel. 1989. *The Periplus Maris Erythraei: Text, with Introduction, Translation, and Commentary.* Princeton, N.J.: Princeton University Press.
Chaillot, Christine. 2002. *The Ethiopian Orthodox Tewahedo Church Tradition: A Brief Introduction to Its Life and Tradition.* Paris: Inter-Orthodox Dialogue.
———. 2005. "Ethiopian Orthodox (Tewahedo) Church: Church Organization Today." EA 2:427–32.
Charles, R. H. 1913. *The Chronicle of John, Bishop of Nikiu: Translated from Zotenberg's Ethiopic Text.* London: Williams & Norgate.
Cohen, John M. 1974. "Peasants and Feudalism in Africa: The Case of Ethiopia." *Canadian Journal of African Studies* 8:155–57.
Colin, Gérard. 2017. *Saints Fondateurs du Christianisme Éthiopien: Frumentius, Garimā, Takla-Hāymānot et Ēwosṭātēwos: Introduction, traduction et notes, avec la collaboration pour l'introduction de Christian Julien Robin et Marie-Laure Derat; Bibliotheque de l'Orient chrétien.* Paris: Les Belles Lettres.
Comboni Missionary Sisters and Comboni Missionaries. 2015. *Evangelizing in Time: New Models of Mission in the Ethiopian Context.* Addis Ababa.
Conference of Major Religious Superiors (of Ethiopia). 2007. *Proceedings of the Symposium, 4th–11th February 2007.* Addis Ababa: n.p.
Cowley, Roger W. 1972. "The Beginnings of the Andem Commentary Tradition." *Journal of Ethiopian Studies* 10:1–16.
———. 1983. *The Traditional Interpretation of the Apocalypse of John in the Ethiopian Orthodox Church.* University of Cambridge Oriental Publications 33. Cambridge: Cambridge University Press.
———. 1988. *Ethiopian Biblical Interpretation: A Study in Exegetical Tradition and Hermeneutics.* University of Cambridge Oriental Publications 38. Cambridge: Cambridge University Press.
Derat, Marie-Laure. 2007. "Lalibäla." In EA 477–80.
———. 2017. "Le développement à l'époque médiévale: Les predications de Takla- Hāymānot et d'Ēwosṭātēwos et le royaume chrétien d'Éthiopie (XIIIe–XVe siècle)." In Colin 2017, LVI–LXXXIX.
Dewel, Serge. 2016. "The Charismatic Movement in Ethiopia: Historical and Social Background for an Identity Problematic." HAL

Archives-Ouvertes. Accessed August 15, 2018. https://hal-inalco.archives-ouvertes.fr/hal-01315593.

Domnic, Negussie Andre. 2010. *The Fetha Nagast and Its Ecclesiology: Implications in Ethiopian Catholic Church Today*. European University Studies. Bern: Peter Lang.

Donzel, E. J. van. 1969. *Ēnbāqom, Anqaṣa Amin (La Porte de las Foi): Introduction, texte critique, traduction*. Leiden: E. J. Brill.

Douglas, Mary. 1966. *Purity and Danger: An Analysis of Concepts of Pollution and Taboo*. London: Routledge & Kegan Paul.

Dunn, James D. G. 1970. *Baptism in the Holy Spirit: A Re-examination of the New Testament Teaching on the Gift of the Spirit in Relation to Pentecostalism Today*. London: SCM Press.

Edemariam, Aida. 2018. *The Wife's Tale: A Personal History*. London: 4th Estate.

Eliade, Mircea. 1959. *The Sacred and the Profane: The Nature of Religion*. New York: Harcourt Brace Jovanovich.

Elliott, John H. 2000. *1 Peter: A New Translation with Introduction and Commentary*. AB 37B. New York: Doubleday.

Engedayehu, Walle. 2014. "The Ethiopian Orthodox Tewahedo Church in the Diaspora: Expansion in the Midst of Division." *African Social Science Review* 6:115–33.

Eshete, Tibebe. 2009. *The Evangelical Movement in Ethiopia: Resistance and Resilience*. Waco, Tex.: Baylor University Press.

———. 2013. "The Early Charismatic Movement in the Kale Heywet Church." *PentecoStudies* 12:161–82.

Esler, Philip F. 1994. *The First Christians in Their Social Worlds: Social-Scientific Approaches to New Testament Interpretation*. London: Routledge.

———. 2014. "An Outline of Social Identity Theory." In *T&T Handbook to Social Identity in the New Testament*, ed. J. Brian Tucker and A. Baker Coleman, 13–40. London: Bloomsbury T&T Clark.

———, ed. 2017a. *The Blessing of Enoch: 1 Enoch and Contemporary Theology*. Eugene, Ore.: Cascade Books.

———, ed. 2017b. *The Early Christian World*. 2nd ed. London: Routledge.

Ethiopian Catholic Secretariat, Pastoral Activities Commission. 2015. *"Get Up and Eat for the Journey Will Be Too Long for You": Proceedings of the Symposium Held to Mark the Golden Jubilee of the Catholic Bishops' Conference of Ethiopia (1964–2014)*. Addis Ababa: n.p.

Fabian, Johannes. 1994. "Jamaa: A Charismatic Movement Revisited." In *Religion in Africa: Experience and Expression*, ed. Walter E. A. van Beek and Dennis L. Thomson, 257–74. London: James Currey and Heinemann.

Fantaw, Alemayehu. 2012. "Ethiopia: Government Increasingly Intolerant of Islam Risks Radicalizing Muslims." *African Arguments Insiders' Newsletter*, November 16, 2012.

Fantini, Emanuele. 2015. "Go Pente! The Charismatic Renewal of the Evangelical Movement in Ethiopia." In Prunier and Ficquet 2015, 123–46.

Fattovich, Rodolfo. 2010. "The Development of Ancient States in the Northern Horn of Africa, c. 3000 BC–AD 1000: An Archaeological Outline." *Journal of World Prehistory* 23:145–75.

Fiaccadori, Gianfranco. 2007. "Kaleb." EA 3:329–32.

———. 2014. "Zagwe." EA 4:107–14.

Finneran, Niall. 2007. "Lalibäla." EA 3:482–84.

Fogg, Sam, and Hosking David. 2001. *Ethiopian Art*. London: Sam Fogg Rare Books and Manuscripts.

Freeman, Dena. 2013. "Pentecostalism in a Rural Context: Dynamics of Religion and Development in Southwest Ethiopia." *PentecoStudies: An Interdisciplinary Journal for Research on the Pentecostal and Charismatic Movements* 12:231–49. https://journals.equinoxpub.com/index.php/PENT/article/view/16952.

Fritsch, Emmanuel, C.S.Sp. 1999. "The Liturgical Year and the Lectionary of the Ethiopian Church." *Warszawskie Studia Teologiczne* 12:71–16.

———. 2001. "The Liturgical Year of the Ethiopian Church." Special issue, *Ethiopian Review of Cultures* 9/10.

Gaertner, S. L., J. F. Dovidio, P. A. Anastasio, B. A. Bachman, and M. C. Rust. 1993. "The Common Ingroup Identity Model: Recategorization and the Reduction of Intergroup Bias." *European Review of Social Psychology* 4:1–26.

Gascon, Alain. 2005. "Geography." In Uhlig 2005, 749–52.

Girma, Mohammed. 2017. *Living Together: The Implications of Christians and Muslims Sharing Territory: Muslim-Christian Relations in Ethiopia; Exploring the Price Tag*. Research Briefings No. 9. Oxford: Centre for Muslim-Christian Studies.

———. 2018a. "Religion, Politics and the Dilemma of Modernising Ethiopia." *HTS Teologiese Studies/Theological Studies* 74.

———. 2018b. "The Promises and Challenges of 'መደመር' (Medemer)." *Gobena Street*, June 30, 2018. http://www.gobenastreet.com/2018/06/30/the-promises-and-challenges-of-መደመር-medemer/.

———. 2018c. "Ethiopia: A Nation in Need of a New Story." *African Arguments Insiders' Newsletter*. Accessed August 16, 2018. http://africanarguments.org/2018/04/18/ethiopia-a-nation-in-need-of-a-new-story-abiy-ahmed-ethiopiawinet/.

Goehring, James. 2017. "Pachomius the Great." In *The Early Christian World*, 2nd ed, ed. Philip F. Esler, 1021–35. London: Routledge.

Goodman, Felicitas D. 1972. *Speaking in Tongues: A Cross-Cultural Study of Glossolalia*. Chicago: University of Chicago Press.

Gorfu, Gebre Eyasus. 2003. "A Brief Introduction to Qene." http://www.meskot.com/qene.htm.

Hahn, Wolfgang. 1999. "Symbols of Pagan and Christian Worship in Aksumite Coins: Remarks to the History of Religions in Ethiopia as Documented by Its Coinage." In Nagel and Scholz 1999, 431–54.

———. 2003. "Coinage." In Uhlig 2003, 766–70.

Haustein, Jörg. 2011. *Writing Religious History: The Historiography of Ethiopian Pentecostalism*. Wiesbaden: Harrassowitz Verlag.

———. 2014. "Pentecostal and Charismatic Christianity in Ethiopia: A Historical Introduction to a Largely Unexplored Movement." In *Multidisciplinary Views on the Horn of Africa: Festschrift in Honour of Rainer Voigt's 70th Birthday*. Studien zum Horn von Africa 1, ed. Hatem Elliesie, 109–27. Cologne: Rüdiger Köppe.

Haustein, Jörg, and Emanuele Fantini. 2013. "Introduction: The Ethiopian Pentecostal Movement—History, Identity and Current Socio-political Dynamics." *PentecoStudies* 12:150–61.

Haustein, Jörg, and Terje Østebø. 2011. "EPRDF's Revolutionary Democracy and Religious Plurality: Islam and Christianity in Post-Derg Ethiopia." *Journal of Eastern African Studies* 5:755–72.

Heldman, Marilyn E. 1994. *The Marian Icons of the Painter Fre Seyon: A Study in Fifteenth Century Ethiopian Art, Patronage, and Spirituality*. Dissertationen zur Kunstgeschichte. Wiesbaden: Harrassowitz Verlag.

———. 2007. "The Churches of Lalibäla." EA 3:484–89.

Henze, Paul. 2000. *Layers of Time: A History of Ethiopia*. New York: Palgrave.

Hogg, Michael A., and Dominic Abrams. 1988. *Social Identifications: A Social Psychology of Intergroup Relations and Group Processes*. London: Routledge.

Horowitz, Deborah E., ed. 2001. *Ethiopian Art: The Walters Art Museum*. Lingfield, UK: Third Millennium.

Huntingford, G. W. B., trans. and ed. 1965. *The Glorious Victories of Amda Seyon, King of Ethiopia*. Oxford: Clarendon Press.

Isaac, Ephraim. 2012. *The Ethiopian Orthodox Täwahïdo Church*. Trenton, N.J.: Red Sea Press.

John Paul II. 1997. "Address of His Holiness Pope John Paul II to the Bishops of Ethiopia on Their '*Ad Limina Apostolorum*' Visit." Libreria Editrice Vaticana. Accessed July 2, 2018. https://w2.vatican.va/content/john-paul-ii/en/speeches/1997/september/documents/hf_jp-ii_spe_19970912_ad-limina-etiopia.html.

Johnson, Edwin Hamilton. 2011. "Patronage and the Theological Integrity of Ethiopian Sacred Paintings in Present Day Addis Ababa." PhD diss., University of London.

Kaplan, Steven. 1992. *The Beta Israel (Falasha) in Ethiopia: From Earliest Times to the Twentieth Century*. New York: New York University Press.

———. 2003. "Beta Israel." EA 1:552–59.

———. 2007. "Lent." EA 3:545–47.

———. 2010. "Solomonic Dynasty." EA 4:688–90.

Kaufman-Shelemay, Kay. 2003. "Aqwaqwam." EA 1:293.

Keller, Edmond J. 1988. *Revolutionary Ethiopia: From Empire to People's Republic*. Bloomington: Indiana University Press.

Launhardt, Johannes. 2010. "Protestantism." EA 4:223–27.

Lee, Ralph. 2014. "The Ethiopic '*Andemta*' Commentary on Ethiopic Enoch 2 (1 Enoch 6-9)." *Journal for the Study of the Pseudepigrapha* 23:179–200.

———. 2017. "The Contemporary Influence of Ethiopian Andemta Traditional Commentary: Examples from the Commentary on 1 Enoch and Other Texts." In Esler 2017a, 44–60.

Leslau, Wolf. 2010. *Concise Dictionary of Ge'ez*. Wiesbaden: Harrassowitz Verlag.

Levine, Donald N. 1972 [1965]. *Wax and Gold: Tradition and Innovation in Ethiopian Culture*. With a new preface. Chicago: University of Chicago Press.

———. ed. 1993. *History of the Galla (Oromo) of Ethiopia: With Ethnology and History of South-West Ethiopia.* Oakland, Calif.: African Sun.

Littmann, Enno, et al. 2005. *Deutsche Aksum-Expedition.* 4 vols. Saarbrücken: Fines Mundi. Originally published 1913, Berlin: Reimer.

Loubser, J. A. 2002. "Two Revolutions Behind: Is the Ethiopian Orthodox Church an Obstacle or Catalyst for Social Development?" *Scriptura* 81:378–90.

Mann, C. Griffith. 2001. "The Role of the Illuminated Manuscript in Ethiopian Culture." In Horowitz 2001, 94–119.

Marcus, Harold G. 2002. *A History of Ethiopia.* Updated ed. Berkeley: University of California Press.

Markakis, John. 2011. *Ethiopia: The Last Two Frontiers.* Woodbridge, UK: James Currey.

Marrassini, Paolo. 2007. "Kebrä Nägäst." EA 3:364–68.

Marx, Annegret. 2010. "Painting: I Technical Aspects of Painting." In EA 4:90–92.

Massaia, Guglielml. 1883–1895. *I miei trentacinque anni di missione nell' alta Etiopia: memorie storiche.* 12 vols. Rome: Società Tipografica A. Manuzio. https://archive.org/details/imieitrentacinqu14mass.

McCrindle, John Watson. 1897. *The Christian Topograpy of Cosmas, an Egyptian Monk.* Number 98. London: Hakluyt Society. https://archive.org/details/christiantopogr00cosmgoog.

McFarland, Michael C., S.J. ca. 2018a. "Ethiopian Catholics' Roots Run Deep for Ge'ez Rite Catholics." Catholics & Cultures. Accessed July 2, 2018. https://www.catholicsandcultures.org/ethiopia/worship.

———. ca. 2018b. "Ethiopia." Catholics & Cultures. Accessed July 2, 2018. https://www.catholicsandcultures.org/ethiopia.

———. ca. 2018c. "Ethiopian Catholic Church." Catholics & Cultures. Accessed July 2, 2018. https://www.catholicsandcultures.org/eastern-catholic-churches/ethiopian-catholic-church.

———. ca. 2018d. "Ethiopia: Catholicism Shaped by Orthodoxy and Ancient Legacies." Catholics & Cultures. Accessed July 2, 2018. https://www.catholicsandcultures.org/ethiopia-catholicism-shaped-orthodoxy-ancient-legacies.

———. ca. 2018e. "Eritrea." Catholics & Cultures. Accessed July 2, 2018. https://www.catholicsandcultures.org/eritrea.

McKenzie, Judith S., and Francis Watson. 2016. *The Garima Gospels: Early Illuminated Gospel Books from Ethiopia.* Manar Al-Athar Monograph 3. Oxford: Manar Al-Athar.

Mercier, Jacques. 1997. *Art That Heals: The Image as Medicine in Ethiopia.* New York: Prestel and the Museum for African Art.
———. 2001. "Ethiopian Art History." In Horowitz 2001, 44–73.
Miran, Jonathan. 2010. "Red Sea Slave Trade in the 19th Century." EA 4:674–76.
Mommsen, Theodor, ed. 1903–09. *Rufin D'Aquilée, Histoire ecclésiastique.* GCS 9, 2. Leipzig: J. C. Hinrichs'sche Buchhandlung.
Munro-Hay, Stuart. 1991. *Aksum: An African Civilisation of Late Antiquity.* Edinburgh: Edinburgh University Press.
———. 2002. *Ethiopia, the Unknown Land: A Cultural and Historical Guide.* London: I. B. Tauris.
———. 2003. "Abeha and Asbeha." In EA 1:45–46.
Munro-Hay, S. C., and Bent Juel-Jensen. 1995. *Aksumite Coinage.* Oxford: Oxford University Press.
Mussie, H. E. Abuna [Eparch of Emdebir]. 2007. "The Future of Religious Life in the Ethiopian Context: Possible Options and Ways Forward." In Conference of Major Religious Superiors (of Ethiopia) 2007, 92–108.
Nagel, Peter, and Piotr O. Scholz, eds. 1999. *Nubica et Aethiopica IV/V. Sonderteil. Äthiopien Gestern und Heute: Akten der 1. Tagung der Orbis Aethiopicus Gesellschaft zur Erhalten und Förderung der Äthiopischen Kultur.* Warzawa: NAZ/PAN.
Nebes, Norbert. 2010. "Die Inscriften aus dem 'Almaqah-Tempel in 'Addi 'Akaweh (Tigray)." *Zeitschrift für Orient-Archäologie* 3:214–37.
Negash, Tekeste. n.d. "The Zagwe Period Re-interpreted: Post Aksumite Ethiopian Culture." Accessed May 14, 2018. http://www.arkeologi.uu.se/digitalAssets/36/c_36108-l_3-k_negashall.pdf.
Núñez, Juan González. 2015. "Reading the Plan of St. Daniel Comboni Today in Ethiopia." In Comboni Missionary Sisters et al. 2015, 66–72.
Østebø, Terje. 2017. "Christianity and Islam in Ethiopia: Orthodoxy, Nationalism and the 'Muslim Other.'" Paper presented at the School of African and Oriental Studies, University of London, March 8, 2017.
Ott, M. 1910. "Blessed Justin de Jacobis." In *The Catholic Encyclopedia.* New York: Robert Appleton. http://www.newadvent.org/cathen/08578a.htm.
Pankhurst, Richard, ed. 1967. *The Ethiopian Royal Chronicles.* Addis Ababa and London: Oxford University Press.
———. 1997. *The Ethiopian Borderlands: Essays in Regional History from Ancient Times to the End of the 18th Century.* Lawrenceville, N.J.: Red Sea Press.

———. 2001. *The Ethiopians: A History*. Oxford: Blackwell.
———. 2005. "Dynasties." EA 2:208–9.
———. 2010. "Slave Trade from Ancient Times to 19th Century." EA 4:673–74.
Pankurst, Rita, and Richard Pankhurst. 2006. "King Lalibela: His Supposed Travels, Tribulations and Achievements." *Annales d'Éthiopie* 22:45–71.
Parry, Ken, ed. 2007. *The Blackwell Companion to Eastern Christianity*. Oxford: Blackwell.
Pedersen, Kirsten Stoffregen. 1999. "Is the Church of Ethiopia a Judaic Church?" *Warszawskie Studia Teologiczne* 12:203–16.
Phillipson, David W. 2009. *Ancient Churches of Ethiopia: Fourth–Fourteenth Centuries*. New Haven, Conn.: Yale University Press.
———. 2012. *Foundations of an African Civilisation: Aksum and the Northern Horn, 1000 BC–AD 1300*. Addis Ababa: Addis Ababa University Press.
Prunier, Gérard, and Éloi Ficquet, eds. 2015. *Understanding Contemporary Ethiopia*. London: Hurst.
Quirin, James. 1992. *The Evolution of the Ethiopian Jews: A History of the Beta Israel (Falasha) to 1920*. Philadelphia: University of Pennsylvania Press.
Roberson, Ronald G., C.S.P. 2018. "The Ethiopian Catholic Church." CNEWA: A Papal Agency for Humanitarian and Pastoral Support. Accessed April 7, 2018. http://www.cnewa.org/default.aspx?ID=64&pagetypeID=9&sitecode=hq&pageno=1.
Robin, Christian Julien. 2017. "L'Arrivée du Christianisme en Éthiopie: La 'Conversion' de l'Éthiopie." In Colin 2017, XXII–LVI.
Romm, James S. 1992. *The Edges of the Earth in Ancient Thought: Geography, Exploration, and Fiction*. Princeton, N.J.: Princeton University Press.
Schaefer, Charles. 2007. "Mahebar." EA 3:649–50.
Schneider, R. 1976. "L'inscription chrétienne d'Ezana en écriture sudarabe." *Annales d'Ethiopie* 10:109–17.
Shinn, David. 2014. "A Look at Muslim-Christian Relations in Ethiopia." *International Policy Digest*, January 21, 2014. Accessed July 6, 2018. https://intpolicydigest.org/2014/01/21/a-look-at-muslim-christian-relations-in-ethiopia/.
Silverman, Raymond. 1999. "Qes Adamu Tesfaw—A Priest Who Paints." In *Ethiopia: Traditions in Creativity*, ed. Raymond Silverman, 132–55 and 261–66. Seattle: University of Washington Press.
Smidt, Wolbert. 2010. "The Slavery Question in Politics." EA 4:680–81.

Stuckenbruck, Loren. 2013. "The Book of Enoch: Its Reception in Second Temple Jewish and in Christian Tradition." *Early Christianity* 4:7–40.

Szymusiak, Jan-M., S.J. 1958. *Athanase D'Alexandrie: Apologie a l'Empereur Constance; Apologie pour sa fuite; Introduction, texte critique, traduction et notes.* Sources Chrétiennes 56. Paris: Les Éditions du Cerf.

Tajfel, Henri. 1978. *Differentiation between Social Groups: Studies in the Social Psychology of Intergroup Relations.* European Monographs in Social Psychology, ed. Henri Tajfel. London: Academic Press.

Tamrat, Tardesse. 1972. *Church and State in Ethiopia, 1270–1527.* Oxford: Clarendon.

Teklehaymanot, Ayele, Donald Crumney, Steven Kaplan, and Kevin O. Mahoney. 2003. "Catholicism." EA 1:699–701.

Thelamon, Françoise. 1981. *Païens et Chrétiens au IVe siècle: L'apport de l'"Histoire ecclésiastique" de Rufin d'Aquillée.* Paris: Études Augustiennes.

Uhlig, Siegbert, ed. 2003, 2005, 2007. *Encyclopaedia Aethiopica.* Vols. 1–3, *A–N.* Wiesbaden: Harrassowitz Verlag.

Uhlig, Siegbert, in cooperation with Alessandro Bausi, eds. 2010. *Encyclopaedia Aethiopica.* Vol. 4, *O–X.* Wiesbaden: Harrassowitz Verlag.

Ullendorff, Edward. 1968. *Ethiopia and the Bible.* Oxford: Oxford University Press for the British Academy.

———. 1990. *The Ethiopians: An Introduction to Country and People.* Reprint of 3rd ed., 1973. Stuttgart: Franz Steiner.

Villard, Ugo Monneret de. 1938. *Aksum: Ricerche di topografia generale.* Rome: Pontificum Institutum Biblicum.

Voigt, Rainer. 2003. "Abyssinia." In EA 1:59–65.

Weldemariam, Alemayehu Tentaw. 2012. "Ethiopia: Government Increasingly Intolerant of Islam Risks Radicalizing Muslims." *African Arguments Insiders' Newsletter.* Accessed July 5, 2018. http://africanarguments.org/2012/11/16/ethiopia-government-increasingly-intolerant-of-islam-risks-radicalization-of-muslim-population-by-alemayehu-fentaw-weldemariam/.

Wolf, Pawel, and Ulrike Nowotnick, with contributions from Catharine Hof, Malgorzata Daszkiewicz, Gerwulf Schneider, Ewa Bobryk, and Alexandra Porter. 2010. "Das Heiligtum des Almaqah von Meqaber Ga'ewa in Tigray/Äithiopien." *Zeitschrift für Orient-Archäologie* 3:164–213.

Wolf, Pawel, Ulrike Nowotnick, and Saskia Schneider. 2015. *The Almaqah Temple of Wukro in Tigrai/Ethiopia.* Berlin: Society for the Promotion of Museums in Ethiopia.

Wondmagegnehu, Aymro, and Joachim Motovu. 1970. *The Ethiopian Orthodox Church*. Addis Ababa: Ethiopian Orthodox Mission.
Wyk Smith, Malvern van. 2009. *The First Ethiopians: The Image of Africa in the Early Mediterranean World*. Johannesburg: Wits University Press.
Ziethen, Gabriele. 2007. "Herodotus." In Uhlig 2007, 19–20.
Zoternberg, H. 1883. "La Chronique de Jean de Nikioû." Edited and translated into French. In *Notices et Extraits des manuscrits de la Bibliothèque Nationale*, XXIV, I, pp. 125–605 (Paris).

Index

Abba Salama: *see* Frumentius
Abgar (King), of Edessa, 109; alleged correspondence with Jesus Christ, 109
Abreha, 33
abuna (head of Ethiopian church), 35; process of appointment 56–57; role and relationship with the king 57; tension with Tewodros II and subsequent emperors, 80–81; replacement with an Ethiopian appointee, 90; the issue of two abunas and schism, 96–98; actions of Abuna Merkorios in New York, 97; resolution of the schism by Ethiopian Prime Minister, 98

abuna (in Catholicism), mode of address for a bishop, archbishop or vicar apostolic, 225
Abyssinia, 7, 51
Acts of Aaron Taumaturg, 115
Acts of Ba-Zalota Michael, 115
Acts of Honorius, 115
Acts of Iyasus Moa, 116
Acts of Lalibela, 53
Acts of Philip, 115
Acts of Samuel, 115
Acts of St. Sebastian, 120
Acts of Takla Alfa, 118
Acts of Takla Haymanot, 116
Adafa, 54
Adal, 64, 65

294 Index

Ad-Din, Shihab, author of account of Muslim invasion, 65
Addis Ababa, 8, 10, 11; establishment as capital, 86; and Protestant missions, 198, 199, 200; opened to Protestantism by Haile Selassie, 201; concentration of Pentecostals, 219
Addis Ababa, Treaty of, 84, 86
Adulis, 19, 43, 46; trade through, 20, 21, 32, 35, 48
Adwa (place), 4, 6, 13
Adwa, Battle of, 4, 83–84
Afar Triangle/Depression, 8, 9
Afse, Abba, one of Nine Saints, 47, 48
Afwerki, Isaias, president of Eritrea, 248
Agaw (people), 53
Agaw (region), 51
Agāzi, the (for Ethiopians), 30
agriculture, pre-historic, 13
Agwezat, the, 37, 41
Ahmed, Abiy (Prime Minister), 7; appointment and career, 96; reconciliation of two branches of Orthodoxy, 98; likely impact on Protestant Churches, 218–19; significance of, 241–43, 245, 246, 247, 248, 253
Aithiopes: in Homer, 12; in Herodotus, 18, 19
Aizanas, 32, 33, 34
Aksum (kingdom of), 4, 8, 12, 16, 20–23, 27, 29, 31, 32, 36, 41, 43, 46, 50, 51, 56, 101, 104, 135
Aksum (place), 4, 13, 20, 31, 32, 33, 34, 35, 38, 40, 45, 48, 72, 107; location of Tablets of the Law, 55, 76
Alef, Abba, one of Nine Saints, 47, 48
Alexander (the Great), legend of expedition to east in the *Zena Eskender*, 114, 156–57
Alexandria, 29, 30, 31, 32, 33, 41, 45, 51, 56, 156, 176

Alexandria, Patriarch of: role in appointing the abunas, 56–57, 66, 69, 80, 90, 107, 108, 109; and the Sabbath Controversy, 60
Al-Ghazi, Ahmad ibn Ibrahim, sultan of Adal, 65; nick-named "the Gragn" (left-handed), 65; leader of invasion of Ethiopia, 65–67, 106, 118, 119, 143; destroyed Aksumite cathedral, 159
Al-Habasa, 7; see also Habasha
Almaqah (god), 17; Great Temple of, 13, 16; a moon god 14; crescent and orb symbol, 14; altar to at Maqaber Ga'ewa, 15; persistence of cult into Aksumite period 19
Alvares, Francisco, chaplain of 1520 embassy, 64; author of *True Relation of the Lands of Prester John* (1540), 64–65; account of Ethiopian religious practices, 65; his work read by Ignatius Loyola, 69
Amba, Alagi, Battle of, 84
Amda Seyon (King), 58–59, 68, 109–10, 115; fostering art, 140
Amhara (ethnic group), 7, 54, 66
Amhara (place), 51, 81; location of Solomonic Dynasty, 56
Ammianus Marcellinus, 30
andemta (commentaries), 132
Angot, 51
animism, campaign of Zara Yaqob against, 61
Anqasa Amin, work by Enbaqom, 118; see also: Enbaqom
Anthony, St., 48; founder of eremitic monasticism, 108
apostolic prefecture, Catholic name for missionary area at pre-diocesan stage, 225; led by prefect apostolic (not usually a bishop), 225

Index 295

apostolic vicariate: Catholic name for missionary area potentially a diocese, 225; led by vicar apostolic (usually a bishop), 225

aqwaqwam, ritual dancing, 130, 168–69; solemn movement, 169

Arabia, 7, 13, 14, 17, 19, 21, 40, 50, 51, 59, 87, 254

Aragawi, Abba, one of Nine Saints, 47, 48; depicted in art, 152; founder of Monastery of Dabra Damo, 160

Aragawi, Mikael, early convert to Protestantism, 197

architecture: types across history, 158–62; Aksumite Cathedral of St. Mary of Sion, 159; destroyed by the Gragn, 159; Aksumite wooden beam and stone technique, 159–60; also at Monastery of Dabra Damo, 159–60; circular churches, 162–63; configuration of churches, 163; *see also* Lalibela (churches)

ark of covenant: *see* Menelik I (King)

Armah (King), 22

Asbeha, 33

Ascension of Isaiah (text), 5, 103

Asmara, 13

Athanasius, 29, 31, 32, 33, 106

Atnetewos II, Abuna, 82–83

Atse Gelawedros High School: *see* Pentecostalism (Protestant)

Awasa: *see* Swedish Philadelphia Church Mission

Awash River, 8, 51

Awash Valley, 9

Bahir Dar, concentration of Pentecostals, 219

Bani al-Hamawiyah, queen of, 51

Baraqish, 14

Baratieri, General, Italian commander at Adwa, 83

Basilios: becomes first Ethiopian abuna, 90; encourages Haymanota Abaw organization, 187

Beja, the, 37

Belate Military Training Camp, 189

Belete, Milion, first pastor of Meserete Kristos Church, 203

Bermudes, João, physician in 1520 Portuguese embassy, 66; suggested Ethiopian Orthodoxy transfer allegiance from Alexandria to Rome, 66; "consecrated" bishop and head of Ethiopian Orthodoxy, 66, 69; organized Portuguese military assistance, 66; had Emperor Gelawedros acknowledge the pope as head of Ethiopian Orthodox Church, 67

Beta Giyorgis (hill at Aksum), 19, 20

Beta Giyorgis, church in Lalibela, 162

beta lahm, building where bread and wine prepared for Eucharist, 165, 182

Beta Madhane Alam, church in Lalibela, 161

Beta Maryam, church in Lalibela, 162

Beza International Church, 216

Bible Churchmen's Missionary Society, 200–201; started in Addis Ababa, 201

Bible Society, The: sole ecumenical entity, 247, 251; sponsor of the Trinitarian Forum, 247

Book of Barlaam and Josaphat, Christianized story of a Buddha legend, 119

Book of Mysteries of Heaven and Earth, 114

Boundary Commission, for Ethiopia and Eritrea, 89–90

Brancaleon, Niccolò, Venetian artist in Ethiopia from late fifteenth century, 143, 146

Bugna, 53
Byzantine Empire, 45, 47, 51

Cairo, 52
Calcutta, 62
calendar, Ethiopian, 176–77; originated in Egypt, 176; modified by Zara Yaqob, 176; a solar calendar of thirteen months, 176; Pagumen, an intercalary month, 177;
candace (title of Kushite queens), 18
canon tables: nature and purpose of, 104; invented by Saint Eusebius, 104; decoration of, 105–6; as evidence of intellectual, theological and aesthetic endeavours in Ethiopia, 106
Capuchin Franciscan Institute of Philosophy and Theology: seminary and institute in Addis Ababa, 235; publishing and conference activities, 235; ecumenical in nature, 247
Catholicism, 6, 7; numbers of, 223; Eastern and Roman rites, 6; promoted by Italians, 88; percentage of Christians, 223; distribution around the country, 224; description of Catholic administrative units, 224–25; number and percentage of Catholics in Eritrea, 225; Cardinal Souraphiel, head of Catholic Church, 225; history since 1837, 226–29; execution and imprisonment of Catholic missionaries in seventeenth and eighteenth centuries, 226; arrival of Giustino de Jacobis, 226; arrival of Guglielmo Massaia, 227; remarkable co-existence of Roman and Eastern rites in Ethiopia, 227–28; arrival of first nuns, (Vincentian) Daughters of Charity in 1878, 228; post World War II need to move out of the north, 228; activity by Eparch Hailemariam Kahsay in the south, 228–29; impact of Catholic religious orders, 229; opposition during time of the Derg, 229; current challenges, 229–33; differences between Catholic Eastern rite and Roman rite, 230; differences between Catholic Eastern rite and Orthodoxy, 230–31; co-existence of the two rites as a cause of tension, 231–32; perceived foreignness of Catholicism, 231–33; Catholic Pentecostalism, 233; current strengths, 233–36; well served by pastoral agents, 233–34; provision of health care and social services, 234–35; educational institutions, 235; openness to ecumenism, 235–36; *see also* Giustino de Jacobis, Guglielmo Massaia
Cederqvist, Karl, Swedish Protestant missionary, 200; attempt to bring Protestants in southern Ethiopia together, 201–2
Cedrenus, 30
cenobitic lifestyle, 48
Ceylon, 46; *see also* Sri Lanka
Chalcedon, Council of, 5, 47, 106
Chapel of the Ark of the Covenant, in Aksum, 113
Christianity, beginnings under Frumentius, 34–35
Christianity, future of in Ethiopia, the context, 239–45; political challenge from EPRDF policies, 239–40; religious freedom and competition, 240; government control efforts, 240; ethnic federalism under EPRDF and globalization, 241; significance of new prime minister, 241–43; prime minister's reform in light of social identity theory, 242; for Orthodoxy,

244–45; for Protestantism, 245–46; recent poor relations between the Christian churches, 246–47; the Bible Society as the sole ecumenical entity, 247; possible change under new prime minister, 247; ecumenism as a way forward, 247–51; drawing inspiration from political initiatives, 248; issues for Orthodox Christians, 249; issues for Protestants, 249–50; possible form of ecumenical discussion, 250–51; role of Catholicism as broker of ecumenism, 251; relations with Islam, 251–56; tradition of peaceful co-existence, 252; popular mutual acceptance, not "toleration," 253; recent increase of tension with Islam, 254–55; violent incidents, 255; scope for Christian-Muslim dialogue; 255–56; *see also ethiopiawinet, medemer*
Chronicle of John, Bishop of Nikiu, 120–21
climatic zones, 10
coinage, 20, 21, 22, 27, 30, 32, 33, 34, 35, 36, 37, 51; imagery on pre-Christian coins, 22, 36; imagery on Christian coins, 36–37, 180
"closed" and "open" areas, established by Haile Selassie re. Protestant missions, 89, 201
Confession of Claudius, work by Gelawedros, 119
Constantine (Emperor), 31, 44; son of Helena, 179
Constantius II (Emperor), 32, 33, 43
Cosmas, 21
Cosmas Indicopleustes, author of *Christian Topography*, 32, 45–46, 87
Council for the Cooperation of Christian Churches, formation, 213–14

Covilhã, Pero da, arrives in Ethiopia, 63; suggests Portuguese alliance, 64
crosses: Greek crosses on coins, 36, 37, 44, 135, 145; devotion to, 180
Cyril (Saint), Patriarch of Alexandria and opponent of Chacedon Christology, 108

Dabra Asbo, original name of Dabra Libanos monastery, 58
Dabra Berhan Selassie, Church of, saved from the Mahdists by bees, 83
Dabra Damo, monastery founded by Abba Aragawi, 48–49; place for isolating Claimants to throne, 56; Aksumite architecture in, 135–36, 159–60
Dabra Gol, monastery founded by Basalota Mikael, 58, 115
Dabra Libanos, monastery founded by Takla Haymanot, 58, 118, 119; renamed and source of clergy, 61
Dabra Selam, Church of, ancient paintings, 138
dabtara/dabtarat, quasi-clerics, 126–27, 165; description of, 126–27; creation and use of prayer scrolls, 154, 220; and aqwaqwam, 169
Dahlak islands, 51, 52
Danel (Abuna), 51
Dawit (King), 60; commissioned translation of *Miracles of Mary*, 140
degwa, songs and chants, 129, 168
Delna'od (King), 52, 54
Derg, the, generally, 90–94, 189; causes of, 92; religious policies, 93; *see also* "Equality for all," "Land to the tiller," Neghele, "villagization"
Dersana Ura'el, 175
Djibouti, 8
Dogali, Battle of, 83
Du Nawas (king of Himyar), 45, 46

Ebana (King), 36
echege, head of Ethiopian monasticism, 118
Edemariam, Aida, author of *A Wife's Tale*, 122
Edesius, 28, 29, 30, 33, 34, 35, 41
Edessa, 109
education of clergy and quasi-clergy, general account, 125–32; devised in Gondar, 126; rural rather than urban pupils, 126; its character, 127; first stage, "house/school of reading" (*nebab bet*), 127; arduous regime for students, 128–29; music school (*zema bet*), the second stage, 129–30; poetry school (*qene bet*), the third stage, 131–32; school of books (*meshafa bet*), the fourth stage, 131–32; *see also zema bet*, *meshafa bet*
Egypt, unsuccessful invasion of Ethiopia 1875–1876, 82
Ella Allada (King), 30, 34
Ella Amida (King), 34, 46
Ella Atsbeha/Asbeha: *see* Kaleb
Emmanuel Fellowship, Pentecostal movement within and then outside Orthodoxy, 191; now a church, 191
encampment (royal), 35, 59; description of, 75–76
Enbaqom, former Muslim, author, Abbot of Dabra Libanos and *echege*, 118; translator of *Book of Barlaam and Josaphat*, 119; *see also echege*
Encomium of St George, 120
Endubis (King), 22–23
Enoch, 1 (text), 5, 114; preservation in Ethiopia, 102–3; influence on prayer scrolls, 156
Entoto, Mount, Menelik II's first capital, 86
eparch: *see* eparchy

eparchy, territory presided over by a bishop called an eparch in Catholic Eastern rite churches, 225
"Equality for all," Derg slogan and policy, 92
eremitic lifestyle, 48
Eritrea, 8, 12, 13; and the Italians, 83, 84; forced federation with Ethiopia, 89; independence, 89
Eritrean War of Independence, 89
Eskender (Emperor), 123, 143
EPRDF: *see* Ethiopian People's Revolutionary Democratic Front
Ethiopian People's Revolutionary Democratic Front ("EPRDF"), generally 94–96, 189; central policy of ethno-regional federalism, 94–95, promoted religious freedom but maintained control, 95; encouraged Islam and Protestantism, 95; new prime minister in 2018, 96
Ethiopian Graduate School of Theology: founded in 1997 in Addis Ababa, 221; graduates undertaking doctorates abroad, 221; hosts annual St. Frumentius Lecture, 221
ethiopiawinet ('Ethiopianness'), existing concept appealed to by Prime Minister, 241–42, 253
Ethiopic Legend of Abgar, 109
Ethiopic: *see* Ge'ez
Ethio-Sabaean period: *see* history
ethnic groups, 7
ethno-regional federalism: *see* Ethiopian People's Revolutionary Democratic Front
eucalyptus trees, introduction to Ethiopia by Menelik II, 86
eunuch, the Ethiopian, 18
Eusebius (Saint): *see* canon tables
Evangelical Association: *see* Heyling, Peter

Evangelical Churches Fellowship of Ethiopia: formation, 215; distance from kept by new independent, neo-Pentecostal Protestant churches, 216; activities of, 220
Evangelical Training College, origin and nature of, 221–22
Ewostatewos (Saint), founder of monasteries, 58; Sabbath controversy, 60; depiction in art, 151
Exodus Apostolic Reformation Church, 216
Ezana (King), 17, 19, 21, 23, 27, 30, 34, 35, 36, 37, 38, 39, 40, 41, 43, 46, 135, 180; conversion to Christianity, 35–41
Ezra, Stephanite monk and artist, 141–43; carver of wooden crosses, 143; *see also* Stephen; Stephanite movement

Falasha, the, 58; origins and character, 59–60, 62; called House of Israel, 59; campaign against by Susenyos, 76; recovery around Gondar, 76; work in building Gondar, 76–77; decline in eighteenth and nineteenth centuries, 78; discovery by outsiders, 79–80; oppressed by the Derg, 94; flown to Israel, 94; Protestant mission under Martin Flad, 198
Fasilidas (Emperor): accession, 72; restoration of Orthodoxy and expulsion of Jesuits, 73; foundation of Gondar as capital, 76, 126, 146; rebuilding of cathedral at Aksum 76; baths in Gondar, 178; arrival of Peter Heyling, 196–97
fasting, 4, 65; central to Ethiopian Orthodoxy, 181, 217; details of, 181–82; fifty-five days fasting for Lent, 181–82; as a means of doing religious work through one's body, 182
Fatimid Dynasty, 52
feast days, 177–81; *see also* Timkat, Festival of; Mesqel, Festival of
Fekkare Malakot, 119
Fetha Nagast, and slavery 87–88; description of, 121–22; and food laws, 185–86
Flad, Martin, Protestant missionary among Falasha, 198
Francis Xavier, co-founder of Jesuits, 68
Fremona, place of Jesuit settlement in northern Ethiopia, 70, 73
Frumentius, 28, 29, 30, 31, 32, 33, 34, 35, 40, 41, 56, 101, 102, 106; Rufinus' account, 28–29; called Abba Salama and Kasate Berhan, 30
Fre Seyon, artist influenced by Western painting, 141

Gabiso, Tesfaye, Protestant singer imprisoned and tortured by the Derg, 214
Gabra Masqal, son of Kaleb 45; king, 46–47; depicted in art with St. Yared, 152, 166
Gabriel (Abuna), 60, 61
gadls, nature of, 115
Gadla Giyorgis, 120
Gadla Lalibela, 109
Gadla Walatta Petros, 120; *see also* Walatta Petros
Galla, the, former (outsider) name for the Oromo, 68
Gama, Cristovão da, son of Vasco and leader of 1541 Portuguese military assistance, 66–67
Gama, Vasco da, 62–63
Gannata Maryam, Church of, rock-cut church, 139–40

Gano, Aster, convert of Swedish missionaries, 199
Garima, Abba, one of Nine Saints, 47, 48; translating Gospels with angelic help, 49; founder of Abba Garima monastery, 103, 116; homily on, 116
Garima Gospels, oldest Ethiopian manuscripts, 50, 107, 116, 151; dating of, 103; illuminated with Ethiopian birds and Aksumite architecture, 104;
Garima, Monastery of, 107; foundation, 48, 103; ancient Gospel books, 50; *see also* Garima Gospels
Ge'ez, 5, 13, 21, 33, 37, 38, 39, 40, 41, 44, 49, 55, 102, 104, 107, 121, 168, 177, 186, 188, 189, 225; continued use in Orthodox liturgy, 217, 219; invention of vocalization of consonants, 101; use in qene, 125; use in Catholic rite, 227
Gelawedros (Emperor): acknowledges Pope as head of Ethiopian Church, 67; opposes Oromo invasion, 68; defender of Orthodoxy, 69; death, 70; as writer, 119
geography (Ethiopian), 8–11; *see also* climatic zones, soil types, topography
George of Cappadocia, 32
Goa, 63, 70, 71
Gobat, Samuel, Anglican missionary, 197; collaborated with Orthodoxy, 197; adapted to Ethiopian culture, 197
Gondar, 3, 4, 8, 59, 73; foundation of, 76, 126; disadvantages of location for royal control, 77, 81; damage by the Mahdists, 83; and clerical education, 126; baths built by Fasilidas, 178; arrival of Peter Heyling, 196
Gospel Books, commissioned in reign of Amda Seyon, 140; *see also* Garima Gospels

Gragn, the: *see* Al-Ghazi, Ahmad ibn Ibrahim
Grat Be'al Gebri, the (palace), 14
Great Rift Valley, 8, 9
Guba, Abba, one of Nine Saints, 47
gult: system of land tenure with arguably feudal aspects, 91; *samon gult*, similar system of ecclesiastical land tenure, 91

Habasha, 51
Haile Selassie (Emperor), 4, 6, 55, 56; pre-regnal name Ras Tafari, 86; as regent, 86; reign of, 87–89; attempt to abolish slavery, 87, 88; failed coup against in 1960, 90; deposition, 90–91,152; initial openness to Protestant missions, 200; deposition by the Derg, 213, 241
Harar (region), 68
Harar (town), site of indigenous Pentecostal outbreak, 207–8
Harbay (brother of King Lalibela), 53
Hatshepsut, Queen, 87
Haymanota Abaw, 119
Haymanota Abaw Ethiopian Students Association, 187–88
heavenly citizenship (*semayawi zeginet*), central to contemporary Protestantism, 218
Helena (Empress), 64; discovery of the Cross, 179
Henotikon, the (Edict of unity), 47
Herodotus, 12, 18
Heyling, Peter, first Protestant missionary, 196–97; aim of revitalizing Orthodoxy, 197; translated Gospel of John into Amharic, 197; founder of Evangelical Association, 197
Himyar, 40, 44, 45

Index

history: pre-Christian, 11–23; pre-literate, 12–13; endogenous culture, 13; Ethio-Sabaean period, 13–17; proto-Aksumite period, 17–20; the rise of Aksum 20–23; period of Frumentius, 27–36; Ezana to Kaleb, 43–46; Nine Saints and Sadeqan, 46–50; decline of Aksum and afterwards, 50–52, Zagwe Dynasty, 52–54; Solomonic Dynasty, 54–62; Muslim invasion, 62–67; Oromo invasion, 67–68; the Jesuits and their expulsion, 68–73; seventeenth to mid-nineteenth centuries, 75–80; 1855 to the present, 80–98
History of the Galla, by Abba Bahrey, 118–19
Hiwot Berhan Church of Ethiopia, number of members, 219
Holy Family, 3
Holy Land (Ethiopia as), 3, 5, 161, 172; Ethiopian pilgrims to, 53
Homiliary of the Archangel Michael, 148
Homily on Garima, 116
House of Israel: *see* Falashas
Horologion, 130

Ifat, sultanate of, 52, 56
Ildephonsus of Toledo, St.: *see* Ta'amera Maryam
incense burner, 15
India, 20, 22, 28, 29, 34, 45, 46, 62, 63, 119, 259
injera (fermented flatbread), 128
inscriptions, 21, 22, 27, 34, 35; Ezana's inscriptions, 37–40
intellectual and literary traditions (of Ethiopian Orthodoxy), in Aksumite period, 102–8; in Zagwe period, 108–9; in Solomonic period, 109–32
Iyoas (Emperor), 149
Israel, son of Kaleb, 45

Islam: *see* Muslims
Italian invasions, 4, 49, 83, 88; defeat of Italians, 89
Iyasus I (Emperor), 78

Jacobis, Giustino de, Vincentian and first Catholic missionary in modern period, 226; adaptation to Ethiopian culture and Orthodoxy, 226; at Rome's direction established a Catholic rite in Orthodox form, 226–27
Jamaa charismatic movement, 191
Jerusalem, 30, 43, 53, 54, 55, 161
Jesus, 3
Jesuits, 6, 41, 143; foundation and character, 68; arrival in Ethiopia, 69; expulsion, 73
Jewish influences: in architecture, 172–76, 185–87; *see also* Orthodox Church (Ethiopian)
Johanson, Donald, 9
John, Prester, 63, 64
Johnson, Samuel, author of *The History of Rasselas, Prince of Abyssinia*, 78
Joseph, 3
Jubilees (text), 5; preservation in Ethiopia, 102–3
Justin I (Emperor), 45
Justinian (Emperor), 45

Kaleb (King), 43, 44–46; throne name Ella Atsbeha/Asbeha, 44; Ethiopian Orthodox saint, 45; hymn about, 110; father of Gabra Masqal, 166
Kale Heywet Church, oppressed by the Derg, 94; formation from Sudan Interior Mission, 202; current position, 216; criticized for social interests, 218
Kasate Berhan: *see* Frumentius

Kassa, pre-regnal name of Yohannes IV, 82
Kebra Nagast: legitimating Solomonic Dynasty, 55, 56, 110, 172; origin, 110; purpose of, 110–11, 112–13; description of, 110–12
Kenya, 8
Khartoum, 8
kings (Ethiopian), ecclesiastical leadership, 57
Koloē, 20
Krapf, Johann: Protestant missionary, 197; went to Shoa and the Oromo, 197; published improved Amharic Bible, 197–98
Kugler, Christian: Anglican missionary, 197
Kush/Kushite, 17, 18, 19
Kushitic population, 61

Lalibela (churches), churches saved from the Gragn, 144; alleged role of angels in construction, 161; built as a new Jerusalem, 161; Aksumite features, 161–62; *see also* Lalibela (place)
Lalibela (cross), 139
Lalibela (King), etymology of his name, 53; later canonization, 115–16; initiates building of rock-cut churches in Lalibela, 138–39, 161
Lalibela (place), 4, 8; modeled on Jerusalem, 54; *see also* Roha
Lambie, Thomas, Protestant missionary, 200
Lamentations of Mary, 148
"Land to the tiller," Derg slogan and policy, 92
languages, diversity of, 7
Lasta (region), 51, 53, 54, 66, 68, 138
Lebna Dengel (Emperor), 64, 65, 66
Lent, 3, 4, 65

Lidj Iyasu (Emperor), accession and claimed descent from Muhammad, and Muslim wives, 86
Life of St Ann, 114
Life of St Anthony, translation into Ge'ez, 107–8
Life of St Paul the Hermit, translation into Ge'ez, 108
Lima, Rodrigo de, leader of 1520 embassy, 64, 66
liq (exalted elder), 132
Liqanos, Abba, one of Nine Saints, 47, 48
Lord of All, 38–40
Lord of Heaven, 38–39
Lord of the Land, 38–40
Loyola, Ignatius, founder of Jesuits, 68; interest in Ethiopia, 68–69; suggested Pope appoint new Ethiopian patriarch, 69; urged respect for Ethiopian Orthodox customs, 69
Lucy, discovery of her remains, 9

Magdala, capital under Tewodros II, 81
Magdala, Battle of, 82; British ransacking of Tewodros' possessions, 82, 121
Mahdists, the (from Sudan), invasion by, 83
Mahfuz of Adal (Emir), 64; governor of Zeila, 64
mahebar, history and nature of, 188
Mahebara Qeddusan, officially sanctioned Orthodox renewal movement, 188–89
Mahrem (Aksumite god), equivalent to Almaqah, 22; god of war, 37, 38
Mai Qoho (hill at Aksum), 20
Malindi, Kenya, 62; Vasco da Gama's pillar, 63
Mani, 21

manuscripts, copying of, 4, 102, 125; arrival and translation in Ethiopia, 102
Maqaber Ga'ewa (place), 15, 17
maqdash, inner sanctuary of a church, 163, 175; *see also qeddesta qeddusan*
Marib, 14
Mark (Abuna), in reign of Gelawedros, 69
Mark (Saint), portrait in Garima Gospel III, 137–38
Maronite Church of Lebanon, 69
Mary, 3; devotion to and miracles of, 62; feasts in honor of, 180
Mary of Zion, St: *see* Maryam Seyon
Maryam Seyon, cathedral in Aksum, 113, 161; and the ark of the covenant, 163, 172
Masafent, the time of, 79
Mashafa Berhan, work by Zara Yaqob, 117
Mashafa Milad, work by Zara Yaqob, 117
Massaia, Guglielmo, Capuchin Franciscan arrived 1846, 227; worked in Oromo area and did not adapt to Orthodoxy, 227; paternalistic, 227; adviser to Menelik II, 227
Massawa, 66; entry port for Portuguese army in 1541, 66; entry port for Pedro Páez, 70; entry port for Italian invasion, 83; start of Swedish Evangelical Mission, 199
Masudi, Al-, Arab writer on Ethiopia, 109
Matewos, Abuna, 86
Mathias (Abuna), appointment 97
Mattson, Anna-Lüsa and Sanfrid, Finnish Pentecostal missionaries 207; establish missions at Wolmera and Mercato (in Addis Ababa), 207
mawasit (memorial services), 130

Mazgaba Haymanot, 119
medemer, concept appealed to by prime minister, 242
Medhane Alam, church in Lalibela, 53
Mehadeyis (King), 43–44
Mekane Yesus Church, oppressed by the Derg, 94; association of Lutheran churches, 202; official recognition in 1959, 202; current position, 216; criticized for social interests, 218
Mendes, Alfonso, Jesuit successor to Páez, 71; disastrous appointment, 71–72, 229; bans Orthodoxy, 72
Menelik I (King), 6, 54, 55; conception and birth, 111; visit to Jerusalem and return with ark of covenant, 111–12, 172, 186
Menelik II (Emperor), 4; king of Shoa, 82; accession, 83; victory at Adwa, 83–84; conquests of, 219
Mengistu (Major Mengistu Haile Mariam), leader of the Derg, 91–92
Mercurius (Saint), 110
Merkorios (Abuna), appointment under the Derg, 93; departure from Ethiopia, 96; move to New York, 97; return to Ethiopia, 98
Meroe (capital of Kush), 18, 19
Meropius, 28, 30, 31
Meserete Kristos Church, formation of, 203; takes in Zion Pentecostal choir and becomes charismatic, 211; persecution by the Derg, 214; current position, 216
meshafa bet (school of books), covers *tergwāmē* and *andemta*, 132
Mesqel, Festival of, 179–80
Metemma, Battle of, 83
Metrodorus, 28, 30, 31
miaphysite/miaphysitism, central theological tenet of Ethiopian

Orthodoxy, 5, 51, 106, 108, 119, 230, 293
Mikael (Abuna), 60, 61
Minas (Emperor), 68, 70
Miracles of Mary: see Ta'amera Maryam
Miracles of St George, 120
missionary activity, recent Orthodox, 189
monarchy (Ethiopian), 4, 6
monasteries, establishment by Nine Saints, 48, 102, 108; in Egypt 48; proliferation in Solomonic period, 56–57; growing power of 58; establishment under Takla Haymanot and Ewostatewos, 58; translation of Egyptian monastic manuals, 107–8
Muhammad, 50; advised some followers to seek safety in Ethiopia, 252
Mulu Wengel Church, formation 209–10; persecution, 210–11; violent incident at Dabra Zeit, 210; "Pente" first applied to Pentecostals, 210; Pente becomes self-designation, 212; persecution leading to spread of Pentecostalism, 212; initial hopes for religious freedom under the Derg, 213; subsequent severe persecution by the Derg, 214; number of, members 219
music (Orthodox), invention by St. Yared, 165–66; the musical notation invented by Yared, 166–67; the three modes of melody invented by Yared, 167; types of hymns, 167–68; Ethiopian music to Western ears, 168; ritual dancing (aqwaqwam), 168–69
Music (Pentecostal), origin and character, 220
Muslims, minority, 7; rise of Islam, 50, 52; favored by the Italians, 89; improvement of position under the Derg, 93; in Eastern Ethiopia oppressed by the Derg, 94; increased influence under the EPRDF, 240–44; arrival in time of Muhammad, 152; Sufi influence, 252; history of relationship with Muslims, 252–53; distinguishing political and popular levels, 252–53; influences from abroad, 254–55; influence of Wahhabi movement, 254; scope for Christian-Muslim dialogue; 255–56
Muslim invasion (seventeenth century), 4, 49, 62–67, 129, 143; destruction wrought by, 118

Najran, 45; martyrs of, 110
nebab bet: see education of clergy and quasi-clergy
Neghele, location of army revolt in 1974 leading to the Derg, 91
neo-Pentecostal churches, arrival in Ethiopia, 216; distance from Evangelical Churches Fellowship of Ethiopia, 216
Nesib, Onesimus, convert of Swedish missionaries, 199; completed first Oromo translation of Bible, 199; worked with Cederqvist, 200
netela (prayer shawl), 3
Nezana (King), 43, 44
Nezoul (King), 43, 44
Nile, the Blue, 8, 10, 19, 20
Nile, the White, 8
Nine Saints, the 46–50, 101, 102; establishment of monasteries, 48–49, 160; miracles of, 49; depicted in art, 152
Nubia, 22; see also Kush
Noba (Nubia), 38, 39, 40

Ogaden Desert, 10
Omahe, Chacha, Kenyan Pentecostal evangelist, 208

Omo River, 51
Ona, 13
Oriental Orthodox Churches, 5
Ormz, 63
Oromo (ethnic group), 7, 11, 77
Oromo migrations, 67–68, 118
Orthodox Church (Ethiopian): theology 5; disputes in seventeenth and eighteenth centuries, 79; introduction of parish councils, 90; extensive land ownership pre-Derg, 92; loss of land and decline of position under the Derg, 92–93; secession of Western Hemisphere branch, 97; long continuity of scholarship, 106; miaphysite theology, 106; meaning of "Tewahedo," 5, 106; antiquity of opposition to Council of Chalcedon, 107; Judaic influences on, 112–13; literary response to Jesuits, 119; *qene* as a sign of intellectual strength of the tradition, 125; recent developments, 187–91; Sunday school movement, 187; missionary activity, 189; preaching, 190; Pentecostalism, 190–91; numbers of Protestants compared with Orthodox, 195–96; Orthodoxy and Protestantism as contrasting modes of ecclesiality, 196; separation of church and date by the Derg, 212–13; nationalization of land under the Derg, 212–13; negative impact of recent politics, 244; anti-ecumenical dimension to response, 244; criticism from Protestant preachers, 244; continuing strategic role, 244–45; *see also* intellectual traditions of Ethiopian Orthodoxy; education of clergy; Mahebara Qeddusan; Emmanuel Fellowship

Orviedo, Bishop Andrew de, Jesuit and leader of mission to Ethiopia in 1557, 69–70
Ousanas (King), 34, 43, 44
Ousas (King), 43, 44

Pachomius, founder of monasteries in Egypt, 48
Páez, Pedro, author of *History of Ethiopia* (1622), 70; Jesuit and successor to Orviedo, 70; departed Lisbon 1588 and arrived in Ethiopia 1603, 70; respectful of Ethiopian customs, 70–71, 226; surveying site for capital, 76
painting, distinctive features, 133–35; periods, 135–50; Christian Aksumite period, 135–38; portraits and decoration in Garima Gospels, 137–38; post-Aksumite period, 138; Zagwe period, 138–39; early Solomonic period, 139–43; arrival of artists from the West, 140–41; influence of Western art on Fre Seyon, 141; Stephanite and Venetian period, 141–43; mid-Solomonic period, 143–46; introduction of Virgin and child image *Salus Populi Romani*, 145; Gondarine period, 146–49; two styles of Gondarine painting, 147–49; period of the Judges, 149–50; late Solomonic period, 150; main subjects of, 150–52; arrangement in churches, 152; prayer scrolls, 152–57; religious art in Ethiopia today, 157–58; involvement of lay artists, 157–58; patronage, 158; *see also* Fre Seyon; Stephanite movement; Ezra; Brancaleon; prayer scrolls
Pantalewon, Abba, and Kaleb, 45; one of Nine Saints, 47, 48

Paulos (Abuna), appointed by Ethiopian Orthodox Church, 96; his career, 96–97

Paul's Areopagus speech, 40

Pearl, the, a tradition concerning Mary, 113–14

"Pente," first applied to Pentecostals, 210; self-designation for Pentecostals, 212; self-designation for all Protestants, 215

Pentecost, in Acts 2, 204

Pentecostalism (Catholic), 233

Pentecostalism (Orthodox), 190–91

Pentecostalism (Protestant), the New Testament basis for Pentecostalism, 204–6; Pentecost, 204; glossolalia not xenoglossy, 205; the evidence in 1 Corinthians 12–14, Galatians 2 Corinthians and Romans, 205–6; its history in Ethiopia, 206–12; first Pentecostal missionaries arrive (Bertha Dommermuth, Ruth Shippey and Ellen French) and leave, 206–7; arrival of Finnish missionaries Anna-Lüsa and Sanfrid Mattson, 207; Swedish Philadelphia Church Mission and beginnings of charismatic manifestations, 207–8; Haile Selassie I University as context for growth, 208; indigenous Pentecostalism in Harar, 208–9; in Nazareth, 209; role of students at Atse Gelawedros High School, 209; debated influence of Mennonites, 209; formation of Mulu Wengel Church, 209–10; persecution of Mulu Wengel Church, 210–11; "Pente" first applied to Pentecostals, 210; appeal of in cities, 211; appeal of in rural areas, 211–12; importance of healing and exorcism, 212; "Pente" becomes self-designation for Pentecostals, 212; movement into mainstream Protestantism, 215, 220; main concentrations of Pentecostals, 219; Pentecostal music in Protestantism, 220; connection of exorcisms with Orthodox practices, 220; challenges to Pentecostalism, 245–46; routinization of charisma, 246; *see also* Mulu Wengel Church

Periplus Maris Erythraei, 20, 21, 87

Persian Gulf, 46, 63

Piedro, Ethiopian monk in Rome known to Ignatius Loyola, 69

Physiologus, The, translation into Ge'ez, 108

Pliny the Elder, 18, 21, 87

Poncet, Charles Jacques, French physician at court of Iyasus I, 78

Portuguese exploration, 62–63

pottery, 13, 17, 19

Prayer of the Hours, 130

prayer scrolls, legend of Alexander in, 114; composed by dabtarat, 131; opposed by Orthodox, 131; description of, 152–57; function of, 154; construction of, 154; role of dabtara, 154; criticism of, 156; common motifs on, 156–57; influence of 1 Enoch, 156

preaching, expansion of in Orthodoxy, 190

prefect apostolic: *see* apostolic prefecture

Protestantism, numbers of Protestants, 6; suppressed by Italians, 88–89; growth during Italian occupation, 89; initial improvement of position under the Derg, 93; oppression by the Derg, 94; numbers of Protestants compared with Orthodox, 195–96; Orthodoxy and Protestantism as contrasting modes of ecclesiality,

196, 217; history of in Ethiopia to 1960s, 196–212; Tewodros' requirement of technical skills, 198; opposition from Yohannes, 199; start of Swedish Evangelical Mission at Massawa in Eritrea, 199; initial acceptance by Menelik, 199; initial acceptance by Haile Selassie, 200; remarkable growth during Italian occupation, 201; beginnings of association of evangelicals, 201; Lutheran Churches form association, 202; Mekane Yesus Church formed, 202; Kale Heywet Church formed, 202; Mennonites in Nazareth, 202; Mennonites' effective *modus operandi*, 202–3; Mennonites' appeal to Orthodox youth, 202–3; formation of Meserete Kristos Church, 203; new Amharic translation of Bible, 203; and the Derg, 212–15; the Derg's separation of church and state, 212–13; initial hopes for religious freedom under the Derg, 213; subsequent persecution by the Derg, 214; growth of appeal of Protestantism under the Derg, 214–15; growing numbers, 215; from a rural to an urban phenomenon, 215; "Pente" as self-designation for all Protestants, 215; position under EPRDF, 215–16; policy of religious freedom, 215; current situation, 216–21; importance of individual responsibility and choice, 217; centrality of notion of heavenly citizenship rather than social interest, 217–18; little theology on social issues, 218; likely impact of new prime minister, 218–19; theological training initiatives, 220–21; current solid position, 245; challenges to Pentecostalism, 245–46; *see also* Heyling, Peter; Gobat, Samuel; Krapf, Johann; Flad, Martin; Swedish Evangelical Mission; Sudan Interior Mission; Evangelical Training College; Ethiopian Graduate School of Theology

Protoevangelium of James, 114

Ptolemy III, 19

qeddase, Eucharistic liturgy, 130, 182; equivalent to ancient Mass of Catechumens, 182; communion infrequently taken, 182; structure of, 183–85

qeddest, middle area of a church, 165

qeddesta qeddusan, inner sanctuary of a church, 163, 175

qene (poetic form), 116, 121; description, 122–25; possible origin in fourteenth century, 123; a largely Amhara phenomenon, 123; explained by metaphor of "wax and gold," 123; forms of, 123; purpose of, 124; examples, 124–25

qene mahlet, vestibule of a church, 165, 175

Qirillos, translation into Ge'ez, 108

Queen Makeda: *see* Sheba, queen of

Qwesqwam, Egyptian town reached by Holy Family, 180, 182

Qwesqwam Abbey, 3

Radio Voice of the Gospel, in Addis Ababa, 203

rainy seasons, 10

Ras Ali (Lord of Begember), 81

Ras Tafari: *see* Haile Selassie

Red Sea, 19, 20, 22, 27, 34, 40, 43, 45, 46, 51, 63, 64, 70, 102

Red Terror, under the Derg, 91–92

Refutation of the Council of Chalcedon, The, ancient Aksumite text, 107
religions, traditional, 7
Roha, Syriac name for Edessa and earlier name for Lalibela, 109, 115
Royal Chronicles, 56
Rufinus of Aquileia, 27, 30, 32, 33, 34, 35, 41
Rule of St Pachomius, translation into Ge'ez, 108

Sabaeans, 16
Sabaean culture, 13, 16–17; integration with Ethiopian culture, 17; persistence, 19, 22
Sabaean writing, 15
Sabbath, the; dispute over observance, 60; observance in sixteenth century, 65
sacred action, 182–87; Eucharistic liturgy, 182–85; practices with a Judaic dimension, 185–87; circumcision 185; food laws, 185–86; some Sabbath observance, 186; explanations for Judaic features, 186–87; Syrian and Solomonic influences, 186–87; see also qeddase
sacred space, 171–76; Jewish features, 170–76; Ethiopia as new Holy Land, 172; churches replicating temple in Jerusalem, 172–73; inaccessibility of a church's inner sanctuary to laity, 173; explaining the similarities, 173–76; relevance of purity issues and Mishnaic tractate *Kelim*, 174–75; concern with threatened boundaries, 175–76
sacred time, 176–82; Ethiopian calendar, 176–77; feast days, 177–81; see also calendar, Ethiopian and feast days
Sadeqan, the, 46, 50
Saladin, 53, 161

Salama, Abuna, 81
Salih, Abu, Armenian writer on Ethiopia, 171
Salome, 3
Salus Populi Romani, painting in Rome copied in Ethiopia, 145–46
samon gult: see gult
Sarsa Dengel (Emperor), opposition to Oromo invasion, 68; accession, 70
Sassanians, 45
Sawana Nafs, 119
Sazanas, 32, 33
Sehm, Abba, one of Nine Saints, 47
Selim I (Sultan), 64
Sheba, queen of, 6, 55, 56, 110, 111, 172, 186; also called Queen Makeda, 111
Shimbra, Kure, battle of, 66
Shoa (region), 51, 52, 56, 58, 66, 68, 81
Simon (Abuna), 71
sistra (handheld instruments), 130, 169
slavery and slave trade, Muslim involvement, 52; attempted abolition by Tewodros, 81; history of it in Ethiopia, 87; attempted abolition by Haile Selassie, 87, 89; acceptance of slavery in *Fetha Nagast*, 87–88; and Ethiopian Orthodoxy, 88; attempt by Italians to abolish, 89
soil types, 10–11
Solomon, King, 6, 55, 56, 110, 111, 172, 187; Net of Solomon in prayer scrolls, 156
Solomonic Dynasty, 52, 57; restoration of, 54; and the *Kebra Nagast*, 55, 172; improvement under Zara Yaqob, 60
soma degwa, hymns for fasting, 168
Somalia, 8, 10
Souraphiel, Cardinal Archbishop Berhaneyesus Demerew, head of Catholic Church, 225
South Sudan, 8
Sri Lanka, 34, 45

stelae, stone (in Aksum), 19
Stephanite movement, prompted by martyrdom of Stephen, 142; Ezra the Stephanite, 142; *see also* Stephen
Stephen, monk executed by Zara Yaqob, 141–42; martydom led to Stephanite movement, 143
stone tool, 13
Sudan, 8, 17, 19, 83
Sudan Interior Mission, 200, 201; established congregations separate from Orthodoxy, 200; transformed into Kale Heywet Church, 202
Supreme Council of Islamic Affairs, relations with EPRDF, 240, 255
Susenyos I (Emperor), accession, 71; faced Ethiopian Church opposition, 71; convert to Roman Catholicism, 71, 143; letter of justification, 72; rebellion against his church policy, 72; abdication, 73; selection of site for permanent capital, 76; opposed by Walatta Petros, 120
Swedish Evangelical Mission, arrival in Massawa, 199; established Bible training school at Imkullu, 199; progress in Addis Ababa and Wellega, 199
Swedish Philadelphia Church Mission, Pentecostal mission and annual conference at Awasa, 207–8
Synaxarium, 114–15
Syria, 47, 48, 102, 108
Syriac loan words, 48

Ta'amera Maryam (miracles of Mary), 116–17; alleged attribution to St. Ildephonsus of Toledo, 117; prescribed for reading in liturgy by Zara Yaqob, 117, 140; translation commissioned by Dawit, 140; dissemination in Gondarine period, 146; in art 146, 151

tabots, 57, 110, 163, 173, 175, 187, 190; essential feature of an Ethiopian church, 164, 172, 185; veneration accorded to, 164–65; taken out for Feast of Timkat, 178; and the Solomonic tradition, 187–88; criticized by Protestants, 190, 244;
Takla Haymanot (Abuna), appointment under the Derg, 93
Takla Haymanot (Saint), 54; founder of monasteries, 58; legends concerning, 116; depiction in art, 151
Tana, Lake, 8, 10, 77
Taytu, Empress, action in Battle of Adwa, 84
Tazena (King), 46
teff, 19
tela, an ecclesiastical umbrella, 164, 182, 184
Tempesta, Antonio, influential in Ethiopia, 146–47
Temro Mastnemar, Sunday school organization, 187
tents: *see* encampment (royal)
tergwāmē (interpretation), 132
Tesfaw, Qes Adamu, a leading contemporary artist, 158
Tewahedo: *see* miaphysite/miaphysitism
Tewodros II (Emperor): accession, 79, 150; reign, 80–82; unification of kingdom, 81; defeat by British and suicide, 82; and Protestants, 198
Theodosius II, 44
Theophilos (Abuna), executed by the Derg, 93; encourages Haymanota Abaw organization, 187
Tigray, 12, 51, 66, 82
Tigrayan People's Liberation Front, dominant group in the Derg, 94
Timkat, Festival of, 178
topography, 8–10
trade, Aksumite period, 20, 21
traders, Muslim, 52

translation, of Bible into Ge'ez, 49
Treasury of Faith, 121
Tsarane, the, 37, 41
tukul huts, 128
Tumsa, Qes Gudina, US trained theologian of Mekane Yesus Church, 213; role in formation of Council for the Cooperation of Christian Churches, 213–14; murder by secret police, 214, 216–17, social justice interest, 217–18
Tyre, 28, 29

Unic 7000 Church, 216

vicar apostolic: *see* apostolic vicariate
"villagization," Derg policy, 93

Wag, 53
Walasma Dynasty, 52
Walatta Petros, nun who defended Orthodoxy against Susenyos, 120; *see also Gadla Walatta Petros*
Waran (Ethiop-Sabaean king), 15–17
Werzelya, child-killing demon, 157
"wax and gold": *see qene*
Wierix brothers, the, their engravings influential in Ethiopian art, 149

Yaqubi, Al-, Arab writer on Ethiopia, 109
Yared (Saint), inventor of Ethiopian church music, 125; life, 165–66; legends concerning, 166; depicted in art, 152
Yeha, 13, 14, 16
Yekunno Amlak (King), 52, 54, 55, 56, 58; fostering literature, art and architecture, 139–40
Yemata, Abba, one of Nine Saints, 47, 48

Yemen, 13, 17, 45, 50, 51, 110; Muslim conquest in sixteenth century, 64
Yeshak I (Emperor), 58; war against the Falasha, 59
Yetbarak (King), 54
Yimreha Krestos (King), links with Egypt, 53
Yishaq (Abba), archbishop of the Western Hemisphere, 97
Yohannes I (Emperor), 78
Yohannes IV: reign, 82–83; opposition to Protestantism, 199; conquests of, 219
You-Go City Church, 216

Za Dengel (Emperor), convert to Roman Catholicism, 70; death 71
Zagwe Dynasty, 52–54, 112; later canonizaton of Zagwe kings, 115–16
Zara Yaqob (King), 58, 60–62, 115, 121; accession, 60; early days, 60; religious leadership and reforms, 61–62; harshness of, 62; encouragement of Marian devotion, and literature, 62, 140; works written by, 117; opposition to prayer scrolls, 156; modification of the calendar, 176
Zawditu, Empress, 86
Zeila, Portuguese conquest of, 64
zema, the music and chant of Ethiopian Orthodoxy, 166
zema bet (music school), 129–30; *see also degwa, zemmare, mawasit, aqwaqwam, qeddase*
zemmare (communion hymns), 129–30, 168
Zena Amda Seyon, 109–10, 115
Zena Eskender, 114; *see also* Alexander
Zeno (Emperor), 47
Zonainos: *see* Pantalewon, Abba
Zōskalēs, 21

www.ingramcontent.com/pod-product-compliance
Lightning Source LLC
Chambersburg PA
CBHW021344300426
44114CB00012B/1073